WORKPLACE RESEARCH

WORKPLACE RESEARCH

Conducting small-scale research
in organizations

ZINA O'LEARY
JENNIFER S. HUNT

Los Angeles | London | New Delhi
Singapore | Washington DC | Melbourne

Los Angeles | London | New Delhi
Singapore | Washington DC | Melbourne

SAGE Publications Ltd
1 Oliver's Yard
55 City Road
London EC1Y 1SP

SAGE Publications Inc.
2455 Teller Road
Thousand Oaks, California 91320

SAGE Publications India Pvt Ltd
B 1/I 1 Mohan Cooperative Industrial Area
Mathura Road
New Delhi 110 044

SAGE Publications Asia-Pacific Pte Ltd
3 Church Street
#10-04 Samsung Hub
Singapore 049483

Editor: Jai Seaman
Editorial assistant: Alysha Owen
Production editor: Imogen Roome
Copyeditor: Elaine Leek
Proofreader: Leigh C. Timmins
Indexer: Silvia Benvenuto
Marketing manager: Sally Ransom
Cover design: Shaun Mercier
Typeset by: C&M Digitals (P) Ltd, Chennai, India
Printed and bound by CPI Group (UK) Ltd,
Croydon, CR0 4YY

Library of Congress Control Number: 2015955560

British Library Cataloguing in Publication data

A catalogue record for this book is available from
the British Library

ISBN 978-1-4739-1320-2
ISBN 978-1-4739-1321-9 (pbk)

At SAGE we take sustainability seriously. Most of our products are printed in the UK using FSC papers and boards.
When we print overseas we ensure sustainable papers are used as measured by the PREPS grading system.
We undertake an annual audit to monitor our sustainability.

CONTENTS

ACKNOWLEDGMENTS

The first note of thanks needs to go to all the workplace-based students, both under-graduate and postgraduate, we have worked with at The University of Sydney and The Australia and New Zealand School of Government. It is incredibly reward-ing to help students navigate the gap between university and the workplace; and it is our shared experiences that have brought this book to life. We'd also like to thank the team at SAGE Publishing, particularly Jai Seaman and Imogen Roome whose support has definitely made this a better work. Thank you also to Dr. Andrew Pratley for his insights on data analytics, and the Experis/Comsys office in Baltimore for lending their expertise in employability skills. Finally, we'd like to give a special note of thanks to Bill Franklin, who at crunch time was ready with a couple of all-nighters and an amazing set of copy-editing skills. The man knows the meaning of the word 'deadline'.

Zina and Jen

PREFACE

A lion lay asleep in the forest when a mouse happened upon him unexpectedly. In her haste to get away the mouse accidentally woke the lion, who caught her in his paw to kill her. The mouse pleaded for her life saying, 'I can be of value to you. If you let me go, I will repay you someday'. The lion roared with laughter: 'I am a lion, the most powerful creature in the forest, and you are just a lowly mouse! What use could you possibly be to me?' Unconvinced but merciful, he let the little mouse go.

A few weeks later, the mouse crossed paths with the lion once again. This time, it was the lion who was in trouble, snared in a hunter's net. Unable to move, his angry roars filled the forest. The little mouse chewed through the ropes, rescuing the lion.

What is the moral of Aesop's fable? Is it that a kindness is never wasted, or perhaps that we should not judge individuals based on their station? One interpretation of Aesop's fable could be not to underestimate others. Another may also be not to underestimate yourself.

When embarking on an industry placement, it may seem that you are the mouse and have little to offer the lion, the organization. How can you prove useful to a team of managers when you're new to the organization and the industry? A workplace-based research project offers you the opportunity to identify interesting problems, collect and analyze data, and sharpen your own marketable skills. It also offers you the opportunity to contribute long-term value to the organization by offering practical recommendations backed by robust research. This book will show you how.

1

UNDERSTANDING SMALL-SCALE APPLIED WORKPLACE-BASED RESEARCH

Chapter preview

What is small-scale applied workplace-based research?

Do we really need a book on this?

What are the challenges of workplace-based research?

How do you best navigate the process?

WHAT IS SMALL-SCALE APPLIED WORKPLACE-BASED RESEARCH?

So what is this long-winded beast, small-scale applied workplace-based research … and why would you ever think about doing it?

Breaking it down

Okay, so we are talking about *small-scale applied workplace-based research*. Well, let's start with **research**. Research can be defined as the systematic study of materials and sources in order to answer a question, establish facts and reach new conclusions – very worthwhile goals.

So let's add ***applied***. Applied research is research with a change-oriented purpose. It is research expressly designed to make things better. Applied research delves into issues in order to form practical recommendations that can lead to problem-solving, opportunities and genuine change – also goals worth striving for.

What about ***workplace-based***, how does research conducted within and for organizations differ from other types of research? Well, workplace-based research still follows the main protocols that give credibility to all types of research, but it does differ in two significant ways. First, workplace-based research is highly 'political'. By this, we mean the context of any and all workplace-based research sits within a political environment. There are actors, players, stakeholders, bosses and boards with a host of varying agendas (as well as a consistent shortage of time and money). So while research still needs to be conducted in objective and scientific ways, it sits within a hot seat of political considerations. Second, the workplace is not a controlled environment. It is an environment full of real-world complexity. In workplace-based research, extraneous variables can pop up in the most unexpected places. We would argue, however, that this political nature and real-world complexity simply add to the excitement of doing grounded research that can make a real difference.

That all makes sense, but why focus on *small-scale*? Sure, organizations face big issues and big problems. And yes, we would all like to be responsible for turning the organization around; for becoming one of the top 500 companies; for reaching all-time highs in customer satisfaction; for winning countless awards; for gaining unprecedented funding. But very few of us are in a position to do that type/scale of research. That type of research is in the realm of PhDs, academics and consultancy firms; in other words, full-time researchers. Further, the reports and papers generated through such processes do not guarantee that large-scale change will occur. Change of that scale is dependent on a host of factors beyond any knowledge that might be generated through such research. So the emphasis here on small-scale is about being practical. It is more realistic to engage in research on problems, or aspects of problems that, while still important and significant, are tangible, local and grounded. Research at this level is about doing research that responds to real and tangible everyday needs.

The benefits

When it comes to the benefits of doing small-scale applied workplace-based research, they can be broken down into two categories ... benefits to the organization and benefits to you.

Benefits to the researcher

Conducting workplace-based research affords you the opportunity to engage in all types of learning. Workplace-based research allows you to:

- *Engage in 'problem-based learning'* – The thinking behind problem-based learning (PBL) is that the best starting point for learning is to work through a problem that needs to be solved in a hands-on fashion. The learning here is 'double loop'. Not only do you learn about a problem you are exploring, you also learn how to tackle that problem, hopefully in a manner that will allow you to transfer problem-solving skills to a variety of new challenges. The nature of conducting workplace-based research embeds problem-based learning into the research process.

- *Engage in 'action learning'* – Kolb (1984) stressed the importance of the creation of knowledge through 'transformation of experience'. He suggested that experiential learning is dependent on cycles that include: (1) engagement in real experiences (concrete experimentation) that need to be followed by (2) thoughtful review and consideration (reflexive observation), as well as (3) broader theorizing (abstract conceptualization) and (4) attempts to improve action (active experimentation). Such processes are embedded in various aspects of conducting research. To 'do' workplace-based research is to engage in cycles of action learning.
- *Enhance communication skills* – Gathering credible data is not a task for the shy or faint of heart. It is a process that is highly dependent on your ability to effectively communicate with others. Whether it is the challenge of gaining access, conducting interviews, or engaging in participant observation, boosting your communication skills is often a side benefit of doing research.
- *Develop research skills* – Even though you are reading our methods text, we are here to tell you that there is only so much you can learn from 'reading' about the conduct of research – the real learning comes from the 'doing'. Without a doubt, it is reflectively conducting research that will teach you how to do it.
- *Produce new knowledge* – You will find out something. You will hopefully get an answer to your research question. You will have produced new knowledge that can make a contribution to problem-solving.
- *Engage in, or facilitate, evidenced-based decision-making* – It is a really good feeling to know that common-sense, practical decisions are being influenced by data you generate.

So those are the learning opportunities, but what about employment opportunities? Does undertaking workplace-based research open up the job market in any way? In a word, 'yes'. Conducting workplace-based research can be a fantastic avenue for improving employment prospects.

- *Improve your chances of getting a full-time job* – In the internship program I coordinate at the University of Sydney Business School, I strongly emphasize that students who undertake research as part of their internship program have a massive advantage over those who do not. Sure, the everyday intern can point to improved teamwork, communication, project management, etc. But the intern who has undertaken research can talk about all of the above, as well as the issues facing their host organization and how they are able to collect and analyze data in order to make robust recommendations for improved decision-making. They are able to talk about their contribution to the organization itself – so much more impressive.
- *Become more valuable in the workplace* – For those who already employed, the conduct of research can set you apart. There are those who get on board with ideas, and those who generate them. Being someone who generates credible data and robust practicable recommendations is undoubtedly the way to go.

Benefits to the organization

The purpose of workplace-based research is simple – to generate data, draw conclusions and offer recommendations that can lead to situation improvement. But, of course, this can occur at varying levels. Situation improvement can involve:

- *Aiding the development of practice* – In this case, your aim is to influence the practices of those within the organization. This can involve: (1) providing an overview of a problem situation with a view to determining the need for new practices; (2) assessing/evaluating 'new' practices, which might involve research that attempts to explore the strengths/weaknesses and costs/benefits of new ways of 'doing' or evaluate the success/failure of new practices.
- *Aiding the development of program* – Here the goal is to influence the organized, structured and defined approaches to the operations, projects and strategies used by the organization. Research at this level can help to make convincing arguments for systemic change. This can involve research that assesses need, i.e. questioning whether there is need for a particular 'change intervention' program; determining feasibility, i.e. exploring the strengths/ weaknesses and costs/benefits of particular programs; reviewing programs to determine effectiveness, i.e. whether the program was successful in meeting its goals: Is it cost-effective; should it be continued; does it require modification; should it be expanded?
- *Aiding the development of policy* – Policy can be defined as 'a plan of action intended to influence and determine decisions, actions, and other matters'. Thus the goal here is conducting research that can impact an organization's strategic plans, aims and objectives, and/or its mission statement. It is research aimed at producing policy recommendations. Now keep in mind that moving from research to policy is not always straightforward. Knowledge, even credible knowledge, is not the only factor in policy development. Power, politics, public will, stakeholder buy-in and, of course, money will all play their part.
- *Improving the 'culture' of the organization* – This can happen in two ways. First, the conduct of research itself can give a sense of empowerment and control in creating futures. In fact, the development of a research culture can be reflective of a move towards a 'learning organization', or an organization where '… people continually expand their capacity to create the results they truly desire' (Senge, 1994: 3). Second, research findings themselves may suggest the downside of the current culture and/or the benefits of an alternative culture. For example, research findings might suggest that a shift from a top-down to bottom-up ethos, from dictatorial to democratic management, or from a profit-driven to a people-driven philosophy are needed for increased productivity and/or job satisfaction.

DO WE REALLY NEED A BOOK ON THIS?

Given that we are writing a book on this, WE certainly feel the answer is 'Yes!'. And we say that for two reasons. The first is that organizations make big and small decisions on a daily basis, and data can be KEY to effective decision-making. The second reason we think an entire book is warranted is that small-scale applied workplace-based research is its own animal it requires a somewhat different research approach and a distinctly different mindset.

Organizations need data

There is no doubt that organizations need data and, therefore, research. Research is the process of gathering data in order to answer a particular question(s); and when conducting workplace-based research, the questions asked generally relate to a need for data that can facilitate decision-making, thereby aiding problem resolution. Research is critical.

Does this then make the data generated by research the answer to an organization's problems? Well, unfortunately not. But research can be an instrumental part of problem resolution. Research can be a key tool in informed decision-making. It can be central to determining what we should do, what we can do, how we will do it and how well we have done it. Research may not be a panacea, but it can supply some of the data necessary for us to begin tackling pressing issues.

Take change management literature as an example. It will clearly tell you that in order to make change happen – in order to solve problems – you need to:

- *understand the problem* – including all the complexities, intricacies and implications;
- *be able to find workable solutions* – vision futures, explore possibilities;
- *work towards that solution* – implement real change;
- *evaluate success* – to find out if problem solving/change strategies have been successful.

Without a doubt, all of these activities can be, and should be, informed by data. Research can be the key to finding out more about pressing issues. It can also help us in our quest for solutions. It can be key to assessing needs, visioning futures, and finding and assessing potential answers. It can also allow us to monitor and refine our attempts at problem-solving. In short, research-driven data may not be the answer – but it can certainly be instrumental in moving towards situation improvement.

How decisions are made

Now you might think that the argument above is pretty good. Organizations need data, therefore organizations need to conduct research. And to be honest, very few would argue with this. It is logical, it is accepted, and it is even seen as best practice.

But do organizations always engage in best practice? Well, no. In reality, there are a number of ways that organizational decisions are made, and many of those are, in fact, data-minimal, if not data-free.

Some of the ways organizations make decisions include:

- *Tradition/legacy/history* – There are a plethora of decisions that are made because 'this is how we've always done it'. And this can be very powerful. Sometimes it's to do with laziness; sometimes it's a complete lack of critical consideration; sometimes it's a comfort zone; sometimes it's a nostalgic connection with the past. But almost always, it's easier. The challenge, however, is avoiding stagnation. Albert Einstein is attributed to having said, 'The definition of insanity is doing something over and over again and expecting a different result'.
- *Personal bias/personal agenda* – There are those who simply 'know'. They know what's best; they know what's needed. Without any data, and based only on their own experience, they know they have the right answer. And if that person is in a position of power – well, that is how a decision can be reached. Also consider whether the needs of the organization come before the needs of the individual. Not always. There is no doubt that people have agendas; agendas that involve power, prestige, desire for promotion – and this can certainly affect decision-making.
- *Ideology/conviction* – Beyond knowing is believing. Some people operate from a space of ideology or moral conviction. Beliefs related to fair trade and environmental sustainability are examples of convictions that may drive decisions, regardless of data.
- *Fear* – 'I don't want to rock the boat', 'I don't want to get in trouble', 'I want this to go away'. Don't underestimate the power of fear in decision-making.
- *Political considerations* – Sometimes a nonsensical decision comes to make sense when you know more of the back story. Organizations are full of power structures and power games – both within and external to the organization. These games and structures can play a large part in how decisions are made.
- *Timelines* – Without a doubt, gathering data can take time; and time can sometimes be a luxury. Management is not always in a position to wait on data, particularly in situations deemed pressing, such as an emergency or something politically hot.
- *Intuition/ heart* – Don't underestimate how many decisions are made from the gut. Following our instincts, good or bad, has always been, and always will be, a decision-making strategy.
- *Religion* – Would Chick-fil-A (for those outside the United States, the US' largest quick-service chicken restaurant chain) make more money if they opened on Sunday? It's hard to see how they wouldn't. But they don't open and haven't since their first restaurant opened in 1946. Time for worship is part of their 'recipe for success' – a terrific example of religion as a driving force in decision-making.

A shift towards evidence

Who would have thought that 'data' would have so much competition in the decision-making stakes? But don't despair, data does have a role, and we'd argue a growing role as accountability becomes ever more in the forefront of private and public sector considerations. Decisions can be influenced by data in the following ways (see Figure 1.1):

- *Data-aware* – To be data-aware means that there is an acknowledgment and consideration of data, but that decisions are being motivated by other forces (see the above list). This is a step above data-free because at least there is no ignorance of the data.
- *Data-influenced* – This is when you have data and a will to act on it, but you are mindful of other considerations as well. In this case, data will influence decisions, but not drive them.
- *Data-informed* – This is where decisions are made in light of data. Decisions are data-driven, but moderated by other considerations.
- *Data-based* – Finally we get to decisions based solely on what the data tells us is most efficacious. The gold medal standard? Sure, but not always realistic. Organizations are complex entities and so are their decision-making processes.

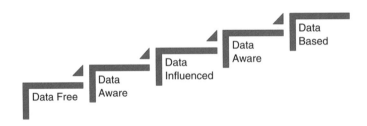

Figure 1.1   Moving up the evidence ladder

Types of decisions that can be data-driven

So we have already talked a bit about how data can influence an organization's practices, programs, policies and culture. But we think it is worth the time to get even more into the nitty-gritty of decision-making. After all, this is where you are likely to jump in with a proposal to conduct research and collect data.

Internal decisions are those that impact an organization's in-house decisions. These are daily business for any organization AND a great starting point for the intern or novice researcher. Examples here include things like whether or not to move from fixed desks to activity-based seating; how to modify employee induction materials; whether the employee award program is worth keeping; how to better share data across the organization; whether to expand the department; whether to allow flexible hours. All are decisions where data would shed light on how to improve the internal machinations of the organization.

External decisions are those that extend outside the organization and are more about enhancing an organization's core business. Examples here might be whether to extend to a new market; whether to launch a new product; whether to take on a new partner; whether to launch an online presence. In these cases, the intern or novice researcher may not be able to provide ALL the data necessary for informed decision-making – but they can provide one or more crucial streams of data that aid the process.

Once you start to think about all the decisions, internal and external, that organizations face on a daily basis, small-scale applied workplace-based research becomes much less intimidating and a whole world of research possibilities begins to open up.

WHAT ARE THE CHALLENGES OF WORKPLACE-BASED RESEARCH?

All sounding good right? Lots of potential, lots of benefits. And not just to the organization, but to you as the researcher as well. So you might be thinking, what's the catch, what's the downside, what challenges am I up for?

Well, there are a few. This type of research is a bit different from traditional social science research. For one, traditional social science research runs on the promise of objectivity. Researchers need to be unbiased entities who close off all personal connection to what they are researching. Being 'political' is absolutely taboo. Second, timeframes are very short – days, weeks, maybe a couple of months, but certainly not years. Decisions need to be made quickly, so data needs to be generated even faster. Third, the research environment is messy. There is nothing controlled about the research setting.

Understanding and appreciating 'political' context

The founding fathers of social science research would roll over in their graves if they knew a text on research was about to say … 'research is highly "political"'. You see, social science research is born of the rules of engagement for the natural sciences. You study the social just as you would study neutrons and protons. That means objectivity and scientific method. To be political is not just taboo, it is wrong. But we are not in a lab; we are not objective scientists seeking knowledge for knowledge's sake. We are employees with an agenda; employees working within an organization full of agendas! Being successful in workplace-based research is highly dependent on understanding and appreciating these agendas.

Knowing what decisions are pressing

As we tell our students, when it comes to workplace-based research, the only real measure of success is whether or not recommendations have been taken up. That's what this is about. It's not about knowledge for knowledge's sake. Research abounds, but change driven by research, not so much. Even in the business world, consultants' reports sit on shelves – with barely an action arising from them. So how do we change that? Well, if it is about generating data to aid informed decision-making, you need to figure out what decisions are pressing.

What decisions are the organization grappling with? Where are they in a bind? Where can't they decide? Where are they unsure of which way to go? Where are the concerns? Are there complaints? Are they facing public pressure? Has the media got onto something and action NEEDS to be taken? What needs are undeniable?

When conducting workplace-based research, the ideal is to have management WAITING on your results. If they have determined that their decisions will be data-informed or better yet, data-based, and it is your data they are waiting on, then your research will have traction. The number one thing you can do to ensure success in workplace-based research is knowing where your contribution is an absolute necessity.

Keeping management interested

In traditional models of research, even consultancy research, there is a tendency to go off and 'do' research and come back later with a report. But in a workplace environment, agendas can shift like the wind. There is no guarantee that what is important to management one day will be important the next. So again there IS a need to be 'political'. You need to be working with decision-makers to ensure that needs and timelines are communicated. You need to keep interest high. You need to do the work so that when data comes in, findings become clear, conclusions are drawn and recommendations are offered, management is still on board, and even better, waiting on your results.

Offering high utility

So we know that if we pick the right research question, in other words one aligned with pressing needs, we will come up with something useful. But high utility is more than that. High utility is not just about the right questions, it is also about offering the right recommendations; that is offering the right decisions/actions for the organization to take.

Recommendations of high utility are those that meet two agendas. First, they need to be efficacious for the organization. What you recommend needs to be based on data and should offer clear guidelines for action. Recommendations should be a logical extension of findings and in the best interest of the organization and its goals. In other words, your recommendations will help the organization make the 'right' decisions. Second, the recommendations need to be *practicable*. Now practicable has a slightly different meaning than practical. If something is practical, it is useful, but if something is practicable it is not only useful, it is also highly feasible or 'doable'. This means that recommendations of high utility are more than a wish list. They are in the realm of distinct possibility, in other words, they can be funded, they are strategically aligned with organizational goals and they have political support. There is no utility in offering the right answers if there is no chance of those right answers being actioned.

The research environment

There is nothing like a controlled environment for conducting research. You can test relationships between certain variables, you can make sure there is nothing that will confound results, and in the end you can make some definitive statements about what's what. But that's not often the case in workplace-based research. This type of research happens in real-world settings where data can indeed be messy.

An organizational setting

When you are conducting workplace-based research, you are (1) working in an organizational setting that you know well; (2) working in a setting in which you are known; (3) working with existing data generally not purpose-built for your research processes. Add to that very tight timelines, and you find yourself with a pressing need for flexibility in your research design. The organizational setting of workplace-based research brings up a number of challenges that need to be managed. Research management techniques include:

- the need to keep methodological designs flexible;
- the need to engage in multiple methods;
- the possibility of not being able to account for all variables;
- the need to manage your own experiences, insights and biases;
- the ability to develop empathetic understanding of various stakeholders;
- prejudices towards you as a 'researcher';
- the need for highly developed social/communication skills;
- being prepared for an array of contingencies without adequate time or money.

There is, however, a big payoff. If you are able to recognize and grapple with multi-dimensionality and messy contexts – and you can still come up with credible findings, conclusions and recommendations – they are much more likely to be realistic, practicable and sustainable than any 'tidy' results produced in a closed environment.

Topics you know

Another big challenge in workplace-based research is that there's a good chance you think you already know the answer to the question you are posing. In fact, you might know EXACTLY what the organization needs in order to move forward. This is especially likely if you have been with the organization for a while. But it can also happen if you are new and you think that the organization's needs are as plain as the nose on your face.

Whoa there. Hold on a minute. How do you expect to come up with anything credible if you carry that much bias? It is an absolute truism that if you are not 'reflexive', that is, you do not take the time to call yourself on your own biases, you will simply seek to confirm those biases through your research. Who you talk to, what you read, how you analyze what is said – unless you are dedicated to finding things out that you do not expect to find, maybe even do not WANT to find, you have very little chance of finding anything but what you already thought. Be ready for the unexpected: that is where the fun is AND it is where the most interesting recommendations are developed.

People you know

There are three messy people-centered situations that can arise in the conduct of workplace-based research. The first is when people you know are part of your research processes. For example, there is often a need to conduct key informant interviews or focus groups when doing this kind of research; and sometimes those individuals are known to you. It takes some forethought to figure out how you can establish researcher credibility and researcher trust in order to get the 'best' data from your informants.

The second challenge is when you are told things about people you know. Say, for example, you are exploring workplace efficiency and your colleague and friend is identified as being a lazy, shifty brown-noser. What do you do? How do you keep your cool, not become defensive? And what do you do with this data? Do you protect your friend? Or do you stay true to the research task? And what if your own department comes under critique? Or your boss, even you yourself? How do you maintain a researcher's perspective, when you are also a colleague, friend or rival? Researchers are expected to take on an 'objective' stance and are not usually involved with research participants outside of their research. This is not always the case in workplace-based research, and represents another layer of complexity to be managed.

A third people-centered challenge is carrying the weight of expectation. You may have a boss who wants you to find and report on only certain things. And while this can be a challenge for anyone doing commissioned research, it is a particularly difficult challenge when you work for the organization. There are plenty of cases where management really wants validation rather than a potentially ugly truth.

But don't despair, there is an upside. Yes, you need to navigate messy context, topics you know too much about and people you know too well. But think of the flipside: who better to undertake research within an organization than some-one with local knowledge; someone who has access; someone who understands the political ins and outs; someone who not only sees problems but tends to be frustrated by them on a day-to-day basis; someone who people already know and trust; someone with something to gain for their own professional practice, or something to gain for their own workplace? The answer here is careful con-sideration of these dilemmas paired with reflexive consideration of how best to navigate the research process with credibility. As shown in Table 1.1, for each advantage there are disadvantages that you will need to carefully consider and thoughtfully negotiate.

Table 1.1   Opportunities and dilemmas in workplace-based research

The researcher's edge	Opportunities	Dilemmas
Experience	• being able to capitalize on a great depth of experiential, local and insider knowledge	• already having the answers, being biased/lacking objectivity
Access	• being able to come and go within an organizational setting	• not being seen or respected as a researcher
Trust	• having people be honest and open because they know and trust you	• being unsure if what is said is to you as a confidential friend or to you as a researcher gathering data • losing trust because you are now a researcher
Political nous	• having a good sense of how the organization operates, and how to best manage politics	• getting on the wrong side of the political machine and having to continue to operate within that political environment after the research is done
Dual role	• being in a position to best see research needs and opportunities	• role conflict as managerial responsibilities can be at odds with researcher objectivity and/or confidentiality
Career opportunities	• making a contribution that will enhance your career	• making a contribution that will undo your career
Improved practice	• evaluating your own practice so that it can be improved	• finding out that what you are doing and what you believe in is not working and/or not appreciated
Organizational change	• being able to make a real contribution to shifting workplace practice, systems and/or culture	• being responsible for an organization needing to go through the upheaval of changing practices, systems and/or culture

Limited resources

This one is pretty straightforward so we will keep it brief. You will not have enough time, or money. Simple. Timelines are tight, resources are limited. And you will think, 'If only … If only I had 2 more weeks; if only I could concentrate on this rather than the other 20 things they expect me to do; if only there were extra funds for … '.

We have two strategies for you here. Strategy one is good research design – a tight research question and very concise and doable, yet credible, methods. The second strategy is political support. If management NEEDS your data in order to make a pressing decision, you just might be able to leverage the support you need.

HOW DO YOU BEST NAVIGATE THE PROCESS?

Given all of the above, you might be wondering just how different is the *conduct* of workplace-based research?

Well the actual *rules* of research are the same. You need to come up with a solid research question; and while you may be more reliant on existing data, your methods of data collection and analysis will still fall within the spectrum of social science research. What is different, however, is the need for 'political' nous.

The 'research' stream

Doing workplace-based research is a stepwise process that involves:

1. *Developing practicable and valuable research questions* (see Chapter 3) – The biggest hurdle for any researcher is question development. This is particularly challenging when the research is conducted not just out of curiosity, but is undertaken in order to add value to an organization in a very tight timeframe. This requires a logical process of understanding the workplace environment; understanding the issues faced by the organization; and understanding the potential for gathering data that can facilitate evidence-based decision-making. It is these understandings that will facilitate the development of a practicable research question.
2. *Doing appropriate prep* (see Chapter 4) – Once a question is developed, there is a tendency to want to jump straight into data collection. But even in small-scale research with truncated timelines, there is still a need to do prep, including reviewing some of the literature that is out there, developing a research plan and preparing a short proposal in an ethical way.
3. *Knowing how to work with existing data* (see Chapter 5) – Nowhere is the need to understand the potential of working with existing data greater than in the conduct of small-scale workplace-based research. Short timeframes, an abundance of organizational data, and the Internet at your fingertips mean existing data is often your first port of call.
4. *Knowing how to gather primary data* (see Chapter 6) – While you may find existing data sufficient, there will be times when primary data is needed. Knowing how to conduct interviews, focus groups and run surveys in a practical way is key.
5. *Engaging in data analysis* (see Chapter 7) – Whether it is numerical data, interview recordings, notes and/or transcripts, or coalescing and synthesizing

existing research, the journey from 'data' to 'story' is something that needs to be tackled in ways that are true to the scale and scope of your project, yet still credible.

6. *Producing and communicating effective deliverables* (see Chapter 8) – When it comes to deliverables, there is often a gap between the academic's expectations and those of organizations. Clear written and oral communication are both important here.

The 'political' stream

So that is the research end of the process. But what about the 'political' end? Well it's actually woven through the research process and manifests something like this:

1. *Orienting yourself to the workplace and its issues* (see Chapter 2) – The most effective way to engage in workplace-based research is to really know that workplace; to understand who's who, what's what and get your head around the lay of the land.
2. *Making sure that the answer to your research question is something the organization really needs* (see Chapter 3) – Research with leverage is research that is needed!
3. *Getting commitment* (see Chapter 4) – One way to get commitment is to write or present a short proposal that really lays out the benefits of your research to the organization.
4. *Collecting data in clever and efficient ways that capitalize on those in the know* (see Chapters 5 and 6) – Existing networks can be key to making workplace-based research happen.
5. *Ensuring take up of recommendation* (see Chapter 8) – While you need to conduct your research with the objectivity of a scientist, you need to advocate your findings and recommendations like a boss!
6. *Leveraging job opportunities* (see Chapter 8) – It is definitely worth considering how to capitalize on your research experience in ways that will help you leverage employment opportunities.

So, that's small-scale applied workplace-based research. Here's hoping that this long-winded beast now makes sense and you are motivated to make things happen!

CHAPTER SUMMARY

- Small-scale applied workplace-based research is the process of developing new knowledge by gathering data that answers a particular question faced by an organization and can offer benefits to both the organization and the researcher.

- Organizations make decisions on a daily basis, and data is often key to effective decision-making. It can be central to determining what an organization should do and can do, how to do it, and how well it's been done.
- There are several challenges in the conduct of workplace-based research, including developing a sound understanding of the political context, maintaining an objective view, dealing with short timeframes and conducting research in a messy real-world environment.
- Successfully navigating the journey involves the need for understanding both the research and political aspects of the process.

FINDING YOUR WAY THROUGH THE WORKPLACE

Chapter preview

Just how green are you?

A brave new world

What's what and who's who

Agendas

JUST HOW GREEN ARE YOU?

For most workplace-based students, the organization where you will be conducting your research project is likely to be a new environment. You may, for example, be an intern who is not only new to a particular organization, but new to organizations in general. Or you might be part of a student group, engaged to conduct research for a particular organization/agency of which you may be only tangentially aware.

On the other end of the spectrum, you may be enrolled in a course designed for professionals who will be conducting research in the organization/agency where you work. And then there is the possibility that you have picked up this book independently and want to know how to conduct, commission and/or manage research within your workplace.

Well, if you are quite green, and the workplace is a fairly new environment, then this is the chapter for you. It covers all the challenges of entering and negotiating a new workplace, including navigating the politics of the organization.

But even if you aren't a novice, it still might be worth browsing through this chapter … if only to remind yourself of politics in the workplace and how, in particular, it can affect the conduct of research.

A BRAVE NEW WORLD

Say for a minute it is day one and you really are quite green. It is the first day you enter your workplace – and for many of you that may mean the first day of an internship.

Well let's step back a second. We'd argue that it really shouldn't be day one at all. Day one should be the day you find out about your work placement. And this is because you would be ill-advised to go into a new work environment without knowing a few basics. Doing your homework is important. Things worth finding out about/considering include basic information such as:

- *The company* – The size/scope of the business/agency; its history; its mission statement; its strategic plan; any challenges it may be facing.
- *The people* – The CEO; the director; your line manager. Have they been in the media? Are there things about them you should know/would be expected to know?
- *Your role and responsibilities* – Are you clear on what role you will have; what you will be doing; what is expected of you?
- *What you want to accomplish* – Have you thought through your goals; what you want to achieve; what you want to learn; what your overall objective might be?

It is intimidating enough starting a new job when you have this background knowledge. But it can be so much worse if you are un- or under-prepared. If you start off on the back foot or give a negative impression, it can be a tough road forward.

BOX 2.1

'Who are you?' Hosei's story

My supervisor was taking me for a tour around the office, showing me where everything was, and introducing me to people along the way. At one stage, we ran into a woman near the kitchen and he warmly introduced her as Sharon Macfarlane. He was immediately interrupted with something that seemed quite urgent, leaving me standing there with her. Being my friendly self, I quickly said, 'Nice to meet you, Sharon. I'm Hosei, the new intern. So what do you do in the company?'. The response was, 'Well, Hosei, I'm actually the CEO'. OMG, I felt *soooo* stupid. I had meant to look at the organization's structure, but I was so busy that first morning thinking about what I would wear, how I was going to get there, making sure I showed up on time … that I never got around to it. What a mistake. All I could think was … there go my job prospects.

Feeling like an imposter

I still believe that at any time the no-talent police will come and arrest me.
Mike Myers

Any new environment has the potential to bring up insecurities and leave you feeling like an imposter. Overcoming these feelings is a challenge that is usually met as you gain experience. For some, however, feeling like an imposter can become a more chronic syndrome.

'Imposter syndrome' as it is called can be defined as a feeling of inadequacy that persists even in the face of information that indicates the opposite is true (see Figure 2.1) This is often coupled with a fear that it's just a matter of time before they've found you to be a fraud and realize management just made a big mistake in hiring you. Those with imposter syndrome believe that luck has a lot to do with where they are. They believe it is their connections, their charm, their timing, or even an administrative mistake that allows them to succeed. And this belief holds true even in the face of evidence to the contrary.

Holding such beliefs can have significant ramifications on the workplace experience. Those with imposter syndrome can struggle to find their way in an organization.

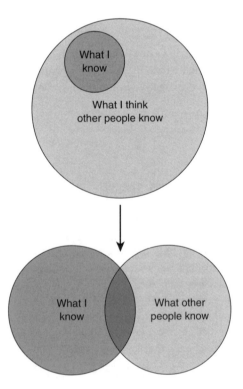

Figure 2.1   The imposter syndrome

In spite of being competent, they are less likely to apply for jobs, less likely to seek promotions, tend not to look for other employment opportunities and are often nervous about talking to others in their field (especially if those others are perceived as highly skilled and/or experienced); they can spend way too much time over preparing and perfecting tasks and can run the risk of letting others take credit for their work.

When you apply these fears and avoidance tendency to the conduct of workplace-based research, the challenge becomes immense. Workplace-based research demands that opportunities are sought; that peers and those senior are addressed with confidence; that timelines are managed; and that researchers see themselves as individuals capable of making a contribution back to the organization. There is a need to own one's competence!

Whether the feeling of being an imposter is brought on by a new challenge or is a much more chronic state of affairs, there are several ways to deal with imposter-type feelings. Some of the strategies that we find work best include:

- *Creating an inventory of strengths and accomplishments* – You may be surprised to see how much you've done, and how much you're doing. Even if it doesn't seem like much now, having it all on paper may amaze you. And if it's written down, you can always refer back when you are feeling insecure.
- *In the words of Nike, 'Just do it'* – Avoidance can cause more stress than tackling something head on. If you are able to cross it off your list, you should let yourself feel the accomplishment.
- *Helping others who are struggling with the same thing* – Not only does it feel good to help others who are dealing with imposter syndrome, it can be a quick way to realise that (1) you're not alone and (2) you're not doing so badly yourself. Helping others overcome their fears will help put your own fears in perspective.
- *Talking to a mentor* – Others tend to be much fairer in their appraisals of us than we are to ourselves. Get some outside perspective. You might be surprised to hear you're actually doing pretty well.
- *Don't make unrealistic comparisons to others* – Sometimes we set ourselves up by thinking about what someone like Steve Jobs was doing when he was our age, or what cousin Vinnie, who got into Yale at 15, is doing now. Don't fall into the trap of making *unrealistic* comparisons. It serves no purpose.
- *Do benchmark yourself against others* – This means referencing yourself to a like group of individuals and doing a reality check to make sure you are not being too harsh (or soft) on yourself. Practice seeing other people as they really are, with their own strengths, but also their own weaknesses.
- *Don't let critique devastate you* – Yes, you need to take advice on board and even accept criticism over things you've done or not done well. This is an important part of work. But if you let yourself be totally shattered by critique, and make it about who you are rather than what you've done, you can actually immobilize yourself. And remember, critiques should not get personal. If they do, it's worth considering whether that critique is more about the person making it, than it is about you.

- *Learn to internalize external validation* – People with imposter syndrome often brush off the compliments they receive. Don't do it. Accept graciously. Let it sink in. Try to own it. After all, chances are you've earned it.
- *Finally, know that you are in good company* – It's worth knowing that imposter syndrome is most common amongst high performers and those deemed gifted!

A word to those who may find the concept of imposter syndrome quite bizarre – hopefully, you can't relate because you are very good at being realistic. You benchmark yourself well and you realize that there is a learning curve you will soon get on top of.

But what if you are just a bit too cocky? Well, there is something called the Dunning-Kruger effect (Kruger and Dunning, 1999) (Figure 2.2). It occurs when individuals fail to adequately assess their level of *in*competence – and see themselves as much more competent than they actually are.

Figure 2.2   The Dunning-Kruger effect

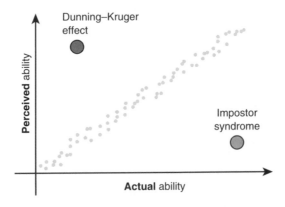

Figure 2.3   Balancing the Dunning-Kruger effect and imposter syndrome

As shown in Figure 2.3, what you are really after is the ability to be quite realistic about where you are and what you do. Treading the line between the Dunning-Kruger effect and imposter syndrome is the quick path to the win.

BOX 2.2

My first day: Torben's story

On my first day on Capitol Hill, I was incredibly nervous. Just the thought of walking into the Congressman's office made me feel sick. I didn't know if I was dressed right, if I should get there early, if I should knock … my stomach was a mess. When I did walk in, I was in total awe, which didn't help. What was I doing here? Everyone seemed so together and confident. I felt hopelessly out of my depth. I thought I was ready, I thought I'd done a good job of researching my internship on the Internet, but I was seriously questioning if being there was nothing but a mistake. That was pretty much how I felt the whole first week of my internship. A big imposter – that was me.

But then week two came around and I realized that it was going to be okay. I paid attention, I asked questions, I laughed, I made friends. Yes, the office was fast-paced, and I had a lot to learn, but I was getting there. I was becoming a part of the team, I was making the shift from imposter about to be exposed to a valued intern!

Making the transition from student to employee

Have a good look at Photo 2.1. Familiar at all? Sadly, it is to the two of us. Apathy, boredom, lack of sleep. These are your rights as a university student.

Photo 2.1

Now look at Photo 2.2. Yes, it is a stock photo with happy young corporates with perversely white teeth, showing the happy gung-ho attitude expected of new recruits. But how, nonetheless, do you make the transition?

Photo 2.2

A student's world is different from the professional one – and making the transition quickly is imperative. Some paradigms that operate differently in the world of work include:

- *Time* – You need to be able to tell it and respect it. Showing up a bit late for a lecture, skipping classes, setting up a 4- or even 3-day schedule, taking a few days off here and there, asking for extensions. We remember those days. Awesome! Not so possible in the 'real world'. Long workdays, overtime – paid and unpaid, projects that need to be finished over the weekend, holidays at the convenience of the organization, scrutiny over time. This is much more the reality. Show up late one too many times and you can find yourself out of a job. Sure, as a student you probably had to do quite a bit of juggling, but undertaking a workplace-based research project and possibly an internship, while doing other units of study, is an extreme time management challenge. And it is critical. Your future with your organization can rest on how well you manage your time.
- *Professionalism* – I'm not even sure how well this word applies to students. Yes, there are codes of conduct and there can be ramifications, but students who come up against this in the system are the minority. In a workplace environment, however, it is an everyday consideration. Professionalism in the workplace requires:

- o *Being a strong reliable team member* – Those you are working with need to know that you will show up, and that you have done what you said you would do.
- o *Being accountable* – Being responsible for adhering to the policies of the organization/company.
- o *Being a self-starter* – It's not just about requirements, it is about making a contribution that gets you noticed.
- o *Being courteous* – Taking the appropriate tone and approach to communicating with others.

- *People skills* – As a student, your people skills are largely social. Yes, it can help if you are able to navigate the administrative and academic worlds of university, but it tends not to be essential. At work it absolutely is. You will need to be able to deal with all types of people and personalities, and your success will be determined by how well you work with others.
- *Influence* – Being influential at university is optional. You are, after all, a student whose job is to learn. But being influential should be a major agenda in the workplace. Ways to become a person of influence include:

- o *Showing up and having a say* – You won't be noticed if you don't put yourself out there.
- o *Learning to speak with presence* – Confidence implies competence. If you are not a strong speaker, it is worth developing these skills, i.e., think about coaching, or joining a group like Toastmasters.
- o *Building strategic relationships* – Know who the power people are, understand the politics of the organization and build strategic alliances.
- o *Being willing to admit and learn from mistakes* – No one expects you to know it all, and admitting you have things to learn will build respect.
- o *Be likeable* – Some people are really awesome to be around; their presence is a good thing. Other people can bring you down, and you don't want that. Sometimes in our quest to do well, to be super competent, we can become demanding, pestering or high-strung. Try to be at ease, and work on developing your sense of humor – and we don't just mean being funny; a good sense of humour is also about being quick to see the humor in others and appreciating it.
- o *Give your full attention* – The best way to have others pay attention to you is to pay attention to them. People want to know they matter. If you are looking bored or texting while listening, you can't complain if the same thing is done to you when it's your time to speak.
- o *Make others look good* – If you want to be influential, you need to make others feel good … and look good! There is no use being right if no one is listening to you. Ideas will only gain ground when they are seen as a win for those who need to get behind them.

Not only are time management, professionalism, people skills and becoming influential important in making your transition to the workplace, they are absolutely essential to the conduct of research. Trust me, you will never be as busy as when you are studying, working and doing a research project (let alone trying to have a life). And you will be navigating various roles including student, employee and researcher, so you will need to be highly professional. You will also need great people skills to be able to collect the research data you require. And finally, you will need to develop the skills related to being influential if you want your research recommendations to be taken up within your organization. If recommendations come from a 'student', they may not be given full and proper consideration. But if they come from someone considered to be a budding professional, they may hold more weight.

BOX 2.3

They were not impressed: Bill's story

So I showed up a bit late on Friday with a great story and a hangover. They were not impressed. Not at all. It wasn't that anyone gave me a hard time, or even sat down and talked to me. It was more that they didn't talk to me. Everyone was busy and I felt I was being ignored. In the afternoon, I finally got a chance to ask one of the people I had become friendly with why I was getting the cold shoulder. He said, 'Look, you left so fast last night, you didn't even realize we were all working late on a short-notice deadline. Fine if you had other plans, but don't think leaving 15 minutes early went unnoticed. Then you show up 30 minutes late this morning, when most of us had gotten in pretty early. You were all red-eyed and looking happy as can be, not even appreciating what was going on here. And it's not the first time'.

What a wake-up call. I wanted this organization to offer me a position after my internship – and I thought I was getting along with everyone really well. But I guess it's more than doing well at happy hour. I needed to change my attitude. So I did. I started coming in on time – sometimes early. I checked in before I left. I became available and interested, I sought work, tried to be there for others. And believe it or not it was really satisfying. I didn't get the job in the end, but I got the next one – and learned a valuable lesson along the way.

WHAT'S WHAT AND WHO'S WHO

Making sense of a new organization – it's a bit like doing a jigsaw puzzle without a clear reference picture. The pieces are scattered everywhere and you are starting to put bits together, but you are not getting a sense of what it will look like when it all comes together. It is hard to see the big picture. Too many players, too many departments, a lot to sort through. But knowing the basics of how the organization runs, its structure, its culture and its people, is critical knowledge. And knowledge, after all, is power.

Becoming familiar with organizational structure

One of the things worth knowing about any organization in which you're working is its organizational structure. In my current job, I came into a particular 'unit', and all my responsibilities sat within that unit. I did my job and I did it well. As my role changed, however, I was expected to start working outside my unit. I was suddenly working with other disciplines, other faculties, other schools. And I was surprised how little I knew about where my unit sat in the bigger picture. I didn't even know who reported to whom. I never sat down and mapped it out, so it took me way too long to understand the power structures in operation. It was only after I had been caught out and my ignorance exposed that I sat down and had a look at how our business operates.

Organizational structure is important – it tells you how the show is run. There are two main organizational structures: tall (see Figure 2.4) and flat (see Figure 2.5). Knowing the difference will tell you a lot about how you can navigate the environment.

Tall organizational structures have more managerial levels than flat structures. There is usually a CEO at the top and several layers of management. Large organizations, particularly ones that are complex, often have a tall hierarchy. Managers are found at various levels and generally have managers above and below them. With tall structures, managers tend to be responsible for smaller subsections of an organization. The military, for example, has a very deep chain of command with a complex vertical (and horizontal) hierarchical structure.

Benefits of tall structures center around managerial control – because of the smaller and tighter lines of responsibility, employees can get more hands-on

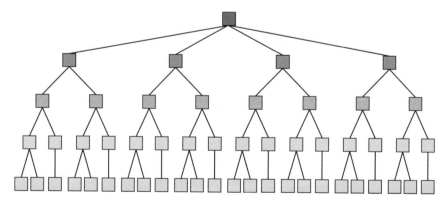

Figure 2.4 Tall organizational structure

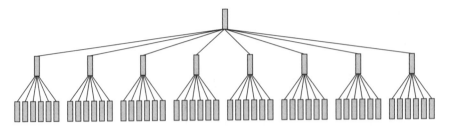

Figure 2.5   Flat organizational structure

supervision. On the downside, however, more hands-on supervision can be seen as overly controlling, and as decisions go up and down the hierarchy, things can take too much time, with red tape becoming a real burden. In terms of employee benefits, there are undeniably promotion opportunities, but the progression to the top can be slow, and influence at the lower levels can be minimal.

When it comes to conducting research in an organization with a tall structure, you are likely to be doing a project with direct benefits to your line manager. Working at the highest level of policy development makes little sense if the chain of command is very deep. The win here will be identifying immediate needs and adding value where you are.

Flat organizational structures have fewer levels of management, with each manager having a broader area of responsibility. There is less emphasis on chains of command and employees often have more autonomy.

Proponents of the flat structure argue that it enhances flexibility and communication tends to run fast – things do not get lost in the chain of command. Flat organizations are also likely to be collaborative and even embed democratic decision-making into their management style. Thus a perceived benefit to employees is a potential sense of empowerment since employees are already near the top of the tree and can have their voices reach upper management. Flat structures, however, can lead to role confusion and high workloads for managers. And while employees in a flat organization may have more direct influence on the organization, they may also consider career paths limited.

When conducting research in organizations with flat structures, there are generally broad opportunities. After all, you are only a step or two from the top. There is, therefore, a real chance that your research can have influence in the organization. The challenge, however, is supervision, i.e. having your manager be able to afford you the time you will need to develop a significant question and a doable research project.

Understanding organizational culture

Okay, so you have got your head around the organization's structure, but what about its culture? And what exactly is organizational culture anyway?

Well, organizational culture is made up of things such as values, beliefs, underlying assumptions, attitudes and behaviors that characterize the workplace environment. In some ways it's like the personality of the organization. And while it can be difficult to name, it is certainly easier to feel. Workplace culture pervades the organization and is critical to how much you enjoy your work, your workplace relationships and your work processes.

Things that can help you understand a workplace's culture include: the use of language (formal vs informal, inclusive or exclusive); dress code; decision-making processes (democratic or authoritarian); the history or 'story' of the organization; types of communication; how meetings are run; how employees keep their desk (lots of personal items or sterile); how common areas are used; levels of autonomy and accountability; dedication to customer/client service; whether employees know about each others' home lives; and attitudes towards work–life balance, etc. You get the picture.

So why is all this important to the new employee, particularly the new employee charged with a small-scale research project? Well there are two main reasons. The first is that, if at all possible, you really you want a good 'fit'. You should be seeking congruence between personal and organizational values. When you have good fit, you are more likely to feel at ease, have greater job satisfaction, be more loyal to the organization and, in fact, feel more competent.

Furthermore, these characterizations of good fit are highly valuable when you are trying to influence the organization through research. The more you feel a part of the organization, the more likely you are to have your finger on the pulse of organizational needs. At the University of Sydney, we know that we have good organizational fit when our interns talk about their host organizations and use the word 'we' instead of 'they'. Without a doubt, this is correlated with a sense of pride over the research they have conducted, and it is even correlated with the likelihood that their research recommendations are taken up by the organization.

The second reason organizational culture is important to the potential workplace researcher is that organizational culture is where many small-scale applied research questions sit. The time you have for conducting your project is highly limited, as is your experience. You may not have the time, access to data, or experience necessary to solve large corporate issues. But organizational culture issues are a good place to cut your teeth on workplace-based research. Research projects that contribute to the understanding of organizational culture might include determining:

- the strengths and weaknesses of hot-desking;
- whether employees see a benefit in flexible hours;
- how a stress-reduction program might be received;
- why turnover of young recruits is so high;
- how to profitably support better work–life balance.

The list is virtually endless.

Knowing who the power people are

Power does not sit only in the organizational hierarchy. Power and power people are everywhere. The CEO, for example, may have formal power, but he or she who controls access to the CEO is a person who wields informal power – a person likely to be formidable in their own right! Here is a quick tip … NEVER patronize ANY administrative person … EVER. For one, patronizing anyone is poor play and mean-spirited; secondly, any attitude of superiority you display over any group of employees will certainly come back to bite you; and finally, you WILL have to navigate the political landscape, making this a very stupid thing to do. Respect of power in all forms is an important lesson to learn.

Power can come from many sources. Some of the more common types of power you are likely to come across in your workplace include:

- *Formal power* – Formal power is generally easy to identify. It is power based on position, i.e. CEO, director, supervisor, manager, etc., which is why it is sometimes referred to as *positional power*. It is also called *legitimate power* because it is power that is recognized by the organizational hierarchy.
- *Informal power* – Informal power is not based on position, but is based on an individual's attributes. In fact, informal power is independent of position so, in theory, anyone in the organization can develop informal power. Most of what follows are forms of informal power.
- *Expert power* – Expert power comes from an individual's experiences, skills and/or knowledge. These attributes become recognized and appreciated within the organization. Keep in mind that having knowledge does not in and of itself guarantee power. It is how knowledge and expertise are capitalized on that confers power.
- *Referent power* – Referent power comes when an individual is trusted and respected by others. People turn to those with referent power because they trust them to give good advice, and believe they will know how to handle difficult situations.
- *Charismatic power* – Charismatic power comes solely from personality. Individuals with charismatic power are those people that colleagues turn to because they inspire them to follow. They often have a personal magnetism and an air of confidence that draws others in.
- *Unstable power* – You won't find this on many lists, but crazy people can have a lot of power. Because they are unstable, they often get their way. Better to placate them than risk them acting irrationally or blowing up.
- *Informational power* – Informational power is where a person has power due to the information they hold, i.e. the person who knows what was done last time around. It is often short-term (the information cannot be held onto for-ever) and may not build the type of credibility associated with expert power.
- *Political power* – Political power comes from connections. It is based on an individual's ability to work with others and gain their allegiance and support.

This can involve trade-offs, i.e. 'you do this for me, and I'll do this for you', whether stated or implied, or by giving preferential treatment to those who are in a position to support you.

Keep in mind that those with formal power are the ones who can offer tangible rewards (things like bonuses, raises, promotions, time off and better work assignments) as well as tangible 'punishments' (things like negative performance reviews, demotions, being fired, lesser responsibilities). But those with informal power can also have an impact. On the positive side they can praise, appreciate, give approval, offer recognition and get in the ear of those with formal power. But on the downside, they can criticize, disapprove, isolate and even shame. And again they have the ability to get in the ear of those with formal power.

Now while it is easy to know who has formal or legitimate power, identifying those with less formal power can be very tricky. But it is well worth being astute and paying attention to who wields what.

There are several benefits to knowing who the power people are in your workplace, not the least of which is lessening the chances of putting your foot in your mouth. But it also facilitates the research process in two ways. For one, it is important to remember that small-scale applied research is always a political endeavor. If you want your research recommendations to be taken on board and for real change to come from your work, it is worth knowing who both the formal and informal power people are.

Secondly, power people are often the ones who can help you answer your research question. Those with power often have access to the data you need, or may be a good source of data in their own right as interviewees. Knowing who is an expert, knowing who holds information, knowing who is politically placed and knowing who knows everyone can help you determine who is best situated to offer you the data you need to answer your research question.

I'd like to put a word in here about networking. One of the best ways to figure out what's what and who's who is by making connections. Yes, you can study the organization but, better still, work to become a part of its nexus. Box 2.4 offers some excellent networking strategies.

BOX 2.4

Networking

Networking, put simply, is making connections with others within your organization and the industry (and beyond if you desire). You can do this casually after meetings, during conferences, company dinners and events. How? Well, first by showing up. Volunteer to

(Continued)

(Continued)

help organize larger events if possible. Once there, have a couple of introduction lines ready – who you are, what you do, etc. If you have not yet started your job placement, consider practicing the art of networking by attending university events, doing volunteer work, or even joining Toastmasters.

Notice that while networking should not be a relentless campaign of self-promotion, you do need to present yourself as professional and capable. 'Well,' you think, 'this will be a short conversation then. I've been at the company for all of 5 minutes.' Perfect! Have you ever heard the saying that 'everyone's favourite word is their own name'? It's true. What do people love talking about more than anything? Themselves! Use this knowledge to ask people about themselves.

Ask people how they got where they are in their professional lives. Odds are, it wasn't a linear path to greatness (which is encouraging for us mortals), but even if it was, that's fine too (take notes). Most people have pretty interesting stories: a consultant may have started out his professional life as a musician, another may have done a work in a remote corner of the globe, a third may be helping a non-profit organization craft their business plan. There is usually a wealth of knowledge with you in the room. However, the bigger the company, the more likely it is to suffer from a lack of coordination across departments as people simply do not know each other.

You can break down these barriers by meeting people and helping them meet each other. 'Oh, you need help with that graph? Stacy in Finance is a whiz with Excel macros.' Connections build a community. The most successful networkers recognize this and try to give as much as they receive. They also realize that you need to network before you actually need it (i.e. before you ask someone else for help). So start building connections and start networking.

AGENDAS

What agendas are in operation? In other words, what are the underlying motives? What are yours? What are theirs? Are agendas out in the open or are they hidden agendas? Is there alignment between yours and theirs?

We all have motives for doing what we do. You have them. We have them. The organization in which you work has them. And these agendas are definitely worth thinking about. It's about being strategic. The more you've thought things through, the more you've considered what you want and what the organization can give you, as well as what the organization wants and what you can give them, the better placed you are to achieve (1) a successful workplace experience and (2) the completion of a successful workplace-based research project.

Setting your agenda

So what do you want to get from your placement? How do you want to develop? What do you want to learn? What do you want to achieve? It is definitely worth considering; it is hard to map out a plan for getting somewhere if you don't know where you want to go.

Professional development

At the University of Sydney Business School, students going into work placements are required to spell out their performance objectives related to their professional development. They are asked to think about *objectives* related to:

- *Knowledge* – What are the things that they want to *learn about* during their placement, i.e. business systems, shared values, organizational hierarchy?
- *Skills* – What are the things they want to *learn to do* while on the job, i.e. presenting powerfully, Excel skills, effective blogging, financial modeling?
- *Values* – What values do they want to develop and experience on the job, i.e. work–life balance, ethics, corporate social responsibility?

Once our students have identified these goals, we then ask them to carefully consider what achieving them will look like in the workplace. In other words, they need to articulate the *strategies* they will employ for achieving each of their goals. For example, strategies for going to meetings; talking to a mentor; taking a course.

Students are then asked about *outputs* of their efforts: in other words, the end result or tangible outcomes of the strategies they put into place to achieve their goals. This might include things like producing sections of a particular report; delivering a presentation; writing four blogs on the company's website.

Assessment criteria are also required – this is evidence that goals have been met. This sometimes can be confused with outcomes. For example, if the goal is to develop writing skills and the output is writing four blogs, then the measure of success might be getting at least three of those published. Take another example: say your goal was to improve time management. Your output might be a well-developed Gantt chart, while your assessment criteria are that your assignments and major workplace projects were all submitted on time.

Goals related to the organization

In addition to your professional development, you may also have an agenda related to the organization. For example, you may want to:

- *Launch a career* – Perhaps this is not a place you see yourself in the long-term. And that's fine. We know that today's graduates are very mobile, with career shifts being a predictable part of the work journey. Nonetheless, a workplace experience, particularly one that affords you the opportunity to do a value-add research project, can strengthen the CV and put you in a better place for exploring career options now and in the future.
- *Apply for a more permanent position* – If you are an intern, there is a pretty good chance that this is a goal. In fact, many organizations are now using

internships as a recruitment strategy. And why not? The organization gets a few weeks to a few months to have a good look at candidates to assess both their competence and their organizational fit. In a sense, you are both trying to get a feel for each other. You need to understand this and act as if you are on an extended interview. There can be huge competition for plum jobs, so yes, certainly assess organizational fit, but do so while keeping options wide open.

- *Get a promotion* – If you are undertaking a workplace-based project in your current organization, it is well worth considering how the conduct of your project can be leveraged into better job prospects (both within and outside the current workplace). We will talk about leveraging the research experience in the last chapter, but keep in mind that being strategic about how you develop and sell your expertise can impact the career journey in very positive ways.

Understanding organizational agendas

Okay, so, that's all about your agendas, but what about organizational agendas? The organization, the CEO, the department head, the line manager, the client – they all have their own agendas. And certainly, it works best when agendas of the various players are public and in-line. But that is not always the case. Agendas can be open or hidden, selfless or selfish, long-term or short-term, holistic or strategic, company-based or individually-based, strategically aligned or at odds. In short, they can be highly confusing and a political minefield.

Organizational agendas related to you

Perhaps the best place to start is understanding organizational agendas as they relate to you – and believe us, this varies. Between the two of us, we coordinate units in which undergraduates need to conduct small-scale research projects while undertaking an internship; experienced Master's students need to do a research project within their current workplace; and Executive Master's students must form working groups and conduct a research project proposed by a particular government agency. This means we work with a host of both public and private agencies, departments and small, medium and large enterprises.

What all these varied placement sites have in common is a stated commitment to student development. Placement providers claim that their goal is investing in the future workforce by offering career-related experiences that provide opportunities for emerging/developing professionals to learn about and within their industry and profession.

But what is said in theory does not always come through in practice. In practice, the agenda, or at least part of the agenda, can include:

- *Maintaining a steady unpaid workforce* – In Washington DC, for example, many of the basic tasks on Capitol Hill are intern-run. Tours of the Capitol and answering congressional and senatorial phones are often the 'bread and butter' of interns.

- *Developing a pipeline of new recruits* – This ends up being a more thorough 'interview process' for the organization that also allows productivity, making recruitment via internships a corporate benefit rather than a cost.
- *Partially replacing external consultants* – In many Master's programs, student groups are engaged to build business plans and/or engage in problem-solving – this type of 'consultancy' can be done at no cost to the organization, or for a highly discounted cost compared to the engagement of external consultants.

As you navigate the workplace and its agendas, these realities bring up challenges that need careful consideration. If the agenda is *maintaining a steady unpaid workforce*, it would be best to see your placement as both an opportunity to learn about a profession or industry as well as a place where you will be expected to make a tangible contribution. The organization will be expecting deliverables, not just your own learning.

If the agenda is *developing a pipeline of new recruits* and you are interested in a future with the organization, then it's best to work towards high-quality deliverables AND to engage in exceptional networking. In this case, it is not only what you do, but who you impress along the way.

If the agenda is *replacing external consultants*, then once again, robust deliverables are important. The real challenge here is making sure that you are clearly negotiating what your team is and is not capable of; what sits within or outside university requirements; and who owns any intellectual property coming from your research. Consultants are engaged to do research for the company, but your research is likely to belong to the university – a contradiction that needs to be negotiated.

In all of these cases (and you probably won't be surprised to hear this coming from us), the conduct of a value-add research project can be critical. Conducting a well-considered research project can find you meeting the dual mandate of rich learning and the production of valuable deliverables.

Broader organizational agendas

But what about broader organizational goals/agendas, i.e. agendas that extend beyond you and your role? Well, as someone engaged within the organization who is expected to conduct value-add research (as well as being someone who might want to enter or move up within that organization), it is well worth knowing what challenges the organization is facing. Being successful has a lot to do with being strategic; and being strategic starts with being in-the-know. Some background knowledge that will help you navigate the workplace includes understanding whether the organization is facing:

- *A period of growth, stagnation or decline* – This is essential knowledge, in fact critical knowledge. Certainly, if you are after a job/promotion, a company in a period of growth would be a good bet. Growth is also a terrific environment for research. A company in a period of growth needs to make strategic decisions about expansion, which opens up a plethora of research questions. That said, a company in a period of decline is also rife with research questions (if not rife with job opportunities). Never is the need for evidence-based decision-making greater than within an organization facing threat.

- *A period of fiscal restraint or prosperity* – If only periods of prosperity were more common these days. If the organization you are working for/with is in a time of prosperity, future job prospects are definitely better. The climate for research can also be strong since resources, both time and money, are more readily available. Unfortunately, it is more likely that it will be a time of fiscal restraint (particularly in Government). In such times, the conduct of research is important, but resources can be scant. The challenge here is designing and conducting small-scale research that may not have all the bells and whistle, but is still robust, credible and useful.

- *A period of change or stability* – They say the only thing constant is change. In a period of stability, the main agenda will be maintaining the status quo and/ or planning for future movements within and by the organization; and this can be an attractive environment to enter into. But change does not have to be a bad thing. For one, change is a reality – get used to it. Second, change often means new employment prospects. Third, it offers wide research opportunities. Restructures, for example, and how to best manage them, set the context for many research questions.

- *Challenges related to their workforce* – Human resource challenges are part of most organizations, but knowing which challenges are most pressing can help you navigate a tricky landscape AND help you target valuable research questions. Today's most common HR challenges include managing the change process; developing effective leaders/managers; developing fair compensation schemes; effective succession planning; managing an ageing workforce; recruiting skilled locals; developing effective training and development materials; increasing workforce retention; improving employee satisfaction/loyalty; promoting employee health and wellness; enriching workplace culture, etc. Knowing priorities can open up a host of well-targeted research opportunities.

- *Challenges related to competition* – Do you know who the main competitors are and what they are up to? A little bit of homework here can go a long way in helping you stand apart from your peers. If you are an intern, do not underestimate how impressed managers will be if you know the competitive landscape. In fact, this is a common theme amongst many workplace-based research projects. Conducting a well-researched competitor analysis can definitely help an organization in their decision-making processes.

- *Challenges related to a changing landscape* – Organizations often face challenges that reach outside the organization or even outside the industry. A framework that can be helpful here is PESTLE, which stands for **P**olitical, **E**nvironmental, **S**ociocultural, **T**echnological, **L**egal and **E**conomic environments. Any of these environments might be presenting management issues for the organization. For example, in the political arena the challenge might be developing a public–private partnership; an environmental concern might be a new plant's environmental impact; a sociocultural concern might be how a proposed plant shutdown will affect the local community; a technological concern might be how smartphone technology can be incorporated into customer service; a legal concern might be how new legislation is impacting the company's ability to import goods; and finally, an economic concern might be how the value of the dollar is impacting trade. Understanding the broader landscape is not only impressive, it sets you apart as a researcher ready to make a valuable contribution.

All of the above point to a need for organizations to engage in complex decision-making or decision-making where evidence can go a long way in both directing and justifying a course of action. The more you know, the more prepared you are, the better placed you are to add value to the organization.

Bringing the two sets of agendas together

A wise goal here is strategic alignment of personal and organizational agendas. In fact, at the University of Sydney, the performance objective framework discussed earlier in this chapter is not just a framework that students use to map out their own agendas and goals. It is actually a negotiation tool. There is a requirement that students seek feedback and sign off on these objectives with their placement supervisor. The idea here is to put development agendas on the table so that expectations can be clarified and any discrepancies brought into alignment.

This can only happen when you can articulate your own agenda and at least be somewhat aware of theirs. Do the work. Thoughtfully consider your goals and do the study required to have insights into your organization, then begin to think strategically about alignment. How can you develop your skills, produce deliverables for the organization, help them face pressing challenges, and maybe even be offered a job?

Well, no surprise here: our answer, or at least one of them, is the design and conduct of a strategically placed small-scale applied research project. A project that will meet varied agendas and will be a win–win for all involved.

So that is the context in which you are working. Now it's time to turn to the development of that all-important research question!

CHAPTER SUMMARY

- Entering the workplace can be an intimidating experience, one that can leave you feeling like quite the imposter. Overcoming those fears and understanding the challenge of transitioning from student to employee is a part of the journey.
- In order to best navigate the workplace, you need to understand it. Getting your head around the organization's structure, its culture and its power people

is basic knowledge any employee, even one just starting out, should have. Not only does it make you less green, it can aid you in navigating the research landscape.

- Everyone has agendas – you, your boss, your co-workers. If you want to reach your goals, you need to know what they are and be mindful of how the agendas of others can impact your journey. Strategic alignment of objectives is the best way forward.
- The more you know, the better placed you are for success; not only success in the research world, but success in your career journey, whatever shape it takes.

DEVELOPING PRACTICABLE AND VALUABLE RESEARCH QUESTIONS

> ## Chapter preview
>
> Issues before questions
>
> Deciding on appropriate evidence-based questions
>
> Getting the research question on target
>
> Pitching your research question

ISSUES BEFORE QUESTIONS

When you are attempting to develop a practical and valuable research question, it pays to first have a look at what types of issues organizations face, and where you might be able to contribute.

Organizations tackle a host of issues – how to allocate resources most effectively, how to build a successful future and how to prioritize among competing demands and challenges. The good news is that issues are everywhere. Indeed, just about anyone who has ever had a job will tell you that workplaces are full of them. For example, what employee doesn't grapple with red tape, inefficiencies, ineptitude, decision-makers not in touch with what's happening on the ground, profit before service, morale and motivation? These are not limited to large multi-national corporations, but are endemic in any complex organization. Even academia is not immune! Your own frustrations are often tied to the frustrations of many – and if they can also be tied to the goals, aims, objectives and vision of the organization, community or institution in which they sit, then there is a good chance those very frustrations will have 'research' potential.

On the other side of the coin are issues that are not so much attributed to inefficiencies or inadequacies within the workplace itself, but are tied to the client groups with which you might work. Some examples here might be unsatisfied customers, communities reluctant to recycle waste, or patients trying to follow dietary guidelines. If these frustrations are widely accepted and can be linked to organizational/community goals, then they are likely to have research potential.

Organizational problems and opportunities

If we get down to it, issues are often problems, but they can be opportunities. Both are rich playgrounds for developing research questions.

Issues as problems

A world without problems … sounds good doesn't it? But if you really think about it, a world without problems would also be a world with no motivation to transform, progress or evolve. It would be stagnant. Surely there would be no need to 'progress' if there were no problems, but perhaps that simply indicates an ambivalent attitude towards change and a framing of the word 'problems' that is less than constructive.

Precisely because (1) there are so many challenges out there, (2) there is a true dedication to problem solving from global to local scales and (3) research is recognized as central for effective and informed decision-making, there is a real call for 'applied' research, or research expressly designed to contribute to solving practical problems. How then do you hone in on a problem conducive to a small-scale workplace-based research project?

Generally speaking, small-scale applied workplace-based research will see you engaged in problems, or aspects of problems, that while still important and significant, are local, grounded and practical. This research responds to real and tangible everyday needs. So whether it is in local or national government, non-government organizations, aid agencies, communities, corporations or, in fact, any workplace, if there are problems to tackle, then there is a need for research that can aid problem resolution.

Perhaps it would be helpful to conceive of problems as a gap between what is real and what is ideal or expected. Of course, 'ideal' is subjective and a matter of some judgment. You might consider some problems as the gap between organizational outcomes and the organizational mission. Where does the organization or department fall short of its ideals and broader goals? What are some of the causes and how can they be tackled? And once there is a design to tackle them, is it a good one?

One of the most woeful research gaps is one on the efficacy of existing solutions to address solutions. As Kurt Vonnegut, Jr wrote, 'A flaw in the human character is that everybody wants to build and nobody wants to do maintenance' (2000: 198).

Finally, broader societal/political problems can illuminate the workplace. For example, timely or contemporary issues, such as an ageing workforce, which intersect with organizational goals are good issues to explore. Growing political interest, sudden media coverage, or even new legal requirements may be enough to motivate a need to conduct research into a particular problem area.

Issues as opportunities

> We are continually faced with a series of great opportunities disguised as insoluble problems.
>
> John W. Gardner

Workplace-based research is not only about problems, but also about opportunities. Yes, we are drawn to problems, for it is problems that motivate change. Perhaps it would be more constructive to see problems as opportunities – to frame problems as potentialities. Problems could then be more than just dilemmas, impediments and obstacles – problems could, in fact, be challenges that open up a world of possibility.

Opportunities abound in organizations, for there is always something that can be improved. Your research question focuses on how to make things better, EVEN if they are fine at the moment. Opportunities, for instance, could include researching how to:

- increase efficiency (processes, systems, etc.);
- improve safety;
- improve sales or marketing of a particular product or service;
- improve training for new recruits;
- boost wellness at work;
- expand the reach of the organization or its mission;
- utilize smarter technology.

These opportunities may be perfect for small-scale workplace-based research projects. Process improvement can produce rapid and visible results with even small tweaks. When done well, updating a training program or improving a tool can save countless hours or dollars.

Every day in organizations we are surrounded by events, situations and interactions that make us wonder, stop, think or become frustrated. If you see something that could be done a better way, perhaps this could be the research opportunity you've been looking for. For an example, see Box 3.1.

BOX 3.1

Seeing opportunities: Keira's story

An experience in my first week with the company helped me select my research topic. There were three 'newbies' in the same department, but we'd showed up right as the team was finishing up a big client project. Apparently someone had volunteered to do our orientation, but had gotten called away and everyone else was busy. Someone set us up in

(Continued)

(Continued)

a separate room with a pile of HR documents including the company policy handbook and a bunch of confidentiality forms and told us to look through them. And then they kind of forgot about us for about a week. Some of us got through the material quickly then just sat around and played online. It was pretty boring and wholly unproductive.

For my research question, I thought about how the intern on-boarding process could be improved to be more engaging and efficient. Clearly, depending on an employee to take time out of their week to voluntarily shepherd us was not ideal, but nor does the company really want to waste a week's worth of labour when new workers could be contributing.

As a result of my research, the company changed its orientation process! Instead of dividing interns up by department, the new process involved all of the interns together across multiple departments. I was tasked with producing a new orientation booklet, highlighting relevant policy and guidelines. I also created quizzes to test knowledge and designed a group activity for confidentiality/ethics training. Another idea I had was to collate a list of tips from previous interns. Since some of the previous interns had gone on to join the company as employees, I arranged for one of them come in to answer questions. Best of all, the new process only took 2 days instead of a week. The company saved time and money by getting their new hires on board quickly and energetically. This was more than a year ago, but I hear the program is still being used!

Perhaps you're thinking, 'Process improvement? I don't even understand the existing processes, like operating the printer!'. First, this is perfectly normal. Everyone hates the printer; in the film *Office Space* the employees celebrate their last day at work by destroying one. It is normal to doubt your ability to impact change at the beginning of your placement, but you'd be surprised how quickly you can adapt and contribute. At first, students tend to stick rigidly to the templates in their organization and double-check everything with their manager. But by the third week or so, students begin to see things slightly differently and offer suggestions about how things can be improved. When processes ossify over time, it sometimes takes just a single individual (like you) to ask 'Why?'. By critically examining processes, reports and tools, you may able to identify opportunities for improvement and, therefore, opportunities for research.

Identifying needs of the organization

A firm's basis of competition ... has changed from tangible products to intangible information.

Kuan-Tsae Huang, Yang W. Lee and Richard Y. Wang

Whether you are looking at problems or opportunities, it's really all about *need*. Your workplace-based research project should take into consideration the needs of the organization (or by extension its customers, clients and constituents).

For example, say your insights suggest that there is a problem – perhaps a sense of dissatisfaction coming from a particular group or from within an organization. It may be worth undertaking a preliminary investigation that can identify the problem or problems from the perspectives of the group. In fact, uncovering these perspectives might end up being a major research question in its own right.

Identifying problems and opportunities might also come from annual reports, media coverage, or listening to stakeholders at various forums including workplace meetings or customer forums. In short, listening to, and identifying, the needs of stakeholders is paramount.

A good strategy here is to undertake a quick stakeholder analysis. This generally includes:

- Identifying the scope, extent, or number of people/organizations likely to be: (1) adversely affected by a problem situation; (2) causal to a problem situation; and (3) involved in potential problem alleviation. For example, if the organization needed to close a lead smelter operating near a residential area due to community protests, stakeholders would include representatives from the parent company and the smelter, employees and local residents, as well as the health department, local government authority, the Environmental Protection Authority, etc.
- Finding out whether, how and why the problem at hand is seen as an issue or priority issue by the various stakeholder groups identified above.
- Recognizing that even within various stakeholder groups there can be a diversity of attitudes and opinions.

The same could be said of opportunities. Say, for example, that the organization wanted to launch a new product. Your stakeholder analysis would include potential consumers, product developers and testers, consumer groups, management, retailers and, depending on the product, regulators. If the product is a child's educational toy, your stakeholder analysis would also include children and their parents, educators or developmental psychologists and consumer groups.

A second strategy to hone in on organizational needs is to examine urgent and important issues.

Identifying urgent vs important issues

What happens when organizations (or individuals) are faced with multiple problems at once? Usually the noisiest problem is dealt with first, while the quieter strategic issues get sidelined. You've probably experienced this. We assure ourselves that important issues in our life will receive due attention 'after this next project is finished', or 'as soon as exams/tax season/the holidays are over'. Companies do the same. Managers even commandeer technological jargon into rationalizing these choices: 'Our team just doesn't have the bandwidth right now.'

In his best-selling time-management handbook *The 7 Habits of Highly Effective People*, Stephen Covey (1989) explains why in our professional and personal lives we tend to prioritize the urgent over the important. Urgent matters are those that solicit and demand our immediate reaction and, certainly, these are appropriate for small-scale applied workplace-based research. But important issues are ones that deal with long-term value – they contribute to the growth, value and mission of the organization and/or individual and are also worth research consideration.

Now by their very nature, urgent issues are aggressively pressing, highly visible and even annoyingly auditory. In short, they are a 'ringing telephone'. Ringing phones are disruptive and hard to ignore, even if you are in the middle of something important. Covey's metaphor is even more apt now that we carry our phones with us literally everywhere we go.

The ringing phone can compel people to disrupt an interview or first date, ignore their partner on holiday, or even enrage a whole audience of movie-goers. There is a reason that film previews now have an announcement to turn off your phone rather than put it on vibrate or silent. If we realize it is ringing, we are drawn to it like a moth to a flame. We've even heard of a wedding where the minister answered his phone in the middle of performing the ceremony!

It appears to be impossible for some people to overcome the allure of the ringing phone, buzzing text message or (ding!) email notification. It is the same with urgent activities. At work, the ringing phone is combined with the bottomless email inbox, a veritable to-do list of the trivial and the impossible as others seek to prioritize our time for us. No one ever got an award for keeping their email inbox clear, much less a promotion. Rather, successful individuals (and organizations) find a way to balance priorities between urgent issues and important long-term issues.

To identify organizational needs, and consequently research questions, it may be worth asking what is not only urgent, but also important. You could be ideally placed to pick up that important issue or initiative that has been languishing on the shelf and move it a few metres down the field. What might some of these important issues look like? They are usually masquerading as unmade decisions. What decisions are the organizations grappling with? Where are the concerns, complaints or pressure from various stakeholder groups that have kept this decision from being made? How can you contribute valuable information to assist with a resolution?

As you are undertaking a small-scale workplace-based research project, you may end up answering only one of these questions through a rigorous research process. But that is okay. Remember small-scale workplace-based research is about gathering data for evidence-based decision-making, so a rigorous contribution, even if offering only one stream of data, can be worthwhile.

Where can you contribute?

Imagination is more important than knowledge.

Albert Einstein

Whether addressing problems or taking advantage of opportunities, your job is to translate an organizational issue into a research project. So, how do you go about doing this? By knowing what is important, what's needed and how data can facilitate a solution. And by keeping in mind how your project can facilitate decision-making and improvements. In Chapter 1, we discussed how evidence-based decision-making can contribute to better policy and outcomes not just for organizations, but also for communities and individuals by:

- highlighting the urgency/importance of an issue and thus helping to secure funding and resources for a solution;
- updating policies, programs and actions so that they respond to needs, and by not creating unintended negative consequences of their own (see Box 3.2);
- enabling information-sharing among key groups within the organization, and between the organization and others (such as clients, customer groups, constituencies, etc.), which can enhance decision-making.

Findings, results and conclusions can lead to practical recommendations, genuine change, great opportunities and real problem-solving. Organizations need your insights. Yes, you! If you are just joining a new organization, you can provide the fresh eyes to see problems and opportunities in a new light. If you have been a part of the organization for a while, you may be well placed to connect the dots between problems spread across departments. Either way, you can add rigor and precision to the process of analyzing organizational needs. Your project could be the first step in a new direction, or the last piece of the puzzle that needs solving. Perhaps your small-scale applied workplace-based research project will have broader ramifications down the road that you might not even be aware of.

BOX 3.2

The Law of Unintended Consequences

Many a product, policy, program or initiative has sought to remedy a problem, only to create another one entirely. This is known as the Law of Unintended Consequences. For instance, in 1990, the Australian state of Victoria made safety helmets mandatory for all bicycle riders. The result was that the number of cyclists actually decreased, a counter-productive outcome in terms of health. Moreover, through a phenomenon known as 'risk compensation', serious injuries for the remaining cyclists actually increased as the helmet encouraged more risky behavior!

Understanding how unintended consequences happen can provide an avenue for research enquiry as you seek to modify policies or create new ones.

(Continued)

(Continued)

There are three types of unintended consequences:

- An *unexpected positive* outcome: Surprise! A drug developed to regulate X is also found to cure Y. Assuming there are more consumers with the Y problem, this could mean a surreptitious profit line. For instance, Listerine was sold as a surgical antiseptic for 40 years before it was found to be a magical cure for bad breath. Viagra, the erectile dysfunction drug, was actually developed to treat high blood pressure and heart disease. During the original clinical trial, the um, side effect was noted and then swiftly marketed. The drug now makes an estimated $1.9 billion dollars annually.
- An *unexpected negative* outcome: Oops! Perhaps the problem has been overcome, but the solution has caused a few ill effects of its own. Sticking with the pharmaceutical theme, a drug designed to help those suffering from depression may also cause side effects (listed in the smallest possible type at the bottom of the advertisement), including drowsiness, itchiness, sensitivity to sunlight, inability to control speech volume and explosive diarrhea. Sounds like you've traded one problem for many others. When these side effects are worse than the disease, we've arrived at the third type of unintended consequences.
- A *perverse* outcome: #$%! The aim has not been achieved, and the solution has compounded the problem, or spawned others far worse. In 2013 it was revealed the National Security Agency had compelled American technology manufacturers such as Apple and Cisco to create 'backdoors' in their products that the government could use to break encryption (*The Economist*, 2015). The goal was to keep Americans safe by foiling terrorist plots. Over several years of this practice, the agency did not stop a single terrorist attack, but it did endanger millions of citizens by creating a systemic vulnerability that has since been exploited by hackers and criminals.

The research potential across all three of these consequences is immense.

The important thing is to recognize that you can contribute something valuable. You don't need to be an expert, but you do need to develop a clear and well-defined research question (more on that in a bit). Once you have that, the second thing you need is confidence. Research shows that confidence is just as important as competence for success (see Box 3.3).

BOX 3.3

Speak up! Clare's story

Though I had a good idea for a research project, I kept putting off discussing it with my manager. I'm a perfectionist and I worried that the project idea wasn't yet ready, and anyway my boss was very busy – directing six new employees, running a large department and shepherding several large projects to an upcoming deadline. 'He doesn't have time for this right now,' I rationalized. 'I don't want to be a bother.' I then watched six weeks sail past! Disappointed that I wasn't really contributing full value to the organization, I finally decided to write my boss a brief email with my idea, and the types of data and reports I would need access to. I fully expected to be dismissed as 'demanding' but to my relief and surprise, I received an enthusiastic reply shortly thereafter. In the subsequent meeting with my boss I received access to the data that I needed to finish the project, and congratulations from my boss on my idea. My advice? Have confidence. Speak up!

Be confident in your intelligence, your problem-solving skills and your ability to rise to the challenge. This is especially true if you are new to the environment. If you are particularly green (see Chapter 2), it is natural to feel a little out of your depth at first. Just remember that every competent and confident professional you see started out exactly where you are.

Just because you are new to research doesn't mean you aren't capable of doing it. Sure it would be easy to say 'Um, actually, I've never done that, I'm really not sure …', and politely suggest a more experienced individual, but why not give it a go! After all, you learn by doing. Project proposals can be reviewed by a manager and revised before they are final. The organization will likely not fold if your research is not PhD level. Don't conflate inexperience with incapability. We are talking about small-scale applied workplace-based research; if something is carefully considered and appropriately managed, it is well within your scope.

DECIDING ON APPROPRIATE EVIDENCE-BASED QUESTIONS

Now you may be thinking, 'I have a pretty good idea about what I want to research. Is working on my actual question so important?'. Well, the answer is an unequivocal 'Yes'. Some people want to jump right into their research project without taking the time to really think through and develop their research question. Some have ideas about their topic, but they are not clear on the aspects they want to explore. Others will have their ideas pretty much narrowed down, but have not clearly articulated this in a researchable question. We are real sticklers for good research questions. Why? Because they are absolutely fundamental to good research; and your ability to articulate one is essential. After all, how will you know when you have found the answer to your question if you can't say what your question is?

Remember: research is a decision-making journey. The process, in fact, demands that you constantly engage in decision-making that is logical, consistent and coherent. And what do you think is the benchmark for logical, consistent and coherent decision-making? It's that the choices you make take you one step closer to being able to answer your research question with credibility. So, without clear articulation of your question, you are really traveling blind.

The value of research questions

Research questions are essential because they:

- *Define an investigation* – A well-articulated research question can provide both you and your eventual readers with information about your project. It can: (1) define the topic; define the nature of the research endeavor – to discover, explore, explain, describe or compare; (2) define the questions you are interested in – what, where, how, when, why; (3) define your constructs and variables – income, age, education, gender, etc.; and (4) indicate whether you foresee a relationship between variables – impacts, increases, decreases, relationships, correlations, causes, etc.
- *Set boundaries* – Along your research journey you are likely to find yourself facing plenty of tangents, detours and diversions; and a well-defined question can help you set boundaries. When faced with an interesting tangent, ask yourself: 'What does this have to do with my question?' There are more potential answers to this question: (1) actually nothing – I will have to leave it and maybe pick it up in my next project; (2) actually it is quite relevant – if you think about it, it really does relate to ... (this can be exciting and add new dimensions to your work); and (3) well nothing really, but I actually think this is at the heart of what I want to know – perhaps I need to rethink my question.
- *Provide direction* – A well-defined, well-articulated research question will act as a blueprint for your project. It will point you towards the topic you need to explore, the information you need to review, the data you need to gather and the methods you need to call on. If you do not know what you want to know, you will not be in a position to know how to find it out.
- *Act as a frame of reference for assessing your work* – Not only does your question provide continuity and set the agenda for your entire study, but it also acts as a benchmark for assessing decision-making. The criteria for all decisions related to your project will be whether or not choices lead you closer to credible answers to your research question.

A research question is therefore crucial to putting you on the right path for your project. But does your research question need to be a simple enquiry or must it be framed as a hypothesis?

Do you need a hypothesis?

A hypothesis is basically a logical conjecture (hunch or educated guess) about the nature of relationships between two or more variables expressed in the form of a testable statement.

The role of a hypothesis is to take your research question a step further by offering a clear and concise statement of what you think you will find in relation to your variables, and what you are going to test. It is a tentative proposition that is subject to verification through subsequent investigation.

For example, let's consider the question 'Is there a relationship between office recycling habits and demographic characteristics?'. Your hunch is that age has a large impact on recycling behavior – basically, you suspect that young people put anything in the recycle bin. Here you have all the factors needed for a hypothesis: logical conjecture (your hunch); variables (recycling behaviors and age); and a relationship that can be tested (recycling behaviors depend on age). It is therefore a perfect question for a hypothesis – maybe something like 'Millennials are more likely than Gen X or Baby Boomers to put inappropriate materials in recycle bins'.

Basically, if you have a clearly defined research question – and you've got variables to explore – and you have a hunch about the relationship between those variables that can be tested, then a hypothesis is quite easy to formulate.

Now not all research questions will lend themselves to hypothesis development. For example, take the question 'How do individuals engage in decision-making processes related to office waste management?'. Remember that a hypothesis is designed to express 'relationships between variables'. This question, however, does not aim to look at variables and their relationships. The goal of this question is to uncover and describe a process, so a hypothesis would not be appropriate.

Generally, a hypothesis will NOT be appropriate if:

- you do not have a hunch or educated guess about a particular situation – your goal may be to build broad understandings;
- you do not have a set of defined variables – your goal might be to simply identify relevant variables;
- your question aims to explore the 'experience' of some phenomena – for example, what is it like to use a new technology product with English as a second language;
- your question centers on developing rich understandings of a group – for example, what it means to be a female CEO;
- your aim is to engage in, and research, the process of collaborative change, making predetermined hypotheses impractical.

In short, whether a hypothesis is appropriate for your question depends on the nature of your enquiry. If your question boils down to a 'relationship between variables', then a hypothesis can clarify your study to an extent even beyond a well-defined research question. If your question, however, does not explore such a relationship, then force fitting a hypothesis simply won't work.

Defining the research topic

All this talk about the need for an appropriate research question is fine, but what if you're not sure what to pursue? Well you're not alone. Yes, there are plenty of students who are quite clear about their topic early on, but there are also a lot of students who really struggle with the idea of generating a research topic. In fact, many feel that coming up with something worthy of research is beyond them. If you are struggling for a topic, try these three suggestions.

- *Listen* – When we are stressed, nervous, tired, or otherwise spending our entire cognitive budget on just keeping up, it can be difficult to notice anything that doesn't immediately impact us. Try to slow down and pay attention. What are the common themes of office conversation – is there a new project under way, or a long-standing problem that appears to be neglected? Could more information assist with resolving the issue? Could evidence communicated to decision-makers facilitate a resolution or improve practice?
- *Read the internal news* – Company newsletters, usually distributed through email, summarize current projects, initiatives or programs. One of them may catch your attention as a research topic, or at least identify the current priorities of the organization in which your data collection efforts could align.
- *Read/watch the external news* – Familiarize yourself with the news around your industry. Watch for how the industry or organization is portrayed in the media. Has part of their work become the focus of global attention? How might government policy or action impact on the company? By gaining a broad understanding of your organization and how it fits within the industry and broader issues you can start to connect the dots regarding what needs may be pressing or just around the corner.

For more ideas on selecting issues suitable for small-scale applied workplace-based research, see Box 3.4. If you're still having trouble, consider setting a deadline for yourself. You may find your mind works best under pressure.

BOX 3.4

Selecting issues suitable for small-scale applied workplace-based research

Below is a list of research topics that some of our students are working on and how/why these issues were selected:

- The cost-effectiveness of brand awareness strategies – selected by a marketing student in a non-profit organization.
- The inclusion of climate change risk as a factor in fire management planning – selected by a manager in the local fire station who recognized the need for currency in planning processes.

- Decision-making in a health promotion center without any evidence base – selected by the new center director who was unsure how to prioritize issues.
- Subcontractors in the construction industry with poor safety records – selected by an occupational health and safety student because of current media coverage related to the topic.
- Underutilization of experiential learning in the classroom – selected by an education student through the literature she came across in the course of her degree.
- Using decision-making frameworks to assess whether the company should invest in the Australian solar industry – selected by a dual science/business major who was placed in the investment arm of a major international research organization in China.
- Adapting the proposed National Disability Insurance Scheme – selected by a student working in a traveling outpatient health care service provider regarding new proposed legislation.
- Risk products to reflect recent changes in the financial industry regulations – selected by a student in the financial industry interested in money-laundering regulations.

Practical questions

As you explore possible research topics and construct a draft research question, make sure you consider practicalities. We know the world is full of problems, but not all of these problems can be solved through research, and fewer still can be solved through short-term, relatively small-scale research projects. For example, the threat of a major currency fluctuation is a real problem for your financial firm, but it's not a problem likely to be solved through the conduct of a small-scale research study with a limited budget. Or say the problem you have identified is a particular manager who is a real work bully! In this case, not only do you have to think about how a research study might or might not inform/help alleviate the problem, but how you might be able to do such research and keep your job at the same time! Now this is not to say that a problem needs to be politically judicious to be researchable. It does, however, highlight the fact that before you decide to research any particular problem, you need to be prepared to carefully consider and sensitively manage political (and financial) realities.

No matter how interesting a topic appears, in the end your project must be 'doable'. Now doability is something we will talk about quite extensively when we look at the potential methods you might use to carry out your study, but even at the point of topic identification it is worth keeping practicalities like appropriateness, supervision and funding requirements in mind:

- *Appropriateness* – There are many students who come up with ideas that are not relevant to the organization they work within, nor relevant to their degree training. What if you're a marketing student who wanted to undertake a research project on financial risk modeling? This may be the time to sit down and really think about your research, academic and career goals … and seek alignment.

- *Organizational support* – If an employer has given you a research area, you may not be able to shift topics. Even within a defined project, however, there can be scope to concentrate on particular aspects or bring a fresh perspective to an issue. Open negotiation and even a 'sales pitch' covering the relevance and potential benefits of your proposed research can give you more creative potential.

- *Academic supervision* – If your research project requires an academic component or is part of an academic program, remember that you may need to seek and secure supervisory support within your university. Finding out whether appropriate supervision for your topic is available before you lock yourself into a project is well advised.

As you select organizational problems and opportunities as research questions, consider the practicalities around the topic. The research question must be a good fit between you, the organization and the resources (including time!) available.

Politically relevant questions

In Chapter 1, we broached the requirement of political relevance. Your research question should be interesting, useful and relevant to the organization. It should speak to an organizational need and build on institutional support from managers, decision-makers and colleagues. Sounds simple, right?

But problems are amazingly complex things. What might appear straightforward at first glance can have a plethora of complexity hidden right below the surface. One level of complexity that you must remain sensitive to is the political landscape. The political landscape is a set of formal and informal hierarchies that describe power and influence within an organization. It's shaped by the size of the organization, whether resources are equitably distributed throughout it, and the personality of key leaders.

This landscape can be thought of like tectonic plates, generally stable but occasionally cataclysmic. You need to be aware of this political landscape and its shifts in the course of your research project. Say that you have started work in a department in which your supervisor has announced that cost-cutting is a priority. You notice some inefficiencies that could be rectified and save the company money so you decide to direct your research effort in that area. A short while later, your supervisor announces she is leaving the company. Should you tweak your research focus simply because the political landscape has changed? The answer may be 'Yes'. If the cost-cutting measure was a personal initiative of your supervisor (and not the broader department or organization) and he/she is the only one with access to the data you require to finish it, or if the successor has different priorities, then you may need to tweak your focus. Why? Because your question is now not as politically relevant.

To be politically relevant, the question should have key decision-makers on-board and even anticipating your results. This involves cultivating and leveraging individual relationships, which can sometimes change. Using the above example, say your supervisor is leaving the department because she has been promoted within the company. Do you still need to redirect your focus? Well, that's a different story. Your supervisor may likely still be very supportive of your project (and thus still able to provide you with resources you require). Moreover, as supervisors/department managers sometimes contribute to hiring their replacement, they may be able to pass along their support of your project to the new manager. If anything, your manager's promotion may make your work even more politically salient, as she is now closer to more powerful decision-makers. For an example of the political landscape in action, see James's story (Box 3.5).

BOX 3.5

A shifting landscape: James's story

I was just a few weeks into my placement when I noticed people in my department behaving strangely. Once open doors were now constantly closed, and colleagues talked in hushed whispers. My boss, the manager, was especially preoccupied, out of the office frequently and then on the phone the rest of the time. What was going on?

Eventually I was told that the manager was moving to another position in another company. The manager left the next day. I was surprised what an impact it made in the office. Apparently his departure was unexpected and it would take a while to find someone else. My research basically stopped. The department was too busy to deal with me and since I was so new, I felt my questions were more of a hindrance than a help.

I had made an effort to make contact with individuals in other departments as part of my research proposal and with their help I was transferred to another department. Looking back, it was the right thing to do. I was able to contribute in the new department without being a burden in a very stressful time.

GETTING THE RESEARCH QUESTION ON TARGET

While expansive questions can be the focus of good research for PhD-level work, there simply isn't time for ambiguous and unwieldy research questions in small-scale applied workplace-based research projects. Being precise makes the research task easier to accomplish within the allotted timeframe. A narrow scope tends to be the number one difference between getting it done on time or not getting the project done at all!

Narrowing the focus

Typically, research questions start out big and need to be wrangled into something manageable. The first step is to clarify your own thoughts through some structured analysis. For narrowing in, try using the four-step question generation process outlined below.

Four-step question generation process

1. Using only one- or two-word responses, write down the answers to the following questions:

    a) What is your topic? That is, client satisfaction, legislative requirements, profit, triple bottom line, etc.

    b) What is the context for your research? That is, a for-profit corporation, non-profit, government office, community body, local authority, etc.

    c) What do you want to achieve? That is, to discover, to describe, to change, to explore, to explain, to develop, to understand …

    d) What is the nature of your question? That is, a who, what, where, how, when, or why question.

    e) Are there any potential relationships you want to explore? That is, impacts, increases, decreases, relationships, correlations, causes …

2. Starting with the nature of the question, i.e. who, what, where, how, when, begin to piece together the answers generated in step 1 until you feel comfortable with the eventual question or questions.

    a) Topic: promotions. Context: HR department of a large organization. Goal: to discover trends in promotion history. Nature of the question: who and what. Relationship: correlation between individuals who get promoted and the results of their previous evaluations.

    b) Question: What is the relationship between employees who get promoted and their evaluation assessments?

    c) Topic: promotions. Context: HR department of a large organization. Goal: to understand how promotion determinations are made. Nature of the question: how. Relationship: none.

    d) Question: How do managers engage in decision-making processes related to employee promotions?

    e) Topic: promotions. Context: HR department of a large organization. Goal: to determine promotion factors aside from evaluation results. Nature of the question: what and why. Relationship: correlation between promotions and a range of factors.

    f) Question: What factors in addition to evaluation results play a significant role in promotion determination?

3. If you have developed more than one question (remember: any one problem can lead to a multitude of research questions), decide on your main question based on interest and practicalities as well as the advice of your supervisor and manager.

4. Narrow and clarify until your question is as concise and well-articulated as possible. Remember: the first articulation of any research question is unlikely to be as clear, helpful and unambiguous as the third, fourth or even fifth attempt.

This generation process should go a long way in helping you define a solid research question. But getting there can be a process.

Assessing your research question

A good question is one that works for you, given your interests, resources and time available. This means doing your due diligence first to ascertain if there is a need, support for and resources accessible to address the problem. You might informally broach the topic with your colleagues and supervisor; see if there's been any other work done in the company that could inform your question. When assessing your research question, ask yourself the following questions.

Is the question right for me?

Common wisdom suggests that setting a realistic research plan involves assessing (1) your level of commitment and (2) the hours you think you will need to dedicate to the task – then doubling both. It is very easy to lose motivation or get distracted with other responsibilities and you are likely to need a genuine interest to stay on track. On the flip side, questions that can truly sustain your interest are usually the ones that best bring out your biases and subjectivities. You may want to give careful consideration to any questions where you know you have an axe to grind. Deep-seated prejudices do not generally lend themselves to credible research.

Is the question right for the organization?

Research questions need to be aligned with organizational needs. An early task in the research process is to be able to clearly articulate a rationale for your study that outlines this connection. You need to be able to articulate why the research question is important, and how the findings might lead to improvements for the organization (or by extension its customers, clients, constituents, etc.).

Is the question well articulated?

A research question should be as clear and specific as possible. This is extremely important in workplace-based research whereby timeframes are short. Say you have an interest in big data, including financial metrics and survey results, and you've noticed what you think is the beginning of a trend. Instead of asking 'Why are profits falling in the third quarter?', try to be more specific – identify a particular product or service that is underperforming. You could examine more closely its targeted customer group, or identify what unsatisfied customers have in common. By narrowing the focus to 'Why are X customer groups leaving Y product?' you can contribute to a targeted resolution.

Is the question doable?

Perhaps the main criterion of any good research question is that you will be able to undertake the research necessary to answer the question. Now that may sound incredibly obvious, but there are many questions that cannot be answered through the research process. Take, for example, the question, 'Do romantic feelings for a manager negatively impact an intern's productivity?'. Not researchable. For one, how do you define romantic feelings? And even if you could define them, you would need to find a way to measure them – not things to which many will want to admit. And even if you could do that, you are left with the dilemma of correlating romantic feelings to productivity. It is an interesting question, but not easily researchable.

Other questions might be researchable in theory, but not in practice. Small-scale applied workplace-based projects are often constrained by:

- a lack of time;
- a lack of expertise;
- a lack of access;
- a lack of funds.

Making sure your question is feasible and that it can lead to a completed project is worth doing early. Nothing is worse than realizing your project is not doable after investing a large amount of time and energy.

Does the question get the tick of approval from those in the know?

When it comes to articulating the final question it makes sense to ask the advice of those who know and do work or research in the area. Most supervisors have a wealth of research and supervisory experience, and generally know what questions are 'researchable' and what questions are likely to be valuable to the organization. Run your question past your academic supervisor, your organizational manager, senior colleagues and any 'experts' you may know.

Once you have an idea for a research question, it pays to run it through the Good Question checklist (Box 3.6).

BOX 3.6

The Good Question checklist

Is the question right for me?

- Will the question hold my interest?
- Can I manage any potential biases/subjectivities I may have?

- Is the question right for the organization?
- Will the findings be considered useful for the organization?
- Does it have the ability to effect change?
- Is the question well articulated?
- Are the terms well defined?
- Are there any unchecked assumptions?
- Is the question doable?
- Can information be collected in an attempt to answer the question?
- Do I have the skills and expertise necessary to access this information? If not, can the skills be developed?
- Will I be able to get it all done within my time constraints?
- Are there any potential ethics problems?
- Does the question get the tick of approval from those in the know?
- Does my supervisor/manager think I am on the right track?
- Do 'experts' in the field think my question is relevant/important/doable?

So you now have the perfect research question; it meets the criteria and you feel you're ready to go. Let's set it in stone. Well maybe not – research questions can, and often do, evolve during the early stages of a project; and not only is this fine, it is actually appropriate as your engagement in the research process evolves both your knowledge and thinking. As you get started on your research, you may come across any number of factors that can lead you to query your aims and objectives, modify your question or even find new questions. The challenge is assessing whether these factors are sending you off the track, or whether they represent developments and refinements that are positive for your work. With workplace-based research, above all, you must be mindful of timeframes. At a certain point, changing the direction of your question is no longer possible, without jeopardizing your chance of finishing your project.

When you're satisfied that you're on the right track with your research question, the next step is getting the organization on board.

PITCHING YOUR RESEARCH QUESTION

In order to move forward and gain approval for your research project, you will need to convince the power people that this is a worthwhile issue. You need to sell your idea, and sell yourself as the right person to implement it. And this might sound a bit uncomfortable.

In *To Sell Is Human*, business author Daniel Pink (2012) identifies three common conceptions of sales:

> To the smart set, sales is an endeavor that requires little intellectual weight – a task for slick glad-handers who skate through life on a shoe-shine and smile. To others it's the province of dodgy characters doing

slippery things – a realm where trickery and deceit get the speaking parts while honesty and fairness watch mutely from the rafters. Still others view it as the white-collar equivalent of cleaning toilets – necessary perhaps, but unpleasant and even a bit unclean. (p. 2)

I certainly felt this way when I first started working. One early pep talk involved the memorable phrase, 'After all, more than 90% of jobs are in sales!'. At the time, I silently wretched, thought 'Not the most interesting jobs!' and aimed to find the elusive 10% within a year. I didn't realize that my boss wasn't referring to *my* conception of sales, which was limited to cheesy car-sale commercials. He meant sales in the form of persuasion, negotiating and exchanging time or money for value.

Selling involves traditional selling of goods and services, but also any exchange of resources. I'm selling when I apply for a job or a promotion – selling my skills as a great investment. I'm selling when I convince a friend (or five friends) to help me move; I'm negotiating for them to exchange their time for a steak dinner. In its most expansive conception, everything is selling: from pitching projects to colleagues, to persuading funders, to negotiating with rowdy toddlers (I'll exchange my time for one more story in order to have the next two hours free while you nap!).

Make no mistake, sales are absolutely necessary and positively booming in unlikely places, like education. When I convince students to part with their resources – time, effort, their smartphones during lecture time – I am selling them the value of the class and its content. Likewise, you'll need to convince your boss (and relevant stakeholders) that they should part with their resources as well. How do you do this? After gathering information on the problem, its urgent or important nature, and possible avenues to research its resolution, you'll need to pitch your idea for the project.

Constructing the elevator pitch

The Otis Elevator Company carries the equivalent of the world's population in its elevators every five days. But even Otis would be surprised to know that his machine carries the potential for real change. What other part of your regular work day gives rise to the opportunity to present your case to those compelled to listen by sheer physical entrapment? Yes, the 'elevator pitch' or 'elevator speech' has long been touted as an opportunity to connect, network and communicate your idea to a host of influential people – all of whom are too lazy to take the stairs.

Now it's more common to hear of the 'elevator pitch' as a concise summary of your value proposition that should take no more time than a theoretical ride with Otis, but it's also perfect for selling ideas.

How you present it is flexible and personal, and completely up to you. Of course, remember timing is important – an elevator pitch shouldn't take more than two minutes. You may need to time yourself. Better yet, pitch it first to your friends, relatives, roommate and your goldfish. There's no set framework for an elevator pitch, but the STAR and SWOT method may be useful in helping you get started.

Using the STAR method

The STAR method is a common business analysis tool. STAR stands for:

S – Situation

T – Task

A – Action

R – Result

This method is commonly used as an interview response technique. A typical interview question is to describe an example of a challenge you overcame in a team project. The STAR method can help you frame your response: 'In the middle of a large group project last year, a group member became extremely ill and was hospitalized with pneumonia (Situation). We had to figure out how to deliver the project, due the following week while missing an important contributor (Task). I approached our manager with a request to borrow a member from another team, while I negotiated a brief extension with the client, and a team member obtained some crucial details from our colleague during his recovery (Actions). As a result, we were able to deliver the project on budget for the client with only a very minimal delay (Result).'

With a bit of tweaking, this framework can be applied to your elevator pitch. Think of the Situation as the problem the organization is facing, the Task is what you've done to look into it so far, the Action is the proposed research project to investigate fully, and the Result is the ways in which you think the research will add value to the company.

For example, say you work in a consulting firm and you notice that client reports feature only basic graphs and charts of the line and bar variety. You think that this diminishes from the hard work that went into the report and makes the findings seem less compelling and memorable overall. You pull some reports from your competitors that are available online and confirm your suspicions that they are moving ahead with more powerful visualizations. Using the STAR method, what would your pitch look like? The Situation is that the company reports are falling behind their competitors in using outdated and basic presentation of findings in the report. The Task is that you've compared the last few reports going out to clients with the samples available online from your two main competitors and found they are blazing ahead with best practice in data visualizations. The Action you propose is to overcome lost ground by conducting a research project on how to skill up some employees in the new techniques. The Result will be knowledge for creating a catchy document to be used to attract new business through advertising.

Using the SWOT method

The SWOT technique was developed by the Stanford Research Institute as part of a research project on why corporate planning fails. It is one of the most widely

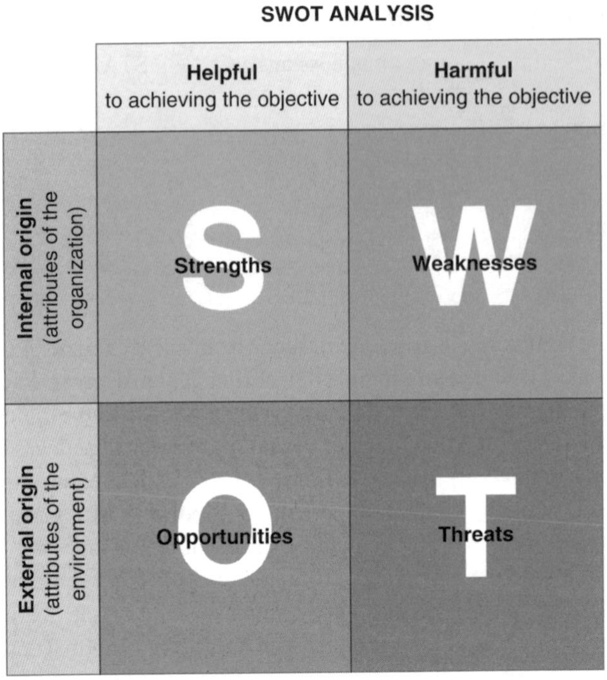

SWOT ANALYSIS

Figure 3.1   SWOT analysis framework

used business analysis frameworks. As illustrated in Figure 3.1, SWOT stands for Strengths, Weaknesses, Opportunities and Threats.

This framework can be utilized in myriad ways. Say a company is trying to choose between three options for its flagship store. For each location, a SWOT analysis would be conducted and then compared. Strengths for one location could be the high visibility on a major city street, Weaknesses could be expensive rent and a lack of parking for customers, Opportunities would be the presence of wealthy foot-traffic customers in a high density area, Threats could be the competition for city retail spots so rents could escalate quickly in the location.

US President John F. Kennedy once said, 'There are risks and costs to a program of action, but they are far less than the long-range risks and costs of comfortable inaction'. Pitching a SWOT analysis can help you make this type of argument. For an example of how SWOT can be used in developing a pitch see Box 3.7.

BOX 3.7

Pitching with SWOT: Max's story

I work in a large multinational corporation which suffers from an email overload problem, a common affliction. Every company announcement, update or policy change is communicated by email, but the volume has grown with the size of the company. Now email policy updates border on the overwhelming. A recent attempt has been made to summarize developments on a weekly basis in the form of a newsletter to cut down on the sheer number of announcements, but these emails are also usually relegated to the 'trash bin' – unread. I decided to research whether there is a better way to distribute new policy updates, rather than email.

To create an elevator pitch, I gathered a couple of examples about mishaps when policies weren't followed – policy updates not received/read were linked to a poor outcome for a particular client, group, or employee. This was a Weakness that threatened to erode the company's Strength (our organization's high safety record). I then pitched my research (Opportunity) by pointing out the continued vulnerability of miscommunication (Threat). The framework helped organize my pitch and present it to decision-makers.

Wading into the political stream

The pitch is the first step in wading into the political stream. In order to get support and resources (including access) to answer your research question, you will likely need to pitch to several different individuals, perhaps in different departments. Start with those in nearest proximity first – your own supervisor, colleagues and manager. These people will likely suggest others who would be interested, helpful or necessary in supporting your project. Think of this process as forming broader and broader concentric circles around you and your research project. The wider the circles you have, the more potential access, support and resources you may be able to call on when things get tough.

Cultivating a multi-stakeholder and organizational perspective

> If there is any one secret of success, it is in the ability to get the other person's point of view and see things from his angle as well as your own.
>
> Henry Ford

In order for your elevator pitch to be persuasive and politically relevant, try to cultivate a multi-stakeholder perspective. The easiest way to conceptualize what that means is to envision its opposite. What is the opposite? One that is focused on *you*, exclusively. You may have heard of Dale Carnegie's book, *How to Win Friends and Influence People*. It's still a bestselling text 80 years after its first publication in 1936, truly unprecedented for a self-help book. Why is it still relevant despite the fact that it was written during the Great Depression? Because it teaches people how to sell by solving problems from the other person's perspective.

If you are considering beginning your elevator pitch with any combination of 'I need to do a project on', 'I am interested in' or 'I think we should …' stop right there. If you want people to approve, sign off on, fund, or otherwise take an interest in your idea, you need to approach it from their perspective. What are their needs, interests and priorities? You need to consider the perspective of the department or the larger company. Once you have an idea, try putting it into different frameworks to see its various sellable angles. You can increase the persuasiveness of your pitch by cultivating a multi-stakeholder perspective and accentuating the benefits to others of your research.

Using the example from the STAR analytical framework, say you would like to research a few training programs that will upskill company employees in new data visualization techniques using open-source technology. You've broached the topic with your manager and the head of several departments and there is enthusiasm for the idea. What could a multi-stakeholder pitch look like?

First, consider organizational goals – to deliver high-quality and cost-effective client consulting reports. High quality visuals would help facilitate this goal but you need to be specific about how this is beneficial to different departments. One strategy is to identify influential groups in the company – typically this is sales (or client facing) and finance. Depending on the type of company, this may also include IT or others. Make sure your proposal meets departmental needs, to increase sales and decrease costs, respectively. For the sales team, you could get their buy-in that high-quality visuals would be a value-add to client reports and a marketing tool to sell more services. For finance, you need to prove cost-effectiveness. The final benefit is the employees themselves; data visualization is a growing market demand and being an organization on the cutting edge could help retain talent. By utilizing a multi-stakeholder perspective, you can get buy-in from various influential groups as well as the decision-makers themselves.

CHAPTER SUMMARY

- Organizational issues can be divided into problems and opportunities, but whichever you pursue, both must respond to an organizational need.
- For a research question to be useful to an organization it must to be practical and politically relevant.
- A good question is one that works for you, given your interests, resources and available time.
- One of the most important parts of your research project is selling it! An elevator pitch is essential for garnering support and resources to address your research question.

DOING THE PREP

Chapter preview

Reading for research

Developing a research plan

Crafting a research proposal

Integrity in the production of knowledge

Once armed with a 'researchable' question, the next stage in the research journey is to work on and develop your *game plan*. There are three distinct stages to the development of this plan. The first is reading. Reading for research is essential. Knowledge builds, and it is virtually impossible for researchers to work towards the utilization of data if they don't have a good handle on what's currently out there.

The second stage is to develop your *methodological design*. This is the 'how' section of your research plan; how you will move from questions to answers, how you will collect your data and how you will analyze that data. It is the nuts and bolts of who, where, when, how and what.

The final stage in developing your game plan is the formal write-up of the plan itself, also known as the *research proposal*. Now when it comes to small-scale applied workplace-based research, very few projects get off the ground without some sort of approval. It may be as simple as verbal approval from your employer and/or academic supervisor. But it might also require a more formal approval process gained through an ethics committee, a corporate executive board, or a funding body. In all of these situations, clear articulation of your plan will be necessary in order for you to sell your project. Specifically, you will need to articulate: (1) what you are trying to find out; (2) why finding it out is useful for the organization; and (3) how you plan to find it out. And the best way to start this process is by reading.

READING FOR RESEARCH

> Reading is a means of thinking with another person's mind; it forces you
> to stretch your own.
>
> Charles Scribner, Jr

Reading acts to both ground and expand your thinking. Reading can help generate ideas, it can be significant in the process of question formation and it is
instrumental in the process of research design. It is also crucial in supporting
the writing process. A clear rationale supported by literature is essential, while
a well-constructed literature review is often a prerequisite in research proposals
and research accounts.

There is really no way around it – reading is an essential part of the research
process. Why? Because you cannot really engage in research from a platform of
ignorance. Research is about responsibility. When you are conducting research
you are attempting to produce knowledge, knowledge that you hope others will
learn from, act on and use toward improvement. The production of new knowledge is fundamentally built on past knowledge. Sure, a lot of knowledge can come
from experience, but even rich experience is likely to be seen as anecdotal if it is
not set within a broader context. Reading is what gives you that broader context.
It educates, inspires and enlightens!

How unfortunate, then, that reading is often seen as an onerous task. The volume
and variety, the difficulty of finding and managing it, dealing with inconsistencies,
the need to review it, and perhaps underpinning this, your own lack of knowledge,
experience and proficiency can make working with literature somewhat daunting.
It's important to keep in mind the role of reading in the research process, and its
utility to your overall project (see Table 4.1).

As highlighted in Table 4.1, reading can help you:

- *Explore a topic* – Not many students, practitioners, or even experienced
  researchers know all they need to know about a particular topic, and reading
  can certainly help you get up to speed. This might involve delving into annual
  reports, texts and media reports, as well as journal-based research studies that
  make up an area's literature.
- *Develop a research question* – As discussed in Chapter 3, a good place to look
  for guidance on the development of your research question is in the literature.
  Popular media that covers current debates, controversy and disputes around a
  particular issue can help generate questions. Finding 'gaps', exploring questions that have not been adequately addressed, or attempting to ask questions
  within a new context are all dependent on 'reading'.
- *Articulate a rationale* – A well-articulated rationale is part and parcel of any
  research proposal, and needs to suggest why time and money should be invested in
  addressing your particular research question. In order to do this, you need to draw
  on literature that can argue the societal and scientific significance of your study.

Table 4.1 Reading for research

Question	Purpose	Reading
What do I know about this topic? How can I find out more?	Exploring a topic	Background reading for your own learning using a broad array of materials including organizational texts, media, trade journals, etc.
What should I read in order to develop an appropriate question?	Developing a research question	Need for more in-depth engagement in research literature so that questions relevant to the organization can be developed
How do I develop a convincing rationale for this study?	Articulating a rationale	Background/contextual readings that put the significance of the research in broader context; can also include media that provides stats/info on 'problems'
What frameworks, models or theory will help my study?	Informing your study with frameworks and models	Reading of contemporary and/or classic frameworks, models and theories may be directly related to the topic or may more broadly inform your analysis strategies
What do I need to read in order to apply suitable methods?	Designing methods	A review of past studies can inform your choice of method; background reading relating to the specific methods may also be necessary
What research has already been conducted in this area?	Writing a literature review	Need for critical review of research studies that have been conducted on this and similar topics – usually journal- or industry-based
Will I use any literature as 'data' that I will explore and analyze?	As a primary source of data	This would be included as part of the study's design; documents must be systematically sourced and analyzed (see Chapter 5)

- *Inform your study with frameworks and models* – There are plenty of business models out there that could assist with conceptualizing the problem and assist with solutions. Reading will help you learn how to use these tools and adapt them to your organization's needs. For some common frameworks, see Box 4.1.
- *Design methods* – Reading can support the design of methods in a number of ways. It can: (1) support learning related to relevant methods; and (2) allow you to critically evaluate, and possibly adopt, methods considered 'standard' for exploring your particular research question. To appropriately design a study, collect the data and conduct analysis, you will need to engage with

broad-ranging methods texts such as this one and books or articles focusing on particular research methods (survey design, focus groups, etc.) you plan to use.

- *Write a literature review* – A formal 'literature review' is a critical review of a body of knowledge including findings, and theoretical and methodological contributions. It reviews past research and relies on articles published in well-established research journals and is usually a distinct and required section of academic research write-up, including grant applications, research reports and journal articles. Check the requirements with your academic supervisor.

- *As a primary source of data* – We generally think of data as something we purposefully generate, i.e. transcripts from interviews or the results of surveys. But all types of literature can be used as primary sources of data. From meta-analysis of past studies, to content analysis of the media, to in-depth analysis of organizational/policy documents, literature can be used to do more than provide context, inform your study and argue the case. It can, in fact, be central to your analysis. More on this in Chapter 5.

BOX 4.1

Analysis frameworks and models for organizations

Frameworks and models are used to clarify thinking, analyze problems, compare solutions, and are useful visuals when persuading decision-makers. A few common ones are listed below, but you will no doubt discover more as you read.

BCG growth share matrix – Developed by Boston Consulting Group, this tool allows decision-makers to assess the relative strengths of their product lines. Each is assigned to one of four quadrants: Cash Cows, Stars, Question Marks and Dogs, as in Figure 4.1.

Core competencies – A core competency is a proficiency in a particular area that is not easily copied by competitors. The process of identifying the company's core competencies can help a company identify and preserve their competitive advantage.

The GE–McKinsey nine-box matrix – Developed by McKinsey to help General Electric prioritize investments in its plethora of business units. This categorization can help companies assess the relative merits of various opportunities.

Benchmarking – the process of comparing metrics. The comparison could be external, i.e. between the organization and other organizations, or between units within an organization. This helps a company establish how they are performing relative to the field.

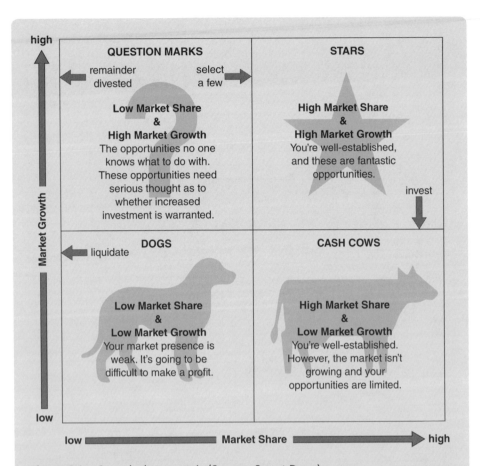

Figure 4.1   Growth share matrix (Source: Smart Draw)

Moore's strategic triangle – This model for positioning public enterprises in complex environments looks at the nexus of public value, organizational capacity and the authorizing environment.

Porter's five forces – This framework is used to identify strategic direction. It outlines the five competitive forces that influence profitability, including competitor rivalry, bargaining power of buyers and suppliers, the threat of new entrants and the threat of substitute products or services. See Figure 4.2.

Innovation adoption curve – When a product or innovation is introduced into the market, it usually takes time to diffuse and penetrate the market. Also called the Roger's model, this curve classifies customers into various categories of adoption to a new product. This strategy could be helpful when deciding which consumer groups to target next. See Figure 4.3.

(Continued)

(Continued)

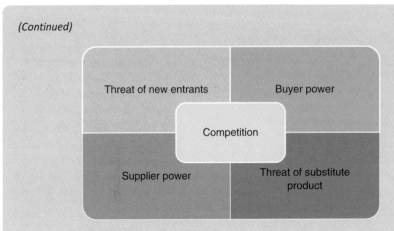

Figure 4.2   Five forces framework

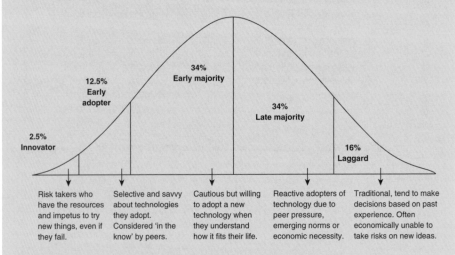

Figure 4.3   Technology innovation adoption curve

Root cause analysis – A useful framework for diagnosing problems or brainstorming ideas is the Ishikawa diagram (sometimes referred to as a 'fishbone diagram' due to its shape). The analysis tool, popularized by Kaoru Ishikawa, helps to identify specific causal factors by category including people (man or manpower), method, machines, materials, management or environment. Cause and effect diagrams such as the one illustrated by Figure 4.4 can reveal key relationships between variables, and provide insight into organizational successes and failures.

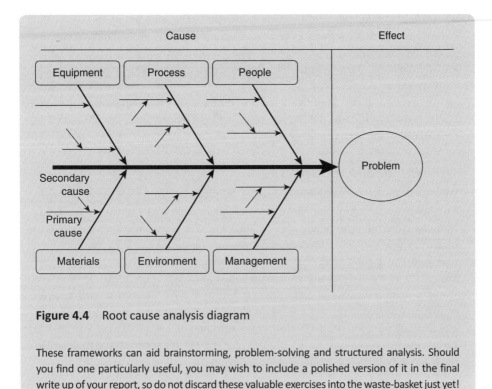

Figure 4.4 Root cause analysis diagram

These frameworks can aid brainstorming, problem-solving and structured analysis. Should you find one particularly useful, you may wish to include a polished version of it in the final write up of your report, so do not discard these valuable exercises into the waste-basket just yet!

Where to start

The good news is that there is a wealth of literature out there that could prove useful to your research project. The bad news is that there is too much of it to read it all. The challenge is finding the right balance between utility and becoming overwhelmed. The key to all research projects, but particularly for workplace-based research projects on tight timeframes, is knowing where to start and when to stop.

Some sources to consider as you begin your literature search include:

- *Organizational materials* – Annual reports, white papers, draft strategy papers, consultant reports, memos, etc.
- *Books and journal articles* – Books tend to be background readings while academic journal articles provide rigorous research accounts. This type of literature is therefore instrumental when you are getting serious about conducting research.
- *Grey literature* – This refers to both published and unpublished materials that do not have an International Standard Book Number (ISBN) or an International Standard Serial Number (ISSN), including conference papers, unpublished research theses, newspaper articles and pamphlets/brochures. Grey literature can be a good source of new ideas, recent trends and current thinking on salient topics.

- *Official publications, statistics and archives* – These materials can be a valuable source of background and contextual information, and often help shape a study's rationale.
- *Writing aids* – This includes bibliographic reference works, dictionaries, encyclopaedias and thesauruses, almanacs, yearbooks, books of quotes, etc. Such resources can offer significant support during the writing-up process, and can be used to: (1) improve the linguistic style of your work; (2) add points of interest to the text; (3) check facts.

Utilizing academic sources

Academic journals are commonly cited as *the* place to start for academic research. For those new to workplace-based research, this can be tricky territory. Academic journals are written *for* academics *by* academics. It is assumed that readers will already have expertise in the subfield including familiarity with key terminology and theoretical constructs. Further, journal articles tend to be dense and quite technical, with only passing explanation of foundational concepts. This means it might seem intimidating and impenetrable, as Calvin and Hobbs will tell you in Figure 4.5. Academic journals are a valuable resource, but going to them first can feel like jumping off the high-dive to learn how to swim! Journal articles can be fascinating and/or insightful, but the 15 minutes you spend trying to decipher the lingo may be better spent elsewhere during the early stages of your project.

Figure 4.5   Academic writing. (Calvin and Hobbes ©1993 Watterson. Reprinted with permission of UNIVERSAL)

For small-scale applied workplace-based research projects, it might be wise to start with accessible literature written by experts for a general audience. A good starting point is sources like *The Conversation* (https://theconversation.com). This website publishes short articles written by academics or other professional researchers to provide context to current headlines within their expertise. It is invaluable in getting up to speed on topical and complex issues quickly. Check out the US, UK, Australia or Africa version. You can sign up to be alerted when particular authors or articles relevant to your research topic are posted.

Once you have a grasp of the basic concepts through a general search, delve into academic research using keywords in either Google Scholar or the library database. A good tactic is to search for 'review' articles. These take a concept, strategy or theory and explore its evolution. It's a good way to get up to speed on developments without having to locate each of the five seminal pieces on the topic and read them from scratch. Expect that there will be some level of to and fro between basic searches and journal readings (theoretical and practitioner) as you explore links and delve deeper.

Academic databases may be divided by discipline, journal collection or both (see Figure 4.6). A good place to start is the 'Web of Science' or 'Web of Knowledge' databases. For business or the social sciences, the SSCI database provides references and keyword-searchable abstracts, with additional links to full text. Of particular use is the Cited Reference Search to search for articles that cite an article you have found valuable. There are a few publishers who now offer full-text versions of articles in their journals through their own website (i.e. without a library subscription). Cambridge University Press (Cambridge Journals Online) and SAGE (Highwire) are two prominent examples. Databases allow you to search within relevant journals. Now there any many databases, and as shown at the very top of Figure 4.6 you can view the databases by title. But if you do not know the names of the relevant data bases you can search by topic area. You simply click on the topic you're interested, say Econometrics and Business Statistics, and all the relevant databases that your library has access to are offered to you.

Many libraries also offer tools like CrossSearch. CrossSearch lets you search all types of material types including print and electronic books, articles, journals, multimedia, theses, newspapers, e-repositories, etc. It ranks them by relevancy and allows to you to limit your search by criteria such as year, format and language.

Academic communities are another useful source. Academia.edu or ResearchGate are the Linkedin of academia. This is a community of scholars online, most of whom regularly update their pages with current research. This is a great place to get the latest research. You can search by topic or author, and ask to be notified of current publications as they happen. Enrolment is free.

Efficiency is absolutely key to a productive academic literature search. This means being able to assess the potential utility of a journal article, book chapter or white paper quickly. If you are reading a journal article, start with the abstract or executive summary before reading the conclusion. This should give you a good sense of relevance without taking the time to read the full script. In a book, peruse the table of contents, the back cover blurb and the introduction. Also have a look at the conclusion offered at chapter ends, as well as the overall conclusion. Within a few minutes you should be able to assess whether a work is likely to be of value to your own research process.

As you get a grasp of the literature, rank the relevance of readings. One strategy is using real or virtual sticky notes. For example, if you are looking at literature related

Databases by Title
A - B - C - D - E - F - G - H - I - J - K - L - M - N - O - P - Q - R - S - T - U - V - W - X - Y - Z -
New - Trials - Alerting services - E-journals - E-books - For mobile devices

Databases by Subject

Accounting
Agricultural Science
Agricultural and Resource Economics
Agriculture – Plant Science
Ancient History
Anthropology
Arabic & Islamic Studies
Archaeology
Architecture, Design and Planning
Art History and Theory
Asian Studies – see also Chinese Studies, Japanese Studies, and Korean Studies
Australian Literature
Behavioral and Social Sciences in Health
Biochemistry and Microbiology
Biological Sciences
Business Information Systems
Business, International and Entrepreneurship
Business Law
Celtic Studies
Chemistry
Chinese Studies – English Language and Chinese Language
Classics
Commercial Law – see Business Law
Computer Science – see Information Technologies
Dentistry
Development Studies
Digital Cultures

Econometrics & Business Statistics
Economics
Education
Engineering
English Literature and Language
Environmental Science
Exercise and Sports Science
Film Studies
Finance
French
Gender and Cultural Studies
Geosciences
Germanic Studies
Government & International Relations
Hebrew, Biblical and Jewish Studies
History
History and Philosophy of Science
Human Resources – see Work and Organizational Studies
Image & online video databases
Indian Sub-Continental Studies
Indonesian Studies
Information Technologies
International Business/ Entrepreneurship
Italian
Japanese Studies
Law
Linguistics
Logistics – see Transport/ Logistics
Management – see Work and Organizational Studies
Marketing

Mathematics and Statistics
Media and Communications
Medical Humanities
Medicine
Modern Greek
Museum Studies
Music
News Services
Nursing and Midwifery
Nutrition
Occupational Therapy
Organizational Behavior
Orthoptics
Performance Studies
Pharmacy
Philosophy
Physics & Astronomy
Political Economy
Project Management
Psychology
Public Health
Religious Studies
Social Work & Policy Studies
Socio-Legal Studies
Sociology and Social Policy
Spanish
Speech Pathology
Statistics – see Mathematics and Statistics
Transport/Logistics
Urban Planning
Veterinary Science
Work and Organizational Studies

Figure 4.6   Electronic resources – databases

to three distinct concepts, you could use three different colour sticky notes, one for each concept, and then rank the overall work, or chapters within a work, with a 1 (minimally relevant), 2 (somewhat relevant) or 3 (highly relevant). It is amazing how much time this can save when you begin a more rigorous review of materials.

Finally, when you find a useful source, check its reference list. There are likely to be a few other articles of interest. Use this resource as a springboard for where to look next. For more strategies see Table 4.2.

Table 4.2 Information-seeking strategies

Strategy	Purpose	Notes
Planning	Brainstorming key terms, synonyms and search tools	Mind mapping may be useful to help generate terms here.
Reconnaissance	Exploratory research to identify key ideas, studies and the overall topic	Useful for getting a sense of possibilities and ideas for your research
Browsing	Process of searching by fairly broad subject or topic. One example is browsing the library shelves for the subject area	Useful to identify sources that will be most helpful for methodical searching
Methodical searching	Using key terms for a deliberate and highly defined search across relevant databases	Remember to keep a record of your searches so you do not duplicate efforts
Citation chaining	Using the reference list of a source to locate other relevant articles and sources	Highly useful when you locate an extremely useful/well-written source
Monitoring	Maintaining awareness of development in the topic by setting up alerts or periodically updating search perimeters to the most recent sources	Depending on the length of your small-scale workplace-based research project, you may not have much time to keep up with developments

Source: Adapted from Phelps et al. (2007: 130).

Utilizing organizational sources

What do we mean by organizational sources? These are sources that are either produced by the organization or written about the organization/industry. Some sources of information that may be useful are:

- annual reports;
- mission statements and strategy documents;
- white papers;
- consulting analysis reports on the industry;
- government reports on the industry.

Organizational sources can be divided into externally available and internal-only sources. Externally available sources are those readily accessible to those outside the organization. This includes annual reports (if the company is publicly listed, annual reports are typically legally mandated), industry analyses or some publicly available consulting reports. Consulting groups such as McKinsey and Co, Bain Consulting Group, Deloitte and others typically have great online resources regarding analysis, forecasts and background on particular industries. Government or consumer groups may also be a helpful source for research, trends and forecasting in a particular industry.

An organization also typically has a rich supply of internal sources. These are company reports, consulting documents, documents, memos, project documentation, strategy and vision papers. Department managers and supervisors may be able to point you in the right direction for this. Be careful when utilizing these sources as they may be subject to commercial in confidence, or other confidentiality protocols. These are usually fine to use for internal analysis and presentation but you may need to seek information to incorporate these into an academic deliverable (essay or report) for your university. This is particularly important for educational institutions that utilize online submission of assessments, and thus are vulnerable to the same data concerns of any online depository. The topic of confidentiality and safe data practice is discussed in more detail later in this chapter when we get to ensuring ethical research practices.

Utilizing social media sources

You might consider using Twitter as a resource to follow experts. By connecting to industry leaders and researchers, you can get a quicker grasp of the organizational environment and its issues and challenges. Best of all, you can join this elite conversation for free, and you don't even have to say a word. As a member of the 'Twitterverse' there is no obligation to publish your own tweet (in fact, perhaps you want to observe a bit before jumping right in). When you follow interesting people from your organization and the industry, you'll be surprised what sort of insights you can bring to bear upon your own research project. (Tip: Avoid following news sources for your first round of following, they quickly crowd your feed.)

Aside from organizational and industry experts, you may also wish to utilize the researcher community on Twitter. Though they are working to a different scale than your small-scale research project, PhD and postgraduate research groups offer useful tips for avoiding procrastination, finding sources and writing up. See Box 4.2 for examples of research communities and business research communities. Likewise, data visualization and big data research groups can point you in the right direction for new online tools that may be helpful for your research project deliverables (more on these in Chapter 8).

BOX 4.2

Research communities on Twitter

Within the Twitterverse is a rich community of researchers. Though the scale of their projects may be different (most are PhD students), you might find their helpful tips and sources relevant to your research project as well. Some examples are included below, but as with all things Internet, check out the latest and greatest from there.

@Thesiswhisperer	@litreviewhq	@HarvardBiz
@Write4Research	@HowToLitReview	@StanfordBiz
@PhDForum	@WriteThatPhD	@Wharton

When to stop reading

Now that we've identified the many possibilities related to reading for research, it may be tempting to try to cover them all. After all, it's good to know everything before you start, right? Well, not quite. The good news is you're not alone, many researchers struggle to know when to stop reading, but at a certain point the 'Just one more report/article/ source' mantra is unhelpful and becomes a crutch for procrastination or perfectionism. The key is to set a time limit and then move on. You will never know everything; moreover, you aren't expected to. Once you have read enough that you have a grasp of the field, additional articles offer only marginal utility. If you find yourself reading more material and thinking 'I've already heard this', you've likely examined the high points. But, of course, this is easiest to do when you are being systematic.

Being systematic

Project management is one of the most marketable skills that you will sharpen during the course of your research project. An important component of project management is documentation. Where did you get the data set that you are using? Which business strategist proved the theory that you are seeking to utilize? (Hint, it was probably Porter. As Michelangelo is to Rome, Michael Porter is to business frameworks.) Nothing is worse than looking for a lost reference that you really need. It could be a quote with a missing page number, or a fact with no citation, or a perfect point that needs to go right there – if only you could remember where you read it. If you can incorporate each of your resources into a management system you will be saving yourself a lot of future heartache.

Being able to locate an important source is time-consuming enough; don't make the mistake of having to locate something twice when managers ask for the basis of your assumptions.

Documentation management

Why is documentation important? Because you need to be able to substantiate the rigor and validity of your project. This is particularly helpful during the question and answer session of your presentation, or when you circulate your research report to management. Without proper documentation, you may run the risk of losing key support for your project (if it is seen to be based on your own opinion versus substantiated evidence).

Additionally, without careful attention to sources and documentation, you may be remiss in proper attribution. Should this research project form part of a degree program, you may put your academic qualification in jeopardy. A few years ago, the German defence minister was forced to resign after parts of his PhD were found to be plagiarized – a problem he put down to a lack of sleep and poor documentation practices (see Box 4.3 on unintentional plagiarism).

How do you go about proper documentation? First, it may be a good idea to keep a copy of sources in digital form. Establish an online folder, and name protocol for documents so that you can keep them organized and accessible. For instance, my pdfs are all named the same way: Author Year Article title (example: Hunt 2014 Has the US Gotten Over the Oil Crisis.pdf). If you find yourself doing a lot of reading, keep a list of the most relevant sources in digital form such as in an Excel spreadsheet. Include not only author, title and date, but also keywords, notes and key quotes. This will making searching for this information during the write-up so much easier. This system is especially helpful for the environmentally conscious who may not be printing out articles, those working with limited shelf space, and/or the perennially disorganized.

There are a few software options to help you manage documentation, the most popular of which are Mendeley or Endnote (these may be available for free download through your university library website). These programs are well integrated into online academic journal subscriptions so they populate some of this information for you at download. Just add keywords and you are well on your way to having a concise research reference, invaluable for small and large-scale projects. These programs also offer add-ins to Word so you can generate a reference list in the finished report in whichever reference style you desire. Alternatively, you can create your own database in Access to store bibliographic details, keep notes and even attach a copy of an annotated article pdf itself.

Staying on top of documentation helps you: (1) save time; (2) locate substantiating evidence quickly; and (3) avoid unintentional plagiarism. Tracking your bibliography in digital reference form so the references are searchable makes finding them during the write-up efficient and easy.

Avoiding plagiarism

Everything is online – and that means a finished literature review can be as close as a few 'cut and paste's away. **Don't do it!** Firstly, it is wrong: you are essentially stealing the work of others. Secondly, it can get you kicked out of your degree program. Thirdly, it simply does not lead to a good finished product. Yes, you can cut and paste and string together bits of abstracts but there will be no arguments running through it. There will be no driving message. You need to write this as a custom piece: a piece that clearly argues the need for, and relevance of, YOUR study.

So what exactly constitutes plagiarism? Plagiarism is when the words, ideas or data of another person are not cited or referenced and are therefore *passed off* as your own. This means you cannot:

- cut-and-paste ideas, phrases, paragraphs, diagrams or images without referencing the source;
- pay someone else to write for you;
- download a paper from an online source and submit it as your own;
- copy from another student's work without acknowledgment;
- change the words of someone else's original idea without referencing;
- quote from a speech or lecture without acknowledging the speaker.

Now it may seem that asking you to do original work by referring to experts may seem like a contradiction. But the key is acknowledgment – in other words, appropriate referencing. You need to be diligent and even pedantic. Find out what referencing style is recommended in your faculty and follow guidelines that can be readily found online or from your institution.

BOX 4.3

The professional consequences of plagiarism

Plagiarism can haunt you long after your university days are over. In 2011, when the German defence minister Karl-Theodor zu Guttenberg was stripped of his PhD, he blamed inadvertent plagiarism on time constraints and poor organization (*The Guardian,* 2011). In 2013, the German education minister also stepped down over charges of plagiarism (Brumfield, 2013). In 2015, a university in Sydney, Australia, revoked degrees from graduates when it was found that they had paid others to do their essay assessments two years previously (Visentin, 2015).

Copyright considerations

Another potential pitfall in working with literature is copyright. When something is copyright protected, it means that the creator of the original work has exclusive rights to it (usually for a limited period of time). You cannot copy copyrighted material unless it falls under the rules of fair dealing (as it is referred to in Commonwealth countries) or fair use (in the United States).

For example, when it comes to study and non-commercial research in Australia, under fair dealing you can copy:

- 5% or one chapter of a book;
- one article from a journal or newspaper issue;
- one paper from a set of conference proceedings;
- one case from a volume of law reports;
- short literary pieces as long as they are less than 10 pages long;
- one (hard) copy of web material (unless otherwise indicated on the site).

In producing a project with photocopied material, you are allowed to make as many copies as needed for assessment as long as there is proper acknowledgment. Fair dealing and fair use have different exclusions and rules in different countries. It is well worth checking copyright laws for your country either by checking with your institution or by googling them.

Annotating references

As you collect sources and material, it is worth developing a systematic approach to note-taking that allows for a methodical and organized review of materials from first read. Many students will read materials without such a systematic approach and later find they need to go back and re-read the material – often when they are short of time and hard pressed to meet deadlines.

A good strategy here is to keep an annotated bibliography or systematic review of your significant literature that can remind you of the relevance, accuracy and quality of sources cited (see Box 4.4). Some academic programs require this element as a first step in the small-scale workplace-based research project. Annotation does not require an onerous volume of notes to be helpful. Annotation should help capture the most relevant elements for further reference and inclusion into your literature review (if you need one) or final research write-up.

- *Author and audience* – The extremely low barriers to entry of posting literature on the Internet have increased the need to assess that literature. The Internet is full of propaganda, uninformed opinion and less than credible research. Ask yourself, who is doing the writing? What are your qualifications? Are they professionals, politicians, researchers or unknown? And who is the work for? Is it for an academic audience, general public, constituents, clients, customers? If the answers to these questions leave you feeling less than comfortable with the source, it is probably best to move on to more credible literature.

- *Summary* – How long should this be? It depends. The aim is to jot down key points that will help you research and write. You may be able to summarize a less relevant work in a sentence or two, while others will be much more instrumental to your own thinking and researching and thus require more in-depth coverage. Write what you think you will want to know later on. Do not fall into the trap of trusting your own memory. What you think you will remember today will likely be forgotten by the weekend, and certainly next week. Keep in mind that you can write annotations in any manner or style that you want: doodles, concept maps, quotes, page numbers, etc.
- *Critical appraisal* – Students generally don't have a problem summarizing information. Where they often struggle, however, is their ability to be critical. In academic reviewing, critical means informed and considered evaluation. As a potential researcher you need to be able to ask and answer the question, 'Was that work persuasive, was the evidence convincing?'. Is this work cutting edge or just a rehash? Is the method clear? Is the argument based on dated evidence or a small sample size? Consider comparing this work with others you have read. How does it sit within the general literature, i.e. compared with other sources?
- *Relevance* – This is where you try to make the connection between what others have done and what you propose to do. Is there anything in the work that turns a light bulb on in your head? Is there some flaw in the thinking/method that makes you want to explore this area/topic/question from a different angle? Is there a quote, passage or section that really gets to the heart of what you're trying to say or do? Look to be inspired. Look to be surprised. Look to be appalled. Use this section to get the creative juices flowing.

BOX 4.4

Sample annotation

Citation

O'Leary, Z. (2001) 'Conversations in the kitchen', in A. Barlett and G. Mercer (eds), *Postgraduate Research Supervision: Transforming (R)elations*. New York: Peter Lang.

Author/Audience

The author is a senior lecturer at the University of Sydney who has written a chapter in a book targeting postgraduate research students and supervisors.

(Continued)

(Continued)

Summary

This is basically an anecdote that discusses and attempts to normalize the emotion and intellectual hardship many research students can go through when trying to juggle family obligations and study.

Critical appraisal

The anecdote is quite short and written in a warm and personal style that makes it very easy to relate to. It is not, however, a research study backed up by any data/rigor and therefore does not allow one to assess the extent of the issues raised to whether the concerns she raises are widespread. That said, it does seem to relate well to the more rigorous research studies conducted by Field and Howard (2002) and Dreicker (2003).

Relevance

This relates quite well to my chapter on 'coping mechanism and strategies for managing role and workloads' and may be good for a quote or two, especially if I feel my text is too dry.

Do you need a formal literature review?

The answer is here is a firm 'maybe'. If your research report is an academic requirement, then yes, a literature review is likely to be required. But if the report is solely for the organization, then the answer is 'possibly not'. While a short review of literature might be useful, a thick academic review may not add value and can, in fact, detract from readability.

The purpose and structure of the review

You'd think that the purpose of a formal literature review would be simply to review the literature. But expectations of what a literature review is meant to achieve go far beyond a simple articulation of what previous researchers have done and found (see Table 4.3). The formal literature review is a purposeful argument that needs to:

- *Inform readers of the state of play of the field* – Not only should a research study inform readers of your particular research question, but it should also inform them of the general topic.
- *Establish researcher credibility* – The literature review allows researchers to establish credibility through a critical evaluation of relevant research works; a demonstrated understanding of key issues.
- *Argue the need for, and relevance of, their study* – The literature review sets the current study within the context of past research. The literature review has the potential to identify 'gaps' that show the appropriate and significant nature of a study's research questions.

Table 4.3   Reviewing the literature vs 'the literature review'

Self-educative reasons for reviewing the literature	What the formal 'literature review' attempts to achieve
<ul><li>Inform yourself of what is happening in the field</li><li>Form a foundation of topical and methodological knowledge and expertise</li><li>Develop skills in critical thinking/analysis</li><li>Find potential gaps in the literature that may point to potential research questions</li><li>Critically evaluate common/typical methods</li><li>Facilitate the development of your own methodological approaches</li></ul>	<ul><li>Inform your audience of what is happening in the field</li><li>Establish your credibility as a knowledgeable and capable researcher</li><li>Argue the relevance and the significance of your research question</li><li>Provide the context for your own methodological approach</li><li>Argue the relevance and appropriateness of your approach</li></ul>

A literature review is, for the most part, an overview of research studies that have been conducted by past researchers. It is a precursor to method designed to open up the space for your research. As such, it should never be included in your methods section.

If, however, you want to explore things like organizational protocols, policy documents, legislation or industry white papers in order to gather data and look for evidence, you are not conducting a literature review. If the exploration of documents is warranted as a credible research method, you are probably conducting document analysis and you need to include this in your methods section.

Once you understand purpose, the question you are likely to ask is 'What exactly needs to go into my literature review?'. The coverage will depend on the requirements of your program. A traditional full literature review should be broad enough to: inform your readers of the nature of the discourse and debate current to your topic; establish your own credibility as a researcher abreast of the field; and demonstrate the need for, and relevance of, your own research. But the depth of the general body of literature, the arguments you are trying to make and the level of the project/thesis will also determine what is both suitable and required. A one-semester undergraduate project may only demand engagement with 15 or so of the most relevant and recent articles, while a PhD thesis may require in excess of 250 or more articles and require you to dig into both theory and seminal works.

A traditional, full-coverage literature review can include:

- *Exhaustive coverage that cites all relevant literature* – This has become almost impossible in the data age.
- *Exhaustive coverage with only selective citation* – This allows you to think broadly but choose wisely.
- *Representative coverage that discusses works that typify particular areas within the literature* – In other words, know your stuff.

- *Coverage of seminal/pivotal works* – Again, a bit old school; seminal or pivotal works can be too vast to cover in one review and you run the risk of your review being dated.
- A combination of the above.

Writing a literature review

There are students who are able to pull together an impressive literature review without too much guidance. They have a sense of the task and tackle it. But this is rare. Most struggle and are looking for a clear way forward. The list below is not the only process that you can follow, but it will get you from A to B. Remember the goal is to inform, establish and argue. To do this, the following steps may be useful:

1. Make doing a literature review an on-going process – your literature review will inform your question and methods. Conversely your question and methods will help set the parameters of your literature review. This is a cyclical process. A literature review is often a moving target that evolves in both thinking and writing as your study develops.
2. Identify the elements and variables in your study and develop a list of synonyms or alternatives.
3. Use a search engine utilizing the variables and alternatives.
4. Select readings starting with the abstracts. Get rid of anything off topic and rank the remaining reading by relevance.
5. Assess whether you need to dig deeper or refocus your review. You may need to add variables or look at studies conducted in the past, say five years ago. Remember that studies do not have to directly explore your particular research question to be relevant, informative and useful.
6. Systematically log your relevant readings. Choices here are to manually construct a bibliography or use software such as ProCite, Endnote or Reference Manager.
7. Read and annotate each relevant article. As suggested earlier in the chapter, comment on author/audience, key points, critical comment and relevance.
8. Sort and organize. Look for themes, issues of concern, common shortcomings. You may find that patterns begin to emerge that can go a long way towards informing your argument.
9. Develop a potential outline for your literature review. Consider what arguments will best convince readers that you are fully engaged with the literature. Your structure can be modified as your thinking evolves, but your main argument should relate to the need for your research study to be undertaken in the way you are proposing.
10. Write purposefully, using the literature to back up your arguments. Rather than review, report or borrow the arguments of others, use the literature to help generate and then support your own arguments. That means each paragraph should make a point that is backed up by the literature. For instance:

'Within the context of climate change, the relationship between knowledge and behavioral change is contentious [the point you are trying to make]. While several studies have shown that knowledge of climate change affects behavior (Jones, 2008; Smith, 2007; Wong, 2002), a new study conducted by Burnie and Powis (2009) argues that knowledge has minimum impact on change and that practices of peers and neighbours are much more influential [the evidence that makes your point].'

11. This is a much more sophisticated approach than leading each paragraph by author, i.e. starting paragraphs with 'Jones (2008) states', 'Wong (2002) found' and 'Smith (2007) argues'.

12. Finally, as with all pieces of writing, get plenty of feedback. Whether you are a student or a professional researcher, you are not likely to get away without a draft or two (or three or four). Drafting and feedback processes will be discussed in more detail in Chapter 8.

DEVELOPING A RESEARCH PLAN

'Would you tell me, please, which way I ought to go from here?'

'That depends a good deal on where you want to get to.'

'I don't much care where –'

'Then it doesn't matter which way you go.'

Lewis Carroll, *Alice in Wonderland* (p. 27)

When it comes to a your small-scale applied workplace-based research project, it may sound incredibly obvious that your goal is to come up with a plan to either (1) answer your well-articulated research question or (2) test your skillfully constructed hypothesis. The research plan is your game plan. Without it, you are like Alice in Wonderland, wandering aimlessly.

Luckily, when you know what it is you want to know, it's generally not too hard to figure out how to get there. As discussed in Chapter 2, a well-articulated research question defines an investigation, sets boundaries, provides direction and acts as a frame of reference for assessing your work. In this way your question acts as a blueprint for decision-making related to method. So if you are still struggling to articulate your question clearly, you really need to go back and work on the question itself. Methods 'depends a good deal on where you want to get to'.

From questions to methods

Following on from the guidelines for question development covered in Chapter 2, it should be quite easy to see how and why questions point to methods. The process of question development should leave you with clear articulation of not only your topic and context, but also your goals, the nature of your question and who might hold the answer to that question.

Decision-making relating to methods is *question-driven*. A well-articulated question should lead you to: who you need to talk to; what you need to ask; and as an extension of this, what data collection methods/tools you might use. For example, imagine you want to research flexible work arrangements. You can do one of two things. You can jump in and begin to design your study – after all, you have it in your mind that you will conduct 'interviews'. Or you can really think about what you know, go through some of the more relevant literature, work on the process of narrowing and clarifying, and maybe even work through a further articulation of your question before you attack the issues of methods.

Students who go for the jump-in approach and work from a topic rather than a question can really struggle. They often end up getting lost and confused. Things take a long time to fall into place (and sometimes never do!) and students can end up with data they don't know how to use. Unfortunately, trying to retrofit a question to your data is not easy – it rarely works!

On the other hand, suppose you have been able to narrow your question. Because you know what you want to know, deciding on the methods is only a small logical step away. For example, you can consider whether you want to get the perspective of other stakeholders. This then clearly points you to both the population and sample you need to target for your data collection.

You can then consider the scale of research that best fits your timeframe – perhaps conducting interviews or a focus group will draw out richer descriptions. You might also consider less obtrusive measures, like observation. No matter what the case, familiarity with the expectations related to methodology, as well as clarity and precision in your question, can readily lead to a range of methods that can be explored and considered on the basis of both their logic and practicality.

For example, say you were interested in the impact of working night shifts on IT system administrators. If you attempted to design your study from here there would be all kinds of possibilities. You could look at stress manifest in the workplace, turnover rates, level/occurrence of 'mistakes', job satisfaction levels etc. And because there are so many possibilities, you don't have enough definition to take you down any particular methods path.

But say you were able to narrow your question to 'Is there a relationship between working night shifts and a tendency to burn out?'. Because this is more clearly defined, it can more readily point to method. Right away you know who you are talking about, that is, IT system administrators who work night shifts – so you have your population. You also know you have to look at the construct of 'burnout'. Now you might be able to retrieve some data from employment records – but you probably need to get some information straight from IT system administrators themselves. So that gives you a couple of choices: you can survey, you can interview, or you can do a bit of both. And this decision will likely depend on your goals, that is, whether you want to assess the extent of a problem and be able to generalize from your sample, in which case a survey approach is likely to work; or whether you are interested in more in-depth exploration and engagement, in which case you would probably want to go with more in-depth interviews.

Working backwards: towards aims and objectives

Another way to hone in on methods is to consider your project's aims and objectives. In small-scale applied workplace-based research projects, you are generally trying to do one or more of the following: (1) understand a problem; (2) find workable solutions; (3) evaluate success and/or failure. As discussed below, each of these distinct goals tends to be aligned with particular methodological approaches.

- *Understanding a problem* – Attempting to develop better understanding of a problem situation might involve looking outwards towards broad societal attitudes and opinions, or inwards using deeper exploration into the intricacies and complexities of your problem situation. Take, for example, the issue of workplace stress. You might want to know, 'How common is stress in the workplace?'. If this were your question, outward exploration, say a population study using a survey approach, might be called for. If, however, your interest was in understanding how a particular staff group reacts to stress, or what it feels like to live with workplace stress, you might look at more qualitative strategies that allow you to delve deeper into complexity.
- *Finding workable solutions* – The quest to find workable solutions might involve: assessing needs and visioning futures; locating potential programs, interventions and/or services; or exploring the feasibility of particular change initiatives. For example, sticking with the issue of workplace stress, your goal might be to understand what can be done to reduce such stress. Specific questions might be, 'Is workplace stress a priority issue for employees?', 'What vision do employees have for a different workplace culture?', 'What programs have been introduced in other settings to reduce stress?' or 'Will program X be suitable/cost-effective for my workplace?'. These types of question are often part of front-end evaluation with strategic visioning being an important part of the process.
- *Evaluating change* – The goal here is to answer the question, 'Has a change initiative/program been successful?'. Now your interest in evaluation might be related to outcomes, that is: Did program X meet its objectives? But it might also be related to a process, that is: How and how well is program X being implemented? So, for example, if you wanted to evaluate a recently introduced stress reduction program you might ask, 'Has program X reduced stress?'. This question would lead you to literature related to 'outcome' or 'summative' evaluation. If, however, you wanted to ask, 'What are the strengths, weaknesses, opportunities, threats, etc. related to the implementation of this program?', you would need to explore 'process' or evaluation literature. See Box 4.5.

BOX 4.5

Evaluative research planning

If there is one thing we are not short of in organizations, it is initiatives. In order to improve a situation, we are willing to try new things: new products, new practices, new policies, new incentives, new legislation, new programs, new strategies, new structures, new routines, new procedures. But how successful are our endeavors – did whatever we tried do whatever it was supposed to do? Have we been able to make some contribution towards positive change? Have we been able to alleviate a problem, improve a process, or more fully satisfy our customer? Answering these questions is the goal of evaluative research.

The need for evaluative studies is increasing. A well-conducted evaluation is now a key strategy for supplying decision-makers with the data they need for rational, informed, evidence-based decision-making. Evaluative studies basically attempt to determine whether an initiative should be modified, expanded or scrapped. This is accomplished by asking various stakeholder groups two types of questions. The first is related to outcomes: Did the initiative meet its objectives? The second is related to process: How successful was a particular initiative and how can it be updated or improved?

In small-scale workplace-based research, you may wish to concentrate on evaluative research of an appropriate scope. This may mean evaluating the experience of the customer: Did our loyalty plan work? How could customer service be improved? What changes would assist in getting back disgruntled customers or avoiding their leaving in the first place?

In applied research, the financial bottom line is almost always a factor, so many outcome evaluations also include data related to cost-effectiveness, often in the form of a cost–benefit analysis. You may also wish to consider the 'triple bottom line'. The triple bottom line is an accounting framework that takes into account externalities and sustainability. It augments the financial considerations with social and environmental costs. These three divisions are sometimes called the 'three P's – profit, people and planet.

The evaluative framework you use will most likely be centered on the organization, but in doing so you will also need to consider the perspective of customers, clients, constituents and the broader community. Methods for doing so are included in Table 4.4.

Assessing the practicality of methods

Once you have worked through research approaches that will fall neatly from your question(s) and meet your objectives, there will still be a need to assess the practicality of your method. By running through the following questions, you can quickly assess the practicality of your methodological plan.

1. *Do you have required access to data?* A major challenge for researchers is gaining access to data. Whether you plan to explore documents, conduct interviews or surveys, or engage in observation, the best-laid plans are worthless if you can't find a way to access people, places and/or records.

2. *Is your timeframe realistic?* If you have not given yourself long enough to do what your design demands, you are likely to: miss deadlines; compromise your study by changing your methods mid-stream; do a shoddy job with your original methods; compromise time that should be dedicated to other aspects of your job/life; or finally, not complete your study at all. (See Box 4.6)

3. *Do you have required organizational support?* Research into any problem, no matter how worthy, will not be practicable or, in fact, possible if there is no audience at the end. Also make sure that, if appropriate, you have organizational support for time to be dedicated to your project, while still meeting your employment responsibilities!

4. *Is your method ethical?* Is it likely to get required ethics approval? A clear criterion of any research design is that it is ethical; and ethicality is likely to be audited by an ethics committee. If a study calls for interaction with people, it may require formal workplace and/or university ethics committee approval. An ethical study takes responsibility for integrity in the production of knowledge and ensures that the mental, emotional and physical welfare of respondents is protected.

Table 4.4   Evaluative methods

	Organizational perspective	Recipient perspective (customer/client)	Wider community perspective
Outcome: Did it work?	Was it cost-effective/ beneficial for the organization?	Was there positive change in the target group?	Did it meet a wider community need or priority?
	Potential methods: • Document review • Key informant • Interviews/ focus groups	*Potential methods*: • Experimental • Focus group/ interview	*Potential methods*: • Surveys • Focus groups
Process: How could it be improved?	What were the strengths/weaknesses? How could the process be made more efficient/ effective for the organization?	What were the strengths/ weaknesses? How could the process be made more efficient/ effective for those it is intended to benefit?	What were the strengths/ weaknesses? How could the process be made more efficient/ effective for the community?
	Potential methods: • Interviews with key organizational stakeholders • Focus groups • Observation • Document review	*Potential methods*: • Surveys • Interviews • Focus groups	*Potential methods*: • Surveys • Key informant • Interviews • Focus groups

BOX 4.6

Is your timeline realistic?

Procrastination and perfectionism

The most well-thought out timelines and deadlines can become impossible burdens if you don't take time to consider how you actually work. For example, are you a procrastinator, a perfectionist or, heaven forbid, both? These afflictions, commonly found together, may severely hamper your progress (and your sanity) during your research project. How do you know if you're at risk? Well, do you need complete information (a thing that does not exist) before you begin a task? Do you find it impossible to begin work until all your emails are answered, your desk is neat and tidy, your hard files are arranged in the appropriate folders and stacks, your template and font are selected, and you have your favorite type of pen at hand?

Dr Jason Fox (2014) calls such perfectionism an 'elite form of procrastination', and it's true. It's also counter-productive. If you wait until you have all the information before beginning a task, you will never start. And if you get caught up in the micro-details, you will never finish. You will be like Douglas Adams, who said, 'I love deadlines. I love the whooshing noise they make as they go by' (1979: 3). But since you are a perfectionist, you won't be so cavalier about it. You'll stay up all night, every night, desperately trying to finish, and still never be truly satisfied with your work. And you'll have an excuse if anyone finds fault with the product. After all, you didn't really have time to finish it to your utmost standard. But there will never be enough time for that. At best, your colleagues and managers will not doubt your intelligence, just your ability to meet a deadline (which is equally important!).

A crucial and painful transition from educational to professional life is the realization that sometimes perfectionism is a terrible habit. In the fast-paced corporate (or even academic) environment, where priorities compete, deadlines are tight and no project can wait for perfect information, perfectionism can be crippling. It's inefficient, unrealistic and unhelpful. Perfectionism actually impedes progress. If we insist on maintaining full-time perfectionist status, we're basically setting ourselves up to burn out. There is nothing wrong with being studious and meticulous, but when it becomes paralyzing, when perfectionism undermines your ability to deliver, then you need to adjust your strategy. After all, intelligence is the ability to adapt!

Getting down to details

Once you feel comfortable with your general research plan – that is, you think your approach will meet your aims and objectives and will answer your research question in a way that is quite practical – it is time to really get down to the nuts and bolts of that plan.

So what constitutes nuts and bolts? As shown in Table 4.5, getting right down to the nitty-gritty is about being able to answer fundamental questions related to

Table 4.5   Getting down to details

Who	
Who do you want to be able to speak about?	This is your population, or the realm of applicability for your results. For example, are your findings applicable to employees of your consulting firm, or more generally?
Who do you plan to speak to/observe?	This is your sample. It is quite rare to be able to speak to every single person you wish to speak about, so the key is ensuring that your sample is either intrinsically interesting/valuable or is representative of a broader population
Where	
What is the physical domain of your sample?	This relates to working out how far afield you need to go in order to carry out your methods. Will you need to travel to different department/office or geographic areas? Are there various sites you need to visit?
Are settings relevant to the credibility of your methods?	This involves considering how place can impact method. For example, if you wanted to conduct job satisfaction interviews with shift workers, you would need to consider whether an informal chat at a pub on a Friday night will generate data distinct from that gathered at a staff meeting
When	
How do your methods fit into your timeframe?	It can take longer than you think to collect, analyze and draw conclusions from data. It is important to make sure your methods fit into your overall timeframe
Is the timing relevant to the credibility of your methods?	This involves considering how timing can impact method. For example, a community survey conducted between the hours of 9 and 5 is likely to lead to a large under-representation of workers, and an over-representation of stay-at-home mothers and retirees
How	
How will I collect my data?	This involves deciding on the methods and tools you will use to collect, gather and/or generate
How will I conduct my methods?	This involves even further consideration of nuts and bolts. For example, considering whether you will tape record your interviews or take notes; or whether your observations will involve you joining an organization, or just sitting in on a number of meetings
What	
What will you look for/what will you ask?	Depending on your methods, this might involve developing questionnaires, drafting interview questions, creating observation checklists, and/or developing frameworks for document analysis. The best advice here is to get support. These tools are difficult to get right, and it may take a few trials or pilots to develop them to a point where you are comfortable with the data they generate

the who, where, when, how and what of your approach. If you can answer these questions, you are well on your way to articulating a clearly defined plan.

Can you over-design?

Before leaving the nuts and bolts of method, let's touch briefly on the issue of over-design. We are strong believers in having a plan and thinking your way through the best possible approach for conducting your study. And most of the time this will mean being able to define and articulate the details that make up your approach. There are, however, several situations where you'll need to leave some give or flexibility in your plan.

Okay, to start with, life is unpredictable, and research really isn't any different. You can have a plan – but that won't stop circumstances from arising to which you will need to be responsive. Whether it's the fact that surveys aren't always returned, or a workplace that suddenly won't give you access, or a key informant that drops out of the picture, hurdles will arise and if you want to get over them you'll need to be flexible.

Another scenario that demands flexibility is when your plan involves developing research protocols based on what emerges from initial data. This is common in phased research or in 'grounded theory' where initial data collection protocols are defined, but subsequent data collection and analysis are highly emergent. In this type of research your plan actually 'evolves as you go'. Finally, if you are working together with stakeholders on a research project, it is important that all stakeholders feel comfortable with, and even have a chance to contribute to, methodological protocols. Keep in mind that due to the tight timeframes in small-scale applied research, you will need to keep on top of these considerations so that they do not end up delaying your entire project.

CRAFTING A RESEARCH PROPOSAL

When it comes to small-scale applied workplace-based research, very few projects get off the ground without some sort of approval. It may be as straightforward as a verbal approval from your manager, or an email version to your boss. But it might also involve a more formal process that includes developing a research proposal.

A research proposal is an opportunity to clarify thinking, provide a study's outline and offer a blueprint for future action. However, the proposal is not merely a reflexive exercise. It is, without doubt, a sales pitch. The role of a proposal is to sell your research project. Your proposal is your opportunity, likely your only opportunity, to demonstrate the usefulness of the research to those who have the power to approve and/or fund it.

Purpose of the proposal

Whether you are looking for permission, backing or funding, the role of the proposal is to convince the powers that be that what you are proposing meets their requirements. Namely, that the research question, the proposed method and the research all have merit. The committee, manager or funding gods will assess whether the project is useful and practicable, yes, but also whether you as the proposer have the ability to carry out the project proposed.

Demonstrating merits of the research question

Essential to any successful proposal is your ability to sell the merit of your research question. Demonstrating merit will rely on two things. The first is that you are able to clearly and succinctly share your research topic and question (generally the work of the title, summary/abstract, aims/objectives, research question/hypothesis). Secondly, you need to demonstrate that your research question is worth answering; that is, your question is significant enough to warrant support either at the level of admission to a program or via funding (generally the work of the introduction/background/rationale).

When it comes to a critical evaluation of your proposal, there are several possible scenarios:

1. The worth of the research question is self-evident, e.g. 'What are the most effective strategies for overcoming high turnover in the workplace?', and you are able to argue the importance and significance of your question to the satisfaction of the assessors. So far so good.
2. The worth of the research question is, as above, self-evident, but you do a lousy job arguing the case and do not convince the assessors that you are capable of mounting what should be a straightforward argument. Major problem.
3. The worth of the research question is not self-evident, but you are able to convincingly argue the case by citing evidence that attests to a real issue and what benefits there might be in conducting research into this area. For example, they may not realize the financial cost of staff turnover.
4. The worth of the research question is, as above, not self-evident, and you do little to help your case. Your arguments are weak so assessors are left scratching their heads and quickly put your proposal onto the reject pile.

The point here is that while the significance of the research question is important, what is actually being assessed is your *ability to argue* the significance. It is therefore crucial that your writing be tight, well structured and well referenced.

Demonstrating merits of the proposed methods

Once your assessors are convinced that your research question has merit, their focus will turn to methods. Here they are looking for several things:

1. Are the proposed methods clearly articulated? If the reader cannot make sense of what you are proposing, your proposal has little chance of getting off the ground.
2. Are the proposed methods logical? In other words, are methods appropriate for the research question?

3. Has the candidate considered the study's boundaries as well as any potential hurdles to effective data collection and analysis? All research is constrained; your job here is to acknowledge this and show the credibility of your methods in spite of any limitations (generally the work of the methods and limitations/delimitations sections).
4. Are the proposed methods ethical? Ethics are central to all research processes (and of course the main focus of an ethics proposal). Your proposal needs to show that the dignity and well-being of respondents, both mentally and physically, are fully protected (the work of the methods and ethical considerations sections).
5. Are the proposed methods practical/doable? It doesn't matter how logical and well considered your methods are if your assessors do not believe their implementation can be achieved. You need to show that you have or can develop the necessary expertise; that you can gain access to required data; that your timeline is realistic; and that you will come in within budget (the work of the methods section as well as, if required, the timeline and budget).

Basically, your methods section needs to convince readers that your approach is an efficient, effective and ethical way to get credible answers to your questions and that you are capable of pulling this off.

Demonstrating merits of the researcher

OK, assume the powers that be are happy with both your questions and your methods. The final question is, are they happy with you? Do they think you are the right person for the job? Do they trust that you can pull this off? Do they believe you have the necessary background knowledge, at least some familiarity with the literature and writing skill commensurate to the task?

Now that's a lot of questions, and it would be great if your assessors could get to know you and get a real feel for what you are capable of. But sometimes that's not possible. When it comes to ethics committees, for instance, there is a good chance your proposal will be reviewed by people you have never met. So what do they use to assess your potential? Simply your proposal. Assessors will judge your ability to engage with the literature through your proposal's short literature review. They will assess your ability to carry out the method, based on the knowledge you show and how well you argue your methodological case. And they will assess your potential to write by the quality of writing in your proposal. It therefore pays to give careful attention to detail and make your proposal one of the tightest pieces of writing you have ever attempted.

Anatomy of a research proposal

The weight given to various aspects of the proposal may vary according to the audience and the type of approval you are seeking. If the research proposal is to your manager, it should focus on the benefits of the potential outcomes and the practicalities of the methods involved. A proposal written for an ethics committee would focus on the relationship between methods and participants. Know your audience, and be sure to speak to their needs and priorities.

Parts of the proposal

A proposal may be a full-length formal document or an informal email responding to your manager who said 'Can you write that up in a page or two?'. Check with your academic supervisor, ethics committee and employer to determine the protocols you should follow. In the absence of direction, it's best to err on the side of formal. The full proposal includes some combination of the following.

Title Go for clear, concise and unambiguous. Your title should indicate the specific content and context of the problem you wish to explore in as succinct a way as possible.

Summary/abstract State the what, why and how of your project in a way that sells it in just a few sentences (yes, this can take some practice). Note that this section is normally referred to as a 'summary' in organizational or business templates, and an abstract for academic ones.

Aims/objectives Most proposals have one overarching aim that captures what you hope to achieve through your project. A set of objectives, which are more specific goals, supports that aim. Aims and objectives are often articulated in bullet points and are generally 'to' statements, for example, to develop, to identify, to explore, to measure, to explain, to describe, to compare, to determine, etc. In management literature you are likely to come across 'SMART' objectives – i.e. **S**pecific, **M**easurable, **A**chievable, **R**elevant results, and **T**ime-bound.

The goal is to keep objectives from being waffly. Clearly articulating what you want to achieve aids your ability to work towards that achievement.

Research question A well-articulated research question defines your investigation, sets boundaries, provides direction and acts as a frame of reference for assessing your work. Any committee reviewing your proposal will turn to your question in order to get an overall sense of your project. Take the time to make sure your question is as well-defined and clearly articulated as possible – and this may involve defining key terms.

Introduction/background/rationale The main job of this section is to introduce your topic and convince your readers that the problem you want to address is significant and worth exploring, and even funding. It should give some context to the problem and lead your readers to the conclusion that, yes, research into this area is absolutely essential if we really want to work towards situation improvement or problem resolution.

Literature, framework and models   This section is likely to be longer for academic proposals than workplace-based proposals. The idea here is to articulate the theory, framework or models that underpin and inform your ideas and your proposed study.

Methods   Some form of 'methods' will be required in all proposals. The goal here is to articulate your plan with enough clarity and detail to convince your readers that your approach is practical and ethical and will lead to credible answers to the questions posed. Under the heading of methods, you would generally articulate:

- the approach/methodology – for example, whether you will be engaged with qualitative and quantitative strategies;
- how you will find respondents – this includes articulation of population and sample/sampling procedures;
- data collection method(s) – for example, surveying, interviewing, document analysis, etc.;
- methods of analysis – whether you will be doing statistical or thematic analysis and perhaps variants thereof.

Ethical considerations   Whenever you are working with human participants there will be ethical issues you need to consider. Now if this were an application for an ethics committee, you would need to focus much of your proposal on ethical issues. But even if this were a proposal for approval or funding, your readers would still need to be convinced that you've considered issues related to integrity in the production of knowledge and responsibility for the emotional, physical and intellectual well-being of your study participants.

Timeline   This is simply superimposing a timeline on your methods, and is often done in a tabular or Gantt chart form (for an example see Figure 4.7); it is particularly helpful for larger projects. The manager or committee reading your proposal will be looking to see that your plan is realistic and can conform to any overarching timeframes or deadlines. Gantt charts can be developed in MS Project, Excel or any of the open source software online such as www.Wrike.com, www.ganttproject.biz/, or http://sourceforge.net/projects/openproj/. There is also a free version on Google charts.

Budget/funding   This is a full account of costs and who will bear them. In workplace-based research, this may be a measurement of your time rather than direct financial outlay. Now it is definitely worth being realistic – it is easy to underestimate costs and time. Software, equipment, travel, transcription, administrative support etc. can add up quite quickly.

	Jan	Feb	Mar	Apr	May	June	July	Aug	Sept	Oct	Nov	Dec
Groundwork	xx	xx										
Submit proposal		xx										
Literature review		xx	xx	xx	xx	xx						
Solidify methods		xx	xx	xx								
Data collection					xx	xx	xx					
Data analysis							xx	xx	xx			
Write first draft		xx	xx	xx	xx	xx	xx	xx				
Write second draft								xx	xx	xx		
Write final draft										xx	xx	xx
Report due												10th
Oral presentation												15th

Figure 4.7   Gantt chart example

References   This can refer to two things. The first is citing references, the same as you would in any other type of academic/professional writing. Believe it or not, it's often missed. Second, is that some committees want a list of say 10 or 15 primary references that will inform your work. This information can help a committee assess your knowledge, your credibility and also give a better indication of the direction your study may take.

Writing the proposal

It is important to recognize that a proposal should never be sloppy, rushed, or thrown together at the last minute. It needs to be a highly polished and well-constructed piece of writing. Remember: the clarity of your thoughts, the veracity of your arguments and the quality of your writing will be used to judge your potential as a researcher. An example of a proposal is included in Box 4.7.

The following tips should help you craft a winning proposal:

- *Get access to a few successful proposals* – The organization or research institution with which you are associated may have proposal examples. If they don't, then google 'research proposal example'. You can combine that with the level of study, i.e. PhD, undergraduate and/or your broad area of study, i.e. business, sociology, policy, etc. But keep in mind that not all proposals up on the Web are good ones!

- *Find a voice* – The convention here is third person; however, using 'I' to state what you will do is now more commonly accepted. Also remember to write in the future tense. A proposal is about what you *will* do, not what you are doing now, or have done in the past.
- *Write tight* – Your writing needs to be concise and succinct, direct and straightforward. Avoid rambling and/or trying to show off by using unnecessary jargon.
- *Write enough* – Somewhat paradoxical to the above, you also need to make sure you write a sufficient amount for assessors to make judgments.
- *Write to the 'non-expert'* – Your proposal needs to be 'stand-alone' and be comprehensible to someone potentially outside your field, industry or organization.
- *Do your homework* – The last thing you want in a short formal proposal is 'mistakes'. Get your facts right, make sure you don't have gaping holes in your literature, and make sure any references are accurate.
- *Don't overquote* – Generally the writing expected is so tight that you probably won't have enough room for too many direct quotes. Keep the words and ideas yours, supported by your reading.
- *Don't let the deadline sneak up on you* – prepare early for the deadline. There's nothing that says not-ready-for-prime-time like missing a deadline.
- *Be prepared to draft and redraft* – Do not underestimate the importance of this step. Leave yourself open to feedback, constructive criticism and improvements, and be ready to make necessary changes

BOX 4.7

Proposal example

Project title: 'Great Speech: De-mystifying Powerful Presentations in the Public Sector'

Project overview (150–250 words)

We all know outstanding presentations and inspirational speakers when we hear them. We know because we are moved. We know because we want to tell others about it. We know because we feel inspired. Yet inspiring can be a difficult objective to reach. In spite of the abundance of advice, dry, tedious, uninspired presentations are often the norm – public sector presentations included. Change within the public sector, however, is generally reliant on cycles of advocacy; and such cycles often culminate in presentations. Reform is often reliant on influence, so the need to drive an idea and inspire an audience is undeniable.

Knowing the best means for influencing an audience through an effective presentation is often challenging, particularly in an information age, where Google and Wikipedia now hold knowledge once the domain of experts.

The goal of this project is to offer recommendations for improved teaching and learning in the space of public sector presentations. Through an analysis of 70 of the best, most inspired presentations of the past decade, with particular reference to the public sector, this project will deconstruct the core elements that underlie truly inspirational presentations. The project will then analyze a cross-section of Trans-Tasman public sector presentations in a bid to identify gaps in best practice and thus training needs.

Project objectives (100–200 words)

The overarching aim of this research project is to offer clear recommendations for improved teaching and learning in the space of public sector presentations.

The objectives of this project are:

- to identify the core elements that make for highly effective, highly motivational presentations;
- to identify core elements and contextual issues of particular relevance to the public sector;
- to create a qualitative matrix for easy identification of core elements;
- to assess the effectiveness of presentations in the Australia/New Zealand public sector or identify gaps in effective Australia/New Zealand public sector presentations in order to develop and enhance teaching and learning development within this space.

Project benefits (100–200 words)

Within the public sector, rarely is there an initiative, project, program or policy reform that does not need to be championed. Advocacy is essential and presentations that fail to motivate can end the run of a potentially good reform. This project, with its goal of improving teaching and learning in the arena of public sector presentation, offers benefits to three stakeholder groups.

The Trans-Tasman Public Sector will benefit via increased ability to influence the policy cycle. Improved presentations can lead to more engaged debate on key public administration issues, and contribute to continuing reform in the public sector. The Funding Institution will benefit through the development of resources for future teaching and applied learning/knowledge activities. The aim is to enhance leadership in public sector communication training, while supporting the development of best practice in government.

Students will benefit from increased skills, confidence and levels of influence.

Methodology – the research method(s) your project will use (50–150 words)

The methodology will rely on a two-phase qualitative approach reliant on both online and 'face-to-face' data.

Phase One – Analysis of 70 highly motivational presentations of the past decade. Population: Online presentations (in English) deemed highly motivational by media/speaking experts. Sampling strategy: Targeted sampling designed to include a wide range

(Continued)

(Continued)

of speaker demographics – with a minimum of 35 public sector presentations. Analysis: Development of a best practice matrix through the use of narrative analysis, content analysis and semiotics.

Phase Two – Analysis of 30 public sector presentations in the Trans-Tasman region. Population: Presentations at ANZSOG's annual conference as well as online presentations. Sampling strategy: Random, cross-sectional. Analysis: Gap analysis via assessment of presentations against the matrix developed in Phase One. All presentations used in this phase will be de-identified and aggregated without identifying data. The aim is to identify common gaps in practice rather than critique individual presentations.

The rationale for using this method/these methods for this project (100–150 words): The methodology for this project does not neatly fall within one particular approach, or even one particular paradigm, but rather represents a question-driven approach that utilizes both traditional social science methods as well as project management tools.

Specifically, this project relies on sampling strategies developed within the quantitative paradigm, data analysis methods such as content analysis, narrative analysis and semiotics drawn from the qualitative school, and a gap analysis more traditionally found in project management. Such mixed methodologies are often advocated for applied research not tied to paradigmatic traditions. The ability to draw from varied schools of thought as well as the ability to leverage the power of the Internet gives veracity to methods and allows for the development of context-driven methods. The particular methods to be employed in this project are those considered most likely to give credible results within the desired timeframe.

When you want to or need to change direction/method

OK, say you are all set to interview 15 department heads, but try as you might, you just can't get more than five to participate. Or imagine that you have undertaken a pilot survey and the responses are completely unhelpful to your research. What do you do? Well, in the words of the US Marine Corps, you 'adapt, improvise and overcome'.

You think about your question, talk to your supervisor or manager, and determine the most 'doable' way to get some credible data. But disappointingly, most students who confront obstacles simply charge ahead and change their study protocols without further consultation. And while this may be the path of least resistance, it is not recommended. If your application represents a 'contract' to do a job, say, for example, to a funding body, you need to inform it of shifts in your approach. Updating ethics applications is equally important. Not only do you want an outside committee to oversee that you will not threaten the dignity and well-being of the researched, but you also want to ensure that you have protected yourself and your institution from potential lawsuits.

INTEGRITY IN THE PRODUCTION OF KNOWLEDGE

How is integrity defined in the research world, and what strategies can you call on to make sure your own small-scale applied workplace-based research project meets this criterion? There are two broad arenas in the research game where you need to consciously work towards integrity. The first is in your quest to produce knowledge – your responsibility here is to make sure you have captured 'truth', reached conclusions not tainted by error and unrecognized bias, and have conducted your research with professional integrity. The second is in working with others – your responsibility here is an ethical one that ensures the rights and well-being of those involved with your study are protected at all times.

Integrity in research

If the goal of conducting research is to produce new knowledge, knowledge that others will come to trust and rely on and maybe even enact change on the basis of, then certainly this production of knowledge needs to be approached with both integrity and rigor.

But this is easier said than done. Most, if not all, organizational research involves working with others – and research that involves people provides a host of challenges to research integrity. In fact, you might say, people are the worst. Bacteria, cells, DNA etc. generally behave in the laboratory – you know what to expect, and the little bacteria are not attempting to consciously or subconsciously throw you. But people are tough. They have hidden agendas, fallible memories and a need to present themselves in certain ways. They can be helpful, defensive and/or deferential – and there will be plenty of times when you won't know when they're being what.

And then there is the researcher – also a fallible, biased or subjective human entity, who is faced with the challenge of producing 'unbiased', trustworthy results. Now when you combine a subjective researcher with an unpredictable 'researched' it makes the production of credible knowledge no easy feat.

So how do you begin to work towards integrity in the production of knowledge? It starts with breaking the job down into manageable tasks, namely:

- recognizing and balancing subjectivities;
- building trust;
- approaching methods with consistency;
- making relevant arguments;
- providing accurate research accounts.

Recognizing and balancing subjectivities

The question here is not *whether* researchers are subjective entities, but rather do they *recognize* themselves as subjective, and can they manage their personal biases? It is imperative that researchers attempt to: (1) recognize their biases and worldview; (2) consider how their worldview may affect the researched and the research process; and (3) balance subjectivities in a manner that ensures the integrity, validity and authenticity of any potential knowledge produced.

Now for traditional scientists, for example those working in a laboratory, this means putting aside any preconceived notions and aiming for pure objectivity. Strict methodological protocols and a 'researched' that is outside the self generally make this a manageable task. For workplace-based researchers, however, the challenge is somewhat more difficult. It is the organization, even society itself, that is being researched, and as products of a society, researchers need to recognize how their own worldview makes them value-bound, and how their values can influence the research process.

It would indeed be nice to think that researcher attitudes and even attributes such as gender, age, ethnicity, religion, education, social class etc., were not factors in conducting research, but they are. You have a gender, you come from a particular place, you have the characteristics of a certain race or races, you have some level of education and you have been socialized in a particular way. And if you as a researcher don't take this into account and work towards 'neutrality', you can readily fall into the trap of judging the reality of others in relation to your own reality. In fact, researchers who do not act to consciously manage their own positioning run the risk of conducting 'self-centric' analysis; that is, being insensitive to issues of race, class or gender, and hearing only the dominant voice.

Conducting 'self'-centric analysis

Without reflective consideration of your own researcher reality, bias can color your interpretations. You have to actively guard against the tendency to understand and judge the things you see according to the rules and guidelines that *you* use to make sense of the world. Others have different rules – and the meanings they associate with particular utterances and events will vary accordingly. For example, suppose you're a well-educated, straight-laced, middle-class man who has just started working in a not-for-profit organization that works to provide after-school activities for at-risk youth. You have become quite interested in attitudes towards drug use, and pick up student conversations about getting high, smoking dope and even doing Ecstasy. Now from your perspective, these students are on the edge of reason, humanity and decency – 'What has the world come to!'. In your world, only those scraping the bottom of the barrel do 'that kind of thing'. But you have to remember that you are not researching your world – you are in the world of the organization, and the challenge facing you is avoiding the temptation to assign the values of your personal world to your research world. For in this world, these might be 'normal' kids – doing 'normal' things.

Being insensitive to issues of race, class or gender

Insensitivity to issues of race, class, gender, etc. refers to the practice of ignoring these constructs as important factors or variables in a study, and can be a by-product of 'self-centric' analysis. Researchers need to recognize and appreciate the reality of the researched, otherwise they run the risk of ignoring unique and significant attributes. For example, a study of student motivation in a multicultural setting would not be very meaningful without ethnicity as one significant variable. Yes, career ambitions, study enjoyment, perceived relevance, etc. can be important predictors of motivation, but all of these factors can be motivated by family and culture. For example, in many Anglo-Asian households, student success and failure are seen as parental success and failure, and this can be a huge student weight and/or motivator.

Insensitivity to issues of race, class and gender can also lead to dichotomization, or the tendency to put groups (such as customers) at two separate ends of the spectrum without recognition of overlapping characteristics. We do this when we talk in absolute terms about 'men' and 'women' or 'young' and 'old'. Research that dichotomizes is often research that has fallen prey to stereotypes.

Finally, insensitivity to race, class and gender can lead to double standards where the same behaviors, situations or characteristics are analyzed using different criteria depending on whether respondents are black or white, male or female, rich or poor, etc. For example, let's say you wanted to explore how generous family leave (paternity) benefits the organization. If you were to use different sets of responses for males and females in which your preconceived notions about work–life balance and family concerns being the exclusive domain of women came through, you would have a double standard. Remember that in the conduct of research, there is an essential need to guard against the assumptions and biases inherent within our society.

Hearing only the dominant voice

For most of history, 'anonymous' was a woman.

Virginia Woolf

It's very easy to listen to those who are speaking the loudest or to those who are speaking your 'language'. But when you do this, you are likely to end up missing an important undercurrent – a whole other voice. We have both struggled with this in our own teaching. We try very hard to relate to our students – to communicate with them rather than lecture at them. This involves engaging in a 'dialogue' to get a two-way conversation going. In every class a core group of students makes this easy.

But who is in this core group? Well, it really can be a mixed bag, but we can tell you who it isn't. It's not generally the international students; they tend to stay in the background. Now there are a number of reasons for this. Many come from an educational system where they are not invited to participate. Others struggle with English as a second language. But another factor could be us. We both like to use personal anecdotes, and may occasionally be considered having an 'in your face' American style (Jen is from North Carolina but Zina, well, she's from New Jersey!). These can all conspire so that those with demographic characteristics similar to ours are the ones who speak up the most. So, it the Asian and Indian students who can go unheard in class (as they are likely to do throughout their Western university careers).

As teachers, the challenge is to find a way to engage the entire class and reach every student, and make sure students can reach the teacher. The challenge for the researcher is similar. If you do not consciously work on strategies for appreciating diversity, you run the risk of gathering data and reaching conclusions that ignore valuable perspectives and inhibit full understanding. An example of how this is relevant for your small-scale workplace-based research is demonstrated in Box 4.8.

BOX 4.8

Hearing only the dominant corporate voice – 'Drinking the Kool-Aid'

In small-scale applied workplace-based research projects, the dominant voice is typically that of the organization itself. The extreme version of this is called 'Drinking the Kool-Aid', a phrase used to refer to an employee's/researcher's unquestioning alliance to the company and its perspective. More recently it has been voted the most annoying example of business jargon by an online poll of *Forbes* readers. The phrase was popularized in a 2000 *New York Times* article about the end of the dot-com bubble which noted that 'The saying around San Francisco Web shops these days, as companies run out of money is "Just keeping drinking the Kool-Aid"'.

However annoying or innocent it may seem, the origin of the phrase is actually quite serious. In the 1970s, a cult leader, Jim Jones, established a base of followers in San Francisco. When he came under investigation for tax fraud, he fled with his flock to South America where he established the community of 'Jonestown'. Later, when a few members tried to revolt, Jones convinced the community of more than 900 people to commit mass suicide by ingesting drinks laced with cyanide. In the ensuing media coverage, this drink was assumed to be Kool-Aid.

'Drinking the Kool-Aid' essentially means the lack of a reflexive process of critical examination. Within an organization, the dominant viewpoint of the corporation can seem like the only perspective. Make sure that you recognize other viewpoints in the course of your research, not only within the company but external to it, such as clients, customers and community stakeholders, not just shareholders.

Building trust

Also crucial to the production of credible knowledge is your ability to get your respondents (including colleagues, clients, customers, community stakeholders, etc.) to talk to you with honesty and openness. Now there could be any number of complex reasons why respondents might be reluctant to fully expose themselves in a research process. But there is one thing we know for sure: if respondents feel intimidated or judged in any way, they will not open up. As a researcher, building trust is absolutely dependent on (1) understanding how research participants are likely to react to you and (2) being able to suspend and withhold judgment.

Researcher attributes

Do you know who in our society generally contributes to the 'scientific' production of knowledge; in other words, who society's researchers tend to be? Well, it is generally those with power, position, privilege and education. Those being 'researched', however, don't necessarily come from that same background, and this can set up a real power divide that can damage trust.

Building trust is reliant on recognizing the power and privilege associated with your own attributes and working to minimize any real or perceived power differential between you and the 'researched'. If you have difficulty doing this, the 'researched' is likely to feel alienated, intimidated and/or uninterested by the research process.

Some of the researcher attributes that need to be considered when attempting to build trust include:

- *Position of power in a particular setting* – This is particularly relevant when you're researching within your own workplace or in another organization where you have a formal role. You need to consider how you might go about building researcher–researched trust when you might be someone's employee in your day-to-day occupational capacity. Will they trust you? Do you think you can get management to give you more than patronizing organizational rhetoric? Will your colleagues trust that there will be confidentiality? There is always an additional dimension in building trust when you are known in a setting and are likely to be perceived as wearing more than one hat (i.e. student, employee and researcher). Clarifying roles and expectations will be crucial.
- *Gender* – The rapport and trust you will build with respondents and the slant on stories you will hear can be very dependent on gender. For example, if you are marketing a feminine hygiene product, be aware that women in your focus group might only feel comfortable talking the product with other women! Or imagine conducting an interview on interoffice relationships; the answers you might elicit could be highly dependent on your own gender. There are no hard and fast rules here. What is important is to consciously think through the issue of gender and whether it is likely to be a factor in building trust.
- *Age* – Trust is often dependent on your ability to relate to your respondents and their ability to relate to you, and age can certainly be a factor here. For example, there are very few parents in the world who can ask their teenagers 'What did you do this weekend?' and get the full story – especially if the weekend was any good! Like it or not, age can be a critical factor in credible data collection. Again, there are no hard and fast rules, just a mandate that you consider how age might influence researcher–researched relationships.

- *Ethnicity* – The ethnic and cultural background of the researcher can certainly influence the research process. It's sad to say that we still have much inequity, suspicion and mistrust running across ethnic and racial lines. But that's a reality – and it's a reality that can affect your ability to gain trust. Say, for example, you wanted to research attitudes towards uptake of a particular product in the Hispanic community. While a 'white' outsider might struggle to gain trust, a Hispanic insider might have an easier time opening up honest and open lines of communication.
- *Socioeconomic status/education* – Societal position can also have great bearing on the research process, with researchers often coming from a position of privilege. As a researcher, you need to think about breaking down barriers, and convincing the 'researched' that you are not sitting in judgment. Being aware of your own socioeconomic status and educational background, as well as that of the researched, puts you in a position to manage any potential power-related issue that might influence your study.

It may seem as though these issues are more likely to be a factor in research that involves close interaction with the researched – and this is true. But it is also worth thinking about how a researcher's attributes can come through even in something like a survey instrument. In a survey, there are unlimited opportunities to leave respondents feeling alienated. An example might be a survey that quizzes knowledge rather than asks opinions. Not many will be willing to take a quiz, particularly if they believe they've been set up to fail.

A classic example here is IQ tests of the 1960s that were clearly based on 'Middle American' assumptions. Back then, it seems that IQ was based in part on knowing how to 'properly' set a table – not likely to be general knowledge for a poor child from the inner city, nor for a child from an Asian background (where do those chopsticks go?). Again, no easy answers. In the end, it is up to individual researchers to consider how 'they' impact the research process and to manage that process in a way that can best yield trustworthy and credible results.

Listening without judgment

This sounds like the job of a therapist, a parent and a best friend. But it's also your job as a researcher. I was reminded of how difficult this task is when I was conducting research interviews with current students about their university experiences. Having fond memories of my own time at university, I was completely unprepared for the litany of complaints I heard in every interview. The list was long: graduate teaching assistants and tutors didn't answer emails in a timely fashion, professors seemed unwilling to provide individual attention, feedback on marked assessments was insufficient.

As the interviewer, I tried to maintain a neutral smile but inside I was starting to seethe. Having been on the other side, I could counter every complaint with a rational (and I thought obvious) explanation. Teaching staff are paid for only a certain amount of hours (usually limited to face-to-face hours) and thus every email outside of office hours is essentially unpaid work – unrelenting unpaid work if students feel entitled to email at 2am on Friday and demand a reply by Sunday afternoon. As for the lack of individual attention, lecturers have no control over class size, it is universities who decide to run enormous classes. It is state and national decision-makers who decide to cut educational funding, and hire academics on meagre part-time contracts to save money. (In the United States a majority of university classes are now taught by adjuncts, some of whom make so little that they qualify for food stamps.) What are lecturers to do when they are overworked and underpaid, and up against students who use the word 'customer'?

As I continued countering these complaints in my own mind, I stopped listening. I could feel my calm smile beginning to crack. I was itching to tell students all the ways in which they were mistaken. I had to remember that my judgment was not what was called for. These are the experiences of the modern student who are honestly convinced that they are customers. Ironically, it was not my place to 'educate' them that society is the customer and they are the product, products branded with the university logo. I had to readjust my strategy. I started with asking interviewees about positive experiences of university first and then building to the negatives. This made for a more balanced interview, more useful insights and helped me listen more carefully and more empathetically.

Like me, you may have to make a conscious effort to suspend judgment. If you are surveying customer experiences, you may be surprised at how difficult it is to please some people. You may come to bemoan human nature, which accentuates the negative over the positive. But beware. People can sniff out judgment from a mile off, and if you don't make an effort to suspend or withhold it, you won't stand a chance at building trust and getting to the heart of an issue. Be conscious of your verbal and non-verbal cues here – what you say, how you say it, your facial expressions and your body language can all work to build trust or alienate the other.

Approaching methods with consistency

Once you have worked through some of the issues related to the management of subjectivities and the building of trust, the quest for integrity in the production of knowledge turns to questions of method. It is important to remember that regardless of scale or approach, researching is not a haphazard activity. Rather, it is an activity that needs to be approached with discipline, rigor and a level of standardization. If the goal is to have your research stand up to scrutiny and be taken as credible, it is important that readers are confident that your methods have been implemented in ways that best assure consistency.

Often consistency in methods is referred to as 'reliability' or the extent to which a measure, procedure or instrument provides the same result on repeated trials. A good example here is bathroom scales. If you were to jump on your scales 10 times in a row and got the same results each time, the scales would be reliable.

The scale could be wrong – it might always be 10 pounds heavy or 10 pounds light, but it would be reliable. A more complicated example might be trying to measure job satisfaction with a questionnaire. The questionnaire would be reliable only if results were not dependent on things like who administered the questionnaire, what kind of day the respondent was having or whether or not it was a weekend.

The flipside of this is that people are complex and multifaceted. At any given time, for any given reason, they may only reveal part of themselves. Say, for example, you wanted to ask about stress – this is something that can, and often does, vary from day to day. So developing methodological tools that are 'reliable' might not be straightforward. But nevertheless, the process of data collection needs to be more than haphazard. In fact, it should be 'dependable'. Methods need to be designed and developed in ways that are consistent, logical, systematic, well-documented and designed to account for research subjectivities.

BOX 4.9

Validity and reliability

There are many who argue that validity and reliability are fundamental indicators of good research. Together, they are seen as what defines scientific proof. When we have validity we know that we are measuring what we intend to measure and that we have eliminated any other possible causal relationships. In other words, we have hit the target.

When we have reliability we know that results are not just one-off. Results will be the same under-repeated trials, given that circumstances stay constant. In other words, we hit the target over and over again.

When we have both validity and reliability, then we have a situation where we are repeatedly not only hitting the target, but hitting the bull's eye each and every time (see Figure 4.8), and this is undeniably a good thing. What is tricky, however, is when you demand validity and reliability as prerequisites to credibility and scientific truth. When we do this, we shut the door to research into the hard-to-pin-down reaches of the human/ social world. And this includes small-scale applied workplace-based research.

If you accept the possibility of multiple realities, varied perspectives, human variability and inconsistency, then it is essential to find indicators of good research that can work within this complex and multifaceted reality. This is why 'post-positivist' researchers call on authenticity alongside validity, and dependability alongside reliability.

Making relevant and appropriate arguments

Assume you now have some great data. You're pretty sure you've been able to manage your biases in ways that really got your respondents to open up, and you've done this using data collection tools and analysis strategies capable of holding up to a good level of scrutiny. The next step is to put forward some credible arguments.

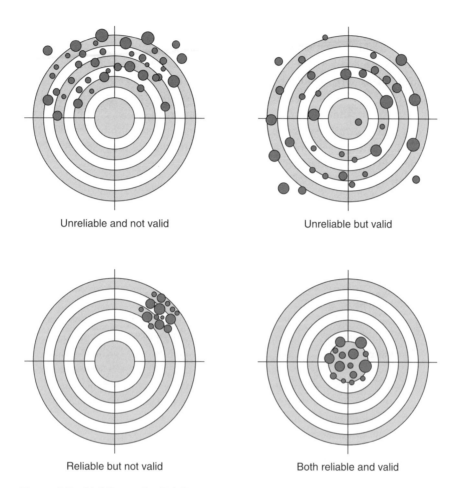

Unreliable and not valid

Unreliable but valid

Reliable but not valid

Both reliable and valid

Figure 4.8   Validity and reliability

Now this will involve a few challenges we've already discussed, i.e. keeping a check on subjectivities and exploring multiple interpretations. But as discussed below, it will also involve weighing up your findings in light of your study's limitations, and being confident that you are speaking for an appropriate group of people.

Being true to your study's limitations

Very few researchers get to conduct their studies in a way they consider ideal: there is rarely enough time or money; the cooperation of others might be less than ideal; and there could be a whole list of things you would have done differently with the benefit of hindsight. So what do you do?

Well, making appropriate arguments is about being able to attest to the credibility of your data and the trustworthiness of your results – in spite of any limitations.

Yes, it can be tempting to downplay difficulties and write up your research as though everything went smoothly in a study that was optimally designed. But if you are challenged here, your ethics and credibility can come into question. As outlined in Box 4.10, a much better approach is to take it in three steps. The first step is to honestly outline the study's limitations or shortcomings. The second step is to outline the strategies that you have employed to gather credible data and generate trustworthy results because of, or in spite of, any limitations. The third step follows from the second and is a 'therefore' type of statement that offers justification or rationalization for the data and findings of your study.

BOX 4.10

Being true to your study's limitations

The following excerpt is a good example of the three-step approach to outlining your study's limitations:

> This study was undertaken by a student who was part of a scientific research organization. He noticed that while the organization itself was highly regarded as meritocratic, public responses to reports and news media coverage of research differed according to authorship. He hypothesized that reports authored by women attracted more online abuse related to credentials and methodology, and that abuse tended to be more sexualized than criticism of male-authored papers.

> While the original data collection protocol was to survey a random sample of the population, preliminary investigation showed that the extent of this population is unknown. A directory of men who have experienced sexualized online abuse/comments on a professional publication simply does not exist [Step 1]. It was therefore decided to divide recent articles by gender and examine the comments for each [Step 2]. While there is no guarantee that the results from this sample will be representative of the greater population, this study does offer valuable insights into the phenomenon, and sheds light on an under-explored area of online harassment in the workplace [Step 3].

Speaking for an appropriate group of people

Also crucial to a good argument is making sure you are speaking for an appropriate group of people. We are talking here about your findings' applicability or the extent to which the findings of your study can extend beyond a particular sample or setting. Now the credibility of a research project relies in part on the broad applicability of its findings. While conclusions relevant to only a particular sample or only within a certain research setting can provide important knowledge for key stakeholders, it does limit the broader generation of new knowledge.

Your goal is wide applicability, but that applicability must be appropriate. Any sample you use should be representative of a wider population and large enough for you to be confident that your findings do reflect larger trends. Meeting these criteria mean that your findings are 'generalizable'. The key is ensuring both adequate and broad representation, and this is generally not too difficult in medium-to-large-scale survey research.

But what if your research project is centered on a particular case, or is designed to collect more in-depth qualitative data that will limit your sample size? Under these circumstances, you may not be able to argue generalizability. Yet broader applicability may still be a goal. If this is the case, your goal will be 'transferability' or highlighting 'lessons learned' that are likely to be applicable in alternative settings or populations. For example, the results of an in-depth case study in any one school will not be representative of all schools – but there will definitely be lessons learned that can illuminate relevant issues and provide rich learning within other school contexts. The key here is providing a detailed description of the research setting and methods so that applicability can be determined by those reading the research account.

Providing accurate research accounts

Conducting research is a highly complex process. Without a doubt, it's hard to get it right. So it is the responsibility of the researcher to consciously minimize the possibility that results are false or misleading. To that end, research approaches are expected to be open and accountable. The physicist Richard Feynman (1997) argues the need to 'report everything that you think might make it [your workplace-based research project] invalid – not only what you think is right about it … Details that could throw doubt on your interpretation must be given, if you know them'. The admission of shortcomings and limitations is encouraged and research is expected to be reproducible. In fact, codes of ethics often require researchers to keep their raw data for a period of 5–7 years, thereby protecting themselves from accusations of fraud or misrepresentation.

Even though the price of fraudulence can be quite high (students shown to be acting fraudulently are often forced to withdraw from their research programs), misrepresentation and fraud are quite rampant. Researchers (and not just students) have been known to:

- blatantly fabricate data or falsify results;
- omit cases or fiddle with numbers in order to show significance;
- plagiarize passages from articles or books without crediting the original author(s);
- misrepresent authorship by using a ghost writer, taking full credit for authorship when more than one author was involved, or naming a co-author who had no involvement in the study.

Verifiable accounts are therefore considered essential. As well as allowing others to attempt to replicate or reproduce findings, verifiable accounts can help establish a study's credibility by making them 'auditable'. It is difficult to blatantly fabricate data, falsify results, omit cases, fiddle with numbers, plagiarize and even misrepresent authorship if your methods are out there for all to see.

Integrity and the researched

Absolutely central to research integrity is ethics. With power comes responsibility. As a researcher, you have an explicit and fundamental responsibility towards the 'researched'.

The dignity and well-being of respondents, both mentally and physically, is absolutely crucial. Understanding how this responsibility is best negotiated at legal, moral, and ethical levels is a prerequisite for any potential researcher.

Commitment to the conduct of ethical research is simply not enough. Most universities and large bureaucratic institutions, such as hospitals or some government departments, require you to obtain official approval that will involve the development of an ethics proposal, including consent forms and information statements in order to undertake a study. This will require you to carefully examine all aspects of your study for ethical implications and work through all the logistics. Ask your supervisor or manager for the process and paperwork, if required.

Legal obligations

In a nutshell, researchers are not above the law. Some might like to be – but clearly they are not. The laws of society stand in the world of research. If it is illegal for the general public, then it is illegal for researchers and research participants. For most researchers, the criterion of non-engagement in illegal activities is not too difficult to appreciate or meet. Most recognize the logic here. But a more common legal dilemma is faced by researchers who come across illegal activities in the course of their investigations.

You may or may not be obligated to report illegal activities, but in most countries the courts can subpoena your data and files. Legal precedents suggest that researcher assurances of confidentiality do not hold up in court. As a researcher, you are not afforded the same rights as a lawyer, doctor or priest.

Moral obligations

When we talk about morals, we are talking about rights and wrongs, societal norms, and values. In research, this boils down to responsibility for the dignity and welfare of both individuals and cultural groups. Put simply, research should not be offensive, degrading, humiliating or dangerous. In fact, it should not be psychologically or physically damaging in any way.

Some moral considerations in the conduct of research include:

- *Conscientiousness* – This refers to a need to keep the interests of respondents or participants at the forefront in any decision-making processes related to the conduct of research. It is important to remember that researchers hold a certain position of power, and being conscious of this power is essential in ensuring the well-being of those involved in your research project.
- *Equity* – Equitable research is concerned with the practice of asking only some segments of the population to participate in research, while other segments are immune from such requests. For example, prisoners, students, children, minorities, etc. may have characteristics that make them targets for research studies, but it is important that particular groups of individuals are not treated as, or made to feel like, 'guinea pigs'.
- *Honesty* – Gone are the days when researchers could 'dupe' respondents and lie to them about what was going to happen, or why a research study was being done in the first place. There is an expectation that researchers are open and honest and that details of the research process are made transparent.

Ethical obligations

Ethics tend to be based on moral obligations, but put a professional spin on what is fair, just, right or wrong. Ethics refers to principles or rules of behavior that act to dictate what is actually acceptable or allowed within a profession. Ethical guidelines for the conduct of research will vary by professional code, discipline area and institution, but generally focus on three elements: informed consent, ensuring no harm comes to participants and ensuring confidentiality.

Informed consent   Participants can only give 'informed consent' to be involved in a research study if they have full understanding of their requested involvement – including time commitment, type of activity, topics that will be covered and all physical and emotional risks potentially involved. Informed consent implies that participants are:

- competent – they have reasonable intellectual capacity and psychological maturity;
- autonomous – they are making self-directed and self-determined choices;
- involved voluntarily – they are not unaware, forced, pressured or duped;
- aware of the right to discontinue – they are under no obligation (or pressure) to continue involvement;
- not deceived – the nature of the study, any affiliations or professional standing, and the intended use of the study should be honest and open;
- not coerced – positions of power should not be used to get individuals to participate;
- not induced – while it may be acceptable to compensate individuals for their time and effort, an inducement should not compromise a potential participant's judgment.

For a good example of what not to do, see Box 4.11 on Facebook's study of 'emotional contagion'.

BOX 4.11

There are no free passes in informed consent

Ethical norms are still being tested when it comes to social media research. In 2014 Facebook was roundly criticized for allowing researchers to manipulate the posts of Facebook users in order test the effects of 'emotional contagion'. These changes were made without users' knowledge or informed consent. Remember, in the words of Dr Max Masnick (cited in Arthur, 2014), 'As a researcher, you don't get an ethical free pass because a user checked a box next to a link to a website's terms of use'.

Ensuring no harm comes to respondents   This includes emotional or psychological harm as well as physical harm. Physical harm is relatively easy to recognize, but risks of psychological harm can be hard to identify and difficult to predict. Whether it be resentment, anxiety, embarrassment or reliving unpleasant memories, psychological 'harm' can be unplanned and unintentional, yet commonplace. Keep in mind that as well as being ethically and morally unacceptable, risks of harm can give rise to legal issues. We are talking about lawsuits here. So even if your conscience or your professional ethics can justify your decisions, the potential for legal action may be enough to make you reassess your approach. For a list of common ethical dilemmas in workplace-based research, see Box 4.12.

BOX 4.12

Ethical dilemmas in workplace-based research

What types of ethics dilemmas are you likely to face when doing workplace-based research? Here are a few examples:

- *Not ensuring confidentiality* – We promise that responses will be confidential, but when reporting on key informant interviews, for example, we give away that person's department and position, such that tracing this individual becomes an easy feat.
- *Putting respondents in a tense situation* – This can happen in ill-fated focus groups. Tensions rise and if conflict is not well managed, it can get ugly. Even

worse, if focus group members are from the same workplace or group, tensions from the research can spill into other parts of their lives. The advice here is never to do your first focus group (particularly on a subject likely to raise debate) on your own.

- *Asking insensitive or potentially threatening questions* – It can be difficult to know what people are sensitive about. We know to be cautious when it comes to certain topics such as sexual assault, domestic violence or experiences of war. But hurt can also arise when people are asked about purchasing habits and procrastination at work. This is where the scrutiny of an ethics committee becomes invaluable – it means that responsibility for unanticipated harm is the burden of the individual researcher.

- *Putting yourself in a situation where you (feel you) need to break confidences* – Dangerous work practices, corruption, fraud, theft – you may come across knowledge of any of these. Do you say 'stuff the research process' and report it? It depends. What about embezzled funds? What about serious breaches of occupational health and safety? What about minor breaches of occupation health and safety? Big dilemma, but not one you need to tackle on your own. Talk to your supervisor, refer it on to the ethics committee. Do not shoulder this burden by yourself.

Confidentiality and other non-disclosure considerations   The third element of ethical considerations is ensuring confidentiality. Confidentiality involves protecting the identity of those providing research data; all identifying data remains solely with the researcher. Confidentiality is of particular importance in an organizational setting, whereby commercial-in-confidence and corporate reputation are paramount. As demonstrated by Dilbert in Figure 4.9, organizations are keen to protect their brand; likewise, employees and other interviewees are keen to protect their jobs!

Figure 4.9   Maintaining confidentiality and anonymity (Dilbert © 2010 Scott Adams. Reprinted with permission of UNIVERSAL)

In order to maintain ethical objectives, you may have to make some compromises at the start, or agree to only limited promulgation of your research findings. For instance, you may agree to release your research report internally or for an academic audience, shield the real name of the organization, or even safeguard the names of interviewees within the organization who may need to be shielded by those higher up. As this represents a high level of responsibility, these issues require careful consideration at the onset. Confidentiality is likely to be a significant issue if you are conducting interviews. You need to negotiate whether quotes will be attributed, that is, whether the name of the person speaking will be attached to their quote. It is good practice to discuss these protocols before you begin the interview. A good compromise is to agree to ask for permission to use any direct quotes as the need arises, and depending on the nature of the quote, to do so with the most basic of identifying information, for instance an 'An experienced member of the finance department said …'. Based on the material discussed, and the hierarchical nature of the organization, lower-level employees may feel particularly vulnerable. These issues should be considered in advance in relation to recording or filming of respondents.

Even if you are not conducting formal interviews, you may be obliged to respect confidentiality in a more general sense. Irving (2003) discusses how conversations in the office, the elevator, over lunch and coffee or in social settings represent environments in which employees are open and frank. Those conversations take place in an environment of trust, and you are morally obliged to respect these boundaries. Similarly, your own observations and meeting notes may reveal individual discussions and disagreements that are not captured in formal organizational documents. These too may require careful use.

As you seek to preserve confidentiality, keep in mind that pseudonyms may not be enough to hide identity. If others can figure out who you are speaking about, or who is doing the speaking, you need to further mask identity or seek approval for disclosure. Anonymity goes a step beyond confidentiality and refers to protection against identification even from the researcher. Information, data and responses collected anonymously should not be identifiable with any particular respondent.

As well as masking identity, protection of confidentiality and anonymity should involve: secure storage of raw data; restricting access to the data; the need for permission for subsequent use of the data; and eventual destruction of raw data. At the very least, data should be preserved on your private laptop (not organizational servers), be password protected and encrypted to ensure high standards of data protection.

While such guidelines may seem straightforward, there's likely to be a trade-off between following such guidelines and the data you want to collect. Ethics, however, must always take precedence, even if this means your design needs to go through a process of modification. Luckily, ethics committees have approval processes that can help you identify and work within the boundaries that define the conduct of ethical research.

Box 4.13 summarizes indicators associated with research integrity.

BOX 4.13

Indicators of research integrity

1. Have subjectivities been acknowledged and managed?

   There are three strategies and associated indicators that reflect the management of subjectivities. These are:

   - *Objectivity* – Conclusions are based on observable phenomena; findings are not influenced by emotions, personal prejudices or subjectivities.
   - *Neutrality* – Subjectivities are explicitly recognized and negotiated in a manner that attempts to avoid biasing results/conclusions.
   - *Subjectivity with transparency* – Acceptance and disclosure of bias or subjective positioning and how it might impact the research process, including conclusions drawn.

2. Are methods approached with consistency?

   The two indicators that are most often used to asses consistency are:

   - *Reliability* – Concerned with internal consistency, or whether data/results collected, measured or generated are the same under repeated trials.
   - *Dependability* – Accepts that reliability in studies of the social may not be possible, but attests that methods are systematic, well documented and designed to account/control for subjectivities and bias.

3. Has 'true essence' been captured?

   Capturing true essence depends on many factors, including your ability to build trust and take your study's limitations into consideration. The following two indicators are often called upon to assess 'truth':

   - *Validity* – Concerned with truth value; that is, whether conclusions are 'correct'. Also considers whether methods, approaches and techniques actually relate to what is being explored.
   - *Authenticity* – Concerned with truth value, but recognizes that multiple truths may exist. Concerned with describing the deep structure of experience/phenomenon in a manner that is 'true' to the experience.

4. Have you spoken for an appropriate group of people?

   Another way to approach this is to ask if your findings are applicable outside your immediate frame of reference. The goal of broad, yet appropriate, applicability is generally assessed by two distinct indicators:

   - *Generalizability* – Whether findings and/or conclusions from a sample, setting or group are directly applicable to a larger population, a different setting or another group.

(Continued)

(Continued)

- *Transferability* – Whether findings and/or conclusions from a sample, setting or group lead to lessons learned that may be germane to a larger population, a different setting or another group.

5. Is the research process open and accountable? Can it be verified?

When you are dealing with a process that has the potential for bias, error, inaccuracy and misinterpretation, it's important to be able to call on indicators related to accountability. Two indicators that attempt to address this issue are:

- *Reproducibility* – Concerned with whether results/conclusions would be supported if the same methodology were used in a different study with the same/similar context.
- *Auditability* – Accepts the idiosyncratic nature of research contexts, and the associated difficulty in aiming for reproducibility. Auditability therefore seeks full explication of methods to allow others to see how and why the researchers arrived at their conclusions.

6. Will the project be considered useful by relevant stakeholders?

This is particularly relevant in applied research where the goal is situation improvement or problem alleviation. The main game is whether or not the research project has been able to make a contribution to the organization (inclusive of its customers, clients, constituents and community).

- *Usefulness* – Concerned with the practical and relevant contribution a research process can have for stakeholders.

7. Have research participants been treated with integrity?

The goal here is to ensure that participants are treated with respect and dignity at all times. Treating research participants with integrity means that all three of the following indicators are met:

- *Legality* – Concerned that the research process is not in breach of the law, including any obligation to report illegal activities that researchers may come to know of in the course of their research.
- *Morality* – Centers on the societal norms that should act to protect research participants. These norms include conscientious decision-making, equity and honesty through full disclosure.
- *Ethicality* – Refers to a professional 'code of practice' designed to protect the researched from an unethical process, and in turn protect the researcher from legal liabilities. Key ethical considerations include informed consent, causing no harm and a right to privacy.

CHAPTER SUMMARY

- The research process demands engagement with literature at every stage. Without this engagement it isn't possible to credibly add to a body of knowledge.
- Designing a research plan involves thinking through how your methods will answer your research question, including who, where, when, how and what.
- Research proposals allow you to give a precise account of your research plan; act as a catalyst for developing ideas; and are an important 'sales pitch' for gaining research support.
- Integrity in the production of knowledge involves both integrity in the conduct of methods and integrity in dealing with the researched.

5

WORKING WITH EXISTING DATA

Chapter preview

What is existing data?

Working with tangible data

Working with online data

Analyzing previous studies

WHAT IS EXISTING DATA?

Existing data is simply data that exists independent of a research project. To say that the amount of existing data is enormous, colossal, maybe even gargantuan, doesn't come close to capturing the nature of what's out there. The Internet has put us well and truly in the information age. We're talking about all the paper-based data that has been digitally rendered and put online. But it's not just paper. Music, movies, artifacts, art … virtually all of our history has been captured for posterity on the Internet. And new data is being generated every day: websites, feeds, blogs, posts, photos and tweets are proliferating at an unfathomable pace.

This makes the Internet an amazing library. Almost every bit of paper that every organization, government agency, NGO, researcher, etc. produces also (and sometimes, only) exists online. Digital photographs, records, databases and government files are available at your fingertips.

Aside from accumulating the vast sum of all human knowledge, the Internet is also an archive of itself. Copies of websites can be captured at specific moments in time. This means that web pages can be viewed as they existed in 1997 or 2006. Think of it as a time machine for the interweb, where the dancing animated clip art of the 1990s comes alive. Websites that would otherwise be overwritten, updated, or deleted are forever preserved.

But the Internet is more than a library and an archive; it's also a source of primary data. Indeed, primary data collection is such an entrenched part of research processes that we sometimes forget that the data we seek may have already been collected. Censuses, large-scale surveys, organizational records and existing research accounts all abound and can potentially hold the answers to research questions. There is a good chance that no matter your topic, somebody has asked it, researched it and collected data on it. Capitalizing on existing data thus makes sense, particularly for small-scale applied research projects.

Benefits and challenges of working with existing data

> I not only use all the brains that I have, but all that I can borrow.
>
> Woodrow Wilson

Using existing data in documents, databases and online resources can undoubtedly save you time, energy and money. Moreover, it provides an objective buffer between the researcher and the researched. Primary research such as interviewing, surveying and even observation studies is driven by the researcher, who undoubtedly has an impact on the reality of the situations, events, or people being explored; researchers and researching have an influence on social environments. However, with existing data interaction does not involve the researcher, so the possibility of tainting data with bias is removed.

A crucial step in using existing data is knowing what you are looking for – that is, having a clearly articulated research question and knowing what types of data might address that question. There are, however, a few caveats even when past this hurdle. Existing data needs to be carefully screened for credibility. Given the profusion of personal websites, blogs and hacks, the trick is not just finding information, but finding accurate and credible information.

Existing data presents further challenges in terms of relevance, currency and methodological issues. Since it is data that has generally been collected for an alternative purpose, it may not be as relevant or current as primary data. Moreover, you may not be aware of methodological flaws in any previous collection methods. Older data sets may suffer from bias inherent in the classification and coding systems that is not immediately obvious. For instance, a longitudinal study of individual time use over the past 50 years suggests that leisure time is increasing, particularly for women. However, embedded in this conclusion is that time spent child-rearing is categorized as *leisure* time (as if!). Nonetheless, the tradeoffs involved with existing data are worth exploring, but it does require an observant researcher.

Benefits

There are some real advantages in exploring existing data. Existing data allows you to:

- explore what people have actually produced;
- capitalize on the vast amount of data already out there;
- collect for rich, in-depth qualitative data and standardized, quantifiable data – as well as both verbal and non-verbal data;

- eliminate the need for physical access to research subjects, which can reduce costs as well as minimize stress for both researchers and research subjects;
- eliminate worries related to: building trust; getting people to act naturally; role playing; and figuring out how attributes such as race, gender, ethnicity, class, and age of researcher and researched might confound data collection;
- be neutral and not a force for change;
- overcome the expectation that 'real' research demands interviews and surveys.

Challenges

That is a pretty long list, but one that will hopefully pique your interest in exploring data that is traditionally underutilized. But there are some challenges associated with working with pre-existing data. Pre-existing data requires you to:

- work through data not expressly generated to answer your particular research question(s);
- ensure your own biases do not color your interpretations and understandings;
- avoid taking records out of context;
- protect the needs of an uninformed research participant, i.e. protection of privacy, anonymity and/or confidentiality;
- question a text's origin/agenda – remember that some sources are by their nature subjective, i.e. media coverage, personal communication, or 'party line' material with an express political agenda, and even authoritative texts with an explicit goal of unbiased knowledge can be tainted by subjectivities.

Photo 5.1   Maintaining a critical eye when using existing data

In fact, because you are working with existing data, assessing credibility is essential. Ask yourself if the pre-existing data you are working with is unbiased, complete and accurate. Does it give a full account? You also need to be able to recognize whether your data was produced with a particular agenda in mind (e.g. promotional materials, or even surveys that have been produced by those with a vested interest). It may be tempting to treat the printed word as truth and to treat artifacts as conclusive evidence, but all data needs to be viewed with a critical eye as per Photo 5.1.

With existing data, the challenge is knowing what you are looking for; knowing options for finding it; knowing whether or not you can trust it; and having some sense of what you can do with it. It starts with identifying exactly what we mean by existing data and where it is found.

Types of existing data

Existing evidence of where we have been and what we have done is absolutely everywhere. We document it in a million ways, we research it, report on it, log it, video it, journal it, blog it, legislate it, develop policy on it, leave our finger-prints on it, draw it, photograph it, write poetry about it, capture it in song, send postcards, write letters, send e-mails and texts, post about it on social media, etc. The physical traces of this activity literally surround us. One way to delineate such data, particularly as related to research methods, is to look at tangible vs. online-generated data.

Tangible data

By tangible data we are referring to documents and data sets that, while often found on the Internet, exist independently of it. One key source of tangible data you are likely to find highly useful is records, both public and private.

Private sector data typically entails communication, documents and records such as:

- databases;
- press releases;
- reports;
- catalogues, pamphlets and brochures;
- meeting agendas and minutes;
- inter- and intra-office memos;
- safety records;
- sales figures;
- human resource records;
- client records (these might be students, patients, constituents, etc., depending on organization type).

Public sector data can include sources such as:

- international data held by organizations such as the World Bank, World Health Organization or United Nations;
- national data held by many federal or national governments and government departments, e.g. National Census data;
- local government data such as state of business registry reports, environment reports, community surveys, water quality data, land registry information, etc.;
- non-governmental organization data collected through commissioned or self-conducted research studies;
- university data, which is abundant and covers just about every research problem ever studied;
- archival data, such as records of births, deaths, marriages, etc.;
- legislation, including local ordinances, and state and federal regulations/laws;
- policy documents from both the public and private sectors.

Given this diversity, the key to success is being prepared. You will need to know well in advance where your data sources are located; who the gatekeepers might be; how to best approach them; whether or not you will need to use a sampling strategy; and whether the collection of sensitive or private data will require ethics approval.

Online data

Online data, on the other hand, is data that is produced on or by the Internet. It includes social data such as Twitter feeds, blogs, Facebook posts, Instagram photos, and Vine and YouTube videos. It also includes websites and their click-throughs. Of course, this pool of data is massive and just waiting to be explored through various means of research.

WORKING WITH TANGIBLE DATA

There are two forms of tangible data that you are likely to analyse in small-scale applied workplace-based research. The first is documents and the second is data sets.

Document analysis

Often the answers to research questions are held in documents, perhaps emails, policy documents and reports. The method we use for analysing such documents is aptly named document analysis. Document analysis is the collection, review, interrogation and analysis of various forms of written text as a primary source of research data. But before jumping in, it is worth exploring bias. In document analysis, pre-existing texts need to be thoughtfully considered in relation to subjectivity. The credibility of the data you generate will, in part, be dependent on recognition of the bias/purpose of the author. It may be tempting to treat the printed word as truth but, if you do, you will need to ask whose truth. A second source of bias lies with you as the researcher. As with any method, how you read and draw from the documents will be colored by your own reality. You will need to consider your biases, your skills, what exactly you are looking for, and how you will ensure credibility for data you did not collect.

In this and in many other ways, using documents as a source of evidence is not that dissimilar from relying on people to answer research questions. Just as you would need to look at the population and select a sample of people, you will need to consider (1) the range of documents you are considering as your pool of potential works, (2) which ones you will you actually look at and (3) how you plan to get your hands on them.

Gathering, reviewing and interrogating 'texts'

So how do you get a document to talk? Once you locate, acquire and assess the credibility of your documents, you will be ready to extract the data. Now the first step is to ask yourself questions about the document. This refers to questions related to the author, audience, circumstances of production, document type, whether it is a typical or exceptional example, the style, tone, agenda, political purpose, whether it contains facts, opinions, or both; basically any background information related to the document. This is sometimes called the latent content or 'unwitting' evidence. Answers to these questions may lie within the document itself, i.e. document type, tone and style, or may require further investigation, i.e. information about the author or the document's genre.

The next step involves exploration of the 'witting' evidence, or the content within the document. There are a couple of ways you can do this. The first is by using an 'interview technique', while the second involves noting occurrences, a method akin to formal structured observation.

- *The interview* – In 'interviewing' your documents, you are, in a sense, treating each document as a respondent who can provide you with information relevant to your enquiry. The questions you ask will be dependent on the nature of your enquiry and on document type. As with an interview, you will need to determine what it is you want to know, and whether your document can provide you with the answers. You then need to 'ask' each question and highlight the passages in the document that provide the answer. Organizing your responses can be done by using a color-coded highlighting system or you can turn to qualitative data management programs such as NVIVO or NUD*IST to help you with document indexing.
- *Noting occurrences* – Noting occurrences is a process that quantifies the use of particular words, phrases and concepts within a given document. As in formal structured observations, the researcher determines what is being 'looked for' and notes the amount, the frequency and often the context of the occurrence.

For example, say you wanted to trace the growth of climate change as a point of reference in US Federal legislation. You would first determine what legislative documents you would want to explore and ensure you have access. Noting occurrences would consist of a search for the phrase 'climate change' and other related terms you feel relevant. Interviewing the document is more in situ and involves 'asking' relevant questions of the document, and exploring them for the answers so that you have better context for how and why the term is used. Box 5.1 will take you through the steps of thorough document interrogation.

BOX 5.1

Gathering, reviewing and interrogating texts

To start the process of interrogating texts you need to:

1. Gather relevant 'texts' – many texts can be collected, but a few will require you to go out in the field; for example, you may want to look at billboards or exhibits.
2. Organize – for collected texts, you will want to develop and employ an organization and management scheme.
3. Copy – make copies of original texts for the purpose of annotation.
4. Confirm authenticity – assess the authenticity and credibility of the 'texts'.
5. Explore the text's agenda – review the texts and consider any inherent biases.
6. Explore background information – extract background information on author/creator, audience, purpose, style as appropriate to the text(s) being explored.
7. Ask questions 'about' the text – Who produced it? What did they produce it for? What were the circumstances of production? When, where and why was it produced? What type of data is it? Basically, you want to explore any background information that is available (sometimes called the latent content or unwitting evidence).
8. Explore content – this will vary by the type of text and, as discussed in the next section, can involve qualitative and quantitative processes. The key to success here is outlining what you plan to extract from the text well in advance.

Reflecting, refining and analyzing

As with any method, good document analysis requires you to reflect, refine and improve as you go. You may also need to be flexible. Because the documents you will be exploring were not written for your express research purpose, each will need a critical eye that can uncover and discover what you are looking for and maybe even relevant information you did not know you were looking for. Once you develop this skill, analysis can be a rich endeavor. Box 5.2 takes you through the steps of reflecting, refining and analyzing, while Box 5.3 offers you an example.

BOX 5.2

Reflecting, refining and analyzing

1. Learn and improve as you go – view document analysis as an iterative and ongoing process.
2. Review the process – reflect on any difficulties associated with gathering the texts, reviewing the sources and exploring the content.
3. Review your notes – reflect on any difficulties you might encounter in making sense of your record.
4. Make modifications – based on your own review of the process and the quality of the data generated.
5. Keep reviewing and refining – keep refining until you are comfortable with the process and data collected.
6. Major issues? – If there are major issues you will need to openly discuss them with your supervisor and consider modifications.
7. Analysis – data collected in textual analysis can be quantitative (through various modes of tallying and more in-depth statistical analysis – see Chapter 7) or can be much more qualitative. Remember: analysis should work towards addressing your research question in insightful ways.

BOX 5.3

An example of document analysis

Halabi, S., Smith, W., Collins, J., Baker, D. and Bedford, J. (2012) 'A document analysis of HIV/AIDS education interventions in Ghana', *Health Education Journal*, published online 10 July 2012.

This document analysis involved using a snowball sampling procedure to gather 24 curricula – seven school-based, 15 adult-based and two multipurpose curricula of prevention programs – and explore them for informational accuracy. Each curriculum was coded independently by two reviewers, who noted specific lines, sections, or images of the curriculum which were problematic. Findings included factual errors; omitted information; oversimplified facts; promotion of fear-based abstinence; confusing condom information; a presentation of infection as women's problem; and misrepresentation of individual risk.

Secondary analysis

The second form of tangible data you will likely be working with is existing data sets. Secondary data analysis is the collection, review, interrogation and analysis of existing data sets in order to answer questions not previously or adequately addressed. In other words it sees researchers answering a new question with old data.

Using secondary data allows you to 'skip' data collection processes and allows you to work with samples that might otherwise have been inaccessible, or samples much larger than you would have been able to generate on your own. But remember: secondary data is only as good as its collection processes – and you have no control over these.

Now perhaps the most crucial step in secondary analysis is knowing exactly what you are looking for – that is, having a clearly articulated research question and knowing what types of data might answer that question. When it comes to secondary analysis, this can actually be more difficult than you might realize. When you are working with an existing data set, you skip the process of design, including working through decisions about population, samples, questions, response categories, etc. You also do not get to explore data as it comes in. And both of these processes offer tremendous opportunity for conceptual work. In secondary analysis, you need to consciously think through such issues, even if design and preliminary data were done by others. Only then will you be in a position to assess the relevance of an existing data set to your research question.

Approach

The basic steps of secondary analysis are:

1. *Determining your research question* – As indicated above, you need to know exactly what you are looking for.
2. *Locating data* – Knowing what is out there and whether you can gain access to it. A quick Internet search, possibly with the help of a librarian, will reveal a wealth of options.
3. *Evaluating relevance of the data* – Considering things like the data's original purpose, when it was collected, population, sampling strategy/sample, data collection protocols, operationalization of concepts, questions asked, and form/shape of the data.
4. *Assessing credibility of the data* – Establishing the credentials of the original researchers, searching for full explication of methods including any problems encountered, determining how consistent the data is with data from other sources, discovering whether the data has been used in any credible published research.
5. *Analysis* – This will generally involve a range of statistical processes.

An example here might be: Step 1, determine what you want to know, 'How have migration rates fluctuated in Canada over the past 30 years?'; Step 2, determine what data sets, including the National Census, might have this information; Step 3, explore relevance by exploring how the question is asked in existing surveys, if there is any bias or assumption in how it is asked, and if it has been asked in the same way over the 30-year period you wish to explore; Step 4, assess credibility – in the case of the Census, methods should be well documented; Step 5, analyze by exploring trends in migration and how this might vary by demographic character-istics like geographic region, age, socioeconomic status, gender, education, etc.

WORKING WITH ONLINE DATA

So much data, so little time. The Internet is a beast when it comes to data genera-tion. Take websites, for example: since 1996, the WayBack Machine has archived more than 450 billion web pages and saved for posterity two petabytes of data (1 petabyte = 1000 terabytes = 1,000,000 gigabytes). This type of data can be extremely useful for analyzing the impact of significant events, movements or technologies. How has financial regulation changed since 9/11 or in the wake of the global financial crisis? Open-source Internet archives hold backups of specific websites, saved periodically over the last two decades. The best part is that these web pages are not a static screenshot, but rather a backup version of the page, meaning some links within it can still be accessed. Two of the best sources for Internet time travel include:

- WayBack Machine – the WayBack Machine, from the Internet Archive, lets you see a particular website's development over time: http://archive.org/web/web.php
- Library of Congress Web Archives – the Library of Congress Web Archives project has archived sites relating to significant events, such as the 9/11 attacks, US elections and the Iraq War: http://lcweb2.loc.gov/diglib/lcwa/html/lcwa-home.html

While this may appear to be a quirky tool with little organizational application, the truth is that opportunities for original organizational research abound. These archived web pages could be used to audit a company's marketing strategy (to determine consistency of brand image and message through their website over time), to research information about the growth of particular private companies (which are not required to publicly file annual reports). Archived websites from the WayBack Machine have even been used as evidence in commercial court cases (such as patent litigation) or to unravel international mysteries (Dewey, 2014) (see Box 5.4). Just as detectives can learn lots from what you throw out in your waste bin, so too can you learn from the discarded remnants of the Internet. New companies can look at their competitors' early designs, strategists can look up failed business ventures, and employers can investigate job applicants' student web pages.

Internet archives like the WayBack Machine are a particularly handy tool for *triangulation*. In research methods, triangulation is locating and validating data through cross-verification with other known (i.e. located) sources. For instance, you have data from a couple of sources (perhaps literature, or interviews) that suggests an early marketing strategy of product X was unabashedly sexist. By looking at the board members listed for the company in that year, you may find that there is no female representation.

If you use online archive tools as part of triangulation, be aware that not everything on the Internet has been archived. The web existed before 1996, and since then various pages may have been excluded. An absence of a website on the archive does not prove that it did not exist at that time. Moreover, more and more sites have sought to exclude archiving. In fact, anyone can use a robots.txt file on the server to exclude the Internet Archive's web crawler. As a result, far too many pages have already implemented this impediment to archiving.

BOX 5.4

Internet sleuthing: the fate of MH17

The WayBack Machine is a non-profit web crawler that archives old versions of Internet pages. In 2014, it preserved this social media posting: 'In the vicinity of Torez, we just downed a plane, an AN-26. It is lying somewhere in the Progress Mine. We have issued warnings not to fly in our airspace. We have video confirming. The bird fell on a waste heap. Residential areas were not hit. Civilians were not injured.'

Only minutes later, international news broke that a Malaysian Airlines commercial flight, MH17 had been downed over Ukraine killing all 298 people on board. Could this be the same plane? Page administrators for the group responsible for the social media posting seemed to think so. When news of the civilian airliner disaster broke, the group tried to delete their post. They could not, however, remove the screen grab from Internet Archive. 'Here's why we exist,' the WayBack Machine wrote on Facebook, with links to earlier versions of the Facebook page. 'A Ukrainian Separatist boasted his pro-Russian Group shot down a Ukrainian plane on his website. When it turned out to be #MH17 #MalaysiaAirlines he erased it, but our WayBack Machine captured the page for history.'

Internet Archive and others like it are powerful testaments for a new wave of pro-transparency bots and tools, all of them dedicated to leveraging technology to expose how governments, politicians and other powerful political figures can manipulate the digital landscape. 'Important work,' one commenter wrote on the Internet Archive page. 'Without it, we're in Orwell's 1984.'

Online databases

Databases offer a wealth of information. Online databases store census information, demographic statistics, conflict data and economic development indicators. This research is useful for nearly every field of inquiry, including business, social sciences and STEM (Science, Technology, Engineering and Mathematical) fields.

Databases parse information by variable and population group. This allows you to capture snapshots (how many people voted for the US Democratic Presidential nominee in 2016) as well as trends over time (how many states changed their party preference over the last four Presidential elections). Some comprehensive national and international databases include:

- World Bank – http://data.worldbank.org
- United Nations – https://data.un.org
- United States – http://fedstats.sites.usa.gov/
- Australian Bureau of Statistics – www.abs.gov.au
- UK – www.data.gov.uk
- Gapminder – www.gapminder.org (For more information see Box 5.5).

How could the type of data found in databases prove useful for decision-making? Perhaps you work for a national bank that wants to roll out a mobile banking application for its customers on smartphones. What information could public databases offer to supplement this business decision? First you could locate the percentage of the population that owns a smartphone. This data is available at the national and the state level. By identifying one or two locations at the state level with high penetration of smartphones (or even a smaller geographic area such as a county or council), you could guide a pilot program whereby one group trials the product and offers feedback for improvements before the final rollout is attempted.

Big data

Big data is information/data sets so large and complex that they cannot be analyzed using traditional databases or data processing applications. The Australian Tax Office, for example, is using the analysis of big data to understand trends in tax evasion. Big data is also associated with social data, data that individuals create that is knowingly and voluntarily shared by them: examples include tweets, posts and videos shared on Twitter, Facebook and YouTube respectively. The unprecedented use of these mediums means that much social data is also big data.

One of the great things about social data is how massive and current it is. It has the ability to give us both a snapshot of now and a look into the future. Understanding travel plans, outbreaks of flu, political opinion, responses to social disasters and, in fact, anything that an Internet community is currently discussing, represents the potential to draw on an extremely large pool of data. This, of course, saves you the time and cost associated with commissioning studies that rely on the collection of primary data.

As pictured in Figure 5.1, Big data means variety, volume, veracity and velocity. With big data technology, we can now harness differed types of data including sensor data, photos, social media messages, email, video, location data, and voice recordings and integrate this information with more traditional, structured data. With this networked data, insights are virtually limitless. This brings us to the fifth

Figure 5.1   Big data

'v' in big data – value. Big data must contribute value to the organization. Without a sound business case for its analysis and application, big data risks becoming a buzzword project that contributes very little to the organization. Aside from the focus on value, there are other significant challenges in using big data. For one, we can become bamboozled by the amount of data and forget that we do not have a representative sample. And we are not just talking about a lack of representativeness within a narrowly defined population; we are also talking about the ability to misrepresent a global population. If, for example, international policy decisions are to be influenced by social data, then developing countries with limited computer and Internet access will not be in a strong position to inform decision-making.

Privacy is another major issue. Is something public just because it is blogged or on Facebook? There is a real blurring of public and private spheres. Additionally, the ability of Internet data to be traced means that researchers are not in a position to ensure anonymity. On the flip side, when there is a need to verify the identity of research subject to ensure credibility, this can be equally difficult to do. One example of the challenge of big data, privacy and targeted marketing, is detailed in Box 5.5.

The sheer volume and rate of change also poses massive challenges for researchers. Traditional research methods were never designed for what the Internet is now delivering and certainly not for what it will be delivering in the future. Our processes of funding, design and conduct, writing up and publication of research studies are undeniably slow. Data collected in one year may not be published in a study until two to three years later – and in that time is likely to be outdated.

User-generated social data is also inherently flawed. We may want to track Twitter followers, Facebook likes and YouTube hits, but these can all be bought. Fake traffic is a reality. If there is a financial incentive to falsify such data, it will happen. We also have to look at the interests of Google, which is there to advertise and make money. Yes, it may be tracking what we do, but through its tracking and targeted ad placements, it also influences what we do. Google has vested interests that have an influence on data. Given all these challenges, what research approaches can help us wade through masses of messy, less than trustworthy data, and what strategies can we call on to ensure credibility of results?

Well, such strategies are ever-developing. What is interesting, however, is that methodological developments in this space are not necessarily being led by academics. It is market researchers and advertising agencies who have come to the fore as they recognize the profits that can come from data mining. Companies like Datasift.com and Gnip.com, for example, build filtered data streams so clients can get answers to their questions from social media in real time. And while they definitely offer information on the retail sector, and in particular brands, they are also in the business of tracking political opinion, emergent health issues and influential people – showing the overlap into traditional academic areas of health, social and political science. Rather than academics, it is private enterprise that is developing the tools needed to mine the web.

BOX 5.5

Big data, privacy, and targeted marketing

The most common commercial application of big data has been to create targeted advertising to customers. In a *New York Times* piece on the how companies use your data, Charles Duhigg shared the story of a Target customer: 'An angry man went to his local Target store in Minneapolis, demanding to speak to a manager: "My daughter got this in the mail!" he said. "She's still in high school, and you're sending her coupons for baby clothes and cribs? Are you trying to encourage her to get pregnant?" The manager looked at the mailer. Sure enough, it was addressed to the man's daughter and contained advertisements for maternity clothing, nursery furniture and pictures of smiling infants. The manager apologized and then called a few days later to apologize again. On the phone, though, the father was somewhat abashed. "I had a talk with my daughter," he said. "It turns out there's been some activities in my house I haven't been completely aware of. She's due in August. I owe you an apology."'

(Continued)

(Continued)

How did Target's algorithms know a customer was pregnant in real-time? Every time you go shopping, you share intimate details about your life with retailers, even more so if you have a customer loyalty card. Each customer loyalty card has a unique identifier that also links to demographic information such as geographic location, family size, spending habits, etc. By analyzing the historical data of mothers in the early months of their pregnancies, analysts at Target discovered buying patterns. That is, women tend to purchase certain products such as unscented lotion and vitamins, in specific trimesters. If a customer starts to buy these items, the company may use this data to presume a baby is on the way and then tailor relevant coupons in their home address mailers. As expectant mothers tend to purchase quite a lot, this represents a lucrative customer segment.

The customer loyalty card and the treasure trove of information it holds represents one of the balancing acts in commercializing big data. The same challenges surround the use of social data. Millions of individuals log their real-time location, vacation plans, purchasing habits, political preferences, list of associates and pictures of breakfast on online social media accounts. Businesses can purchase access to some of this data to provide targeted advertising, thereby enabling service providers such as Facebook to offer free social media accounts and still make a profit (Facebook had revenues of roughly 12 billion US$ in 2014, up from nearly 8 billion US$ in 2013). As a consumer in the age of big data, one caveat appears to be necessary: if the product is free, then *you* are the product.

Web mining

Web mining is the process of discovering patterns in web-based large data sets involving methods that call on artificial intelligence, machine learning, statistics and database systems. When it comes to the web, there are actually three distinct things you can mine for: web usage, which looks at users' history and tells us what people are looking at on the Internet; web content, which extracts and integrates data from web page contents; and web structure, which analyzes the connection structure of a web site by exploring hyperlinks. Because of structural diversity and ever-expanding sources, it is getting more and more difficult to mine effectively with current search tools. This has led to the quest for intelligent web agents, basically, a sophisticated artificial intelligence system that can autonomously extract and organize web-based information.

The benefits here constitute information that can aid targeted marketing. Government agencies, for example, are using this technology to identify criminal activities and even classify threats of terrorism. In the public sector, web mining can help pinpoint public perception and needs. In health care, it can uncover outbreaks as well as health fears.

As a research strategy, however, there are methodological concerns related to data quality and representativeness that need to be approached with transparency, as well as concerns related to ethics. Mining usage, for example, is an invasion of privacy. There are plenty of places we go on the web that we might not want others to know about, and the process of de-individualization is not foolproof. Ethics committees will need to develop and redevelop their policies as academic research becomes ever more common in this space.

Strategies for productive online research

Thus far, we have looked at what is available on the Internet, but not how to get the most out of it. Small-scale applied workplace-based research projects demand discipline and efficiency. The Internet is a tremendous research tool, but it can be a virtual rabbit hole that you will emerge from hours later with nothing accomplished!

Remember the programmers' mantra: GIGO (Garbage In = Garbage Out). A tool is only as useful as the typing fingers wielding it. Search engines will try to place the most relevant results at the top of the list, but if search terms are too broad or ambiguous, the results will be unhelpful. The most productive searches are those that use engines to filter suitable results. For example, Google Scholar returns results from peer-reviewed academic journals and scientific papers. Box 5.6 details some ways to narrow search results to the most relevant for your small-scale workplace-based research project.

BOX 5.6

Refining your online search

- Put the tilde operator '~' before your search term to return results that include synonyms.
- Use the term 'OR' or search for either of two terms.
- Use the minus '–' sign to identify terms you don't want in your results.
- Put quotation marks around words '' to search for that exact phrase.
- Use the wildcard operator * – Google calls it the 'fill in the blank' operator. For example, amusement* will return pages with amusement and any other term(s) the Google search engine deems relevant. You can't use wildcards for parts of words. So for example, amusement p* is invalid.
- Start your search with 'site': this limits your search-specific sites or types of site (.org, .edu).
- Add 'filetype:' and the three-letter file abbreviation to limit your search to only that type of file, e.g. pdf or ppt.
- Use the Google Goggles app and take a photo instead of typing a search.
- Add a zip code/postcode to the end of a search to get local offerings.
- Use 'Related sites:' For example, related:www.youtube.com can be used to find sites similar to YouTube.

Assessing credibility of online data

As you work with existing data, particularly online data, issues of credibility are paramount. In the uncharted waters of the World Wide Web users must develop a critical eye to evaluate the quality of information found. For existing data to be useful for research, it must be credible and current. So you need to ask: (1) Where did this information come from? (2) Is the original data replicated or interpreted through a second lens? (3) What are some useful strategies to ascertain this?

A useful strategy is to deconstruct the web address. Web addresses, or URLs, provide one of the most obvious hints about source origin of information and thus credibility contained therein. For instance, if there is a tilde (~) in the URL, the web site is probably a personal web page or blog and should be used only with extreme scrutiny.

BOX 5.7

Caveat: domain names matter! Ben's story

I was conducting some research for the organization about government policy in the industry and I was looking for a particular executive statement. I typed it into Google and clicked on the first link. I immediately knew I had made a mistake. Apparently www.whitehouse. com was pornography! I tried the second result, www.whitehouse.net. Now that my guard was up, I looked more carefully than usual. I noticed that instead of the bald eagle, the government seal featured a vulture. Though the page formatting looked legit, the content was all wrong. A statement against Hispanic immigrants? Apparently I had stumbled into a white supremacist group! I was still reeling when I remembered that the real White House URL is www.whitehouse.gov. Wow, those domain names really matter!

As Box 5.7 suggests, the domain suffix can provide a clue about the purpose, authorship and audience of a website. Search engines rank material according to their idea of relevance (usually by keyword and date), but that does not mean it meets the high bar set for research use. Table 5.1 lists some of the common domain names and the corresponding level of credibility.

Credibility of information is inextricably linked to who is providing it. Pay attention to clues such as connection of the author to the subject, the audience, as well as the documentation of supporting evidence.

- *Credentials* – What is the authority of the author? What are the author's qualifications or credentials?
- *Motive/Intention* – Affiliation or sponsorship. What organization are they associated with? Is there a link to a contact number or email address associated with that organization? A link to an association does not necessarily mean that the organization has approved the content.

Table 5.1   Examining domain names

Suffix	Use	Credibility
.com .net	Most common, commercial or personal site	Low
.org	Traditionally a non-profit organization. Purpose is advocacy so may be rich information on specific issues, but also a particular bias. Note that .org is becoming increasingly common as a generic domain extension	Low to medium
.edu	Educational institution. Sites using this domain site range from primary through postgraduate. Students affiliated with a university may also receive web space with an .edu domain suffix so check whether individual pages are faculty or students in the department	Medium
.mil	Military. Good luck getting past the glossy recruitment page without some clearance credentials. Depending on the branch, there are reports or study findings that may be useful on the public pages	Medium
.gov	Government websites, usually at the federal/national level. Information typically includes official statistics, department portals and judicial rulings	High

- *Recognised authority* – Has the author published in scholarly or professional publications? These publications are peer-reviewed by other experts, meaning that mistakes are caught and usually ruthlessly exterminated by a community of scholars.
- *Objectivity* – Are there clues of author bias? Are they promoting a product?
- *Verifiability* – Does the author provide a complete list of works cited? If so, whom do they reference and are they experts in their field?
- *Currency* – Is the web information current? Are links missing or broken? Poor web maintenance may mean the site has been abandoned and it may be difficult to determine whether information presented is current.

Other strategies to critically access websites include triangulation. As mentioned, do not rely on a single online avenue; rather, look for evidence from multiple sources.

Aside from existing sources found one at a time, there may be existing sources that bundle multiple studies together. The last part of the chapter details how to analyze previous studies, including systematic analysis and meta-analysis.

ANALYZING PREVIOUS STUDIES

Finally, in the existing data stakes we get to explore existing research studies – of which there are plenty! Research abounds: there are over 3 million new journal articles produced every year. And a solid research question is one that asks whether there are any definitive results we can draw from a range of similar studies. There are two strategies for working with existing studies and existing data. Systemic reviews are used to assess and synthesize a range of studies to determine more definitive results. Meta-analysis is the result of running combined data sets through analysis to synthesize or confirm results. Let's start with systematic reviews.

Systematic review

A systematic review is an overview of primary studies on a particular topic. It relies on transparent, reproducible methods to locate, critically appraise and synthesize the findings and results of credible studies. But take care not to confuse systematic reviews with a literature review. A literature review is a critical review of a body of knowledge, including findings and theoretical constructs. It is an overview of a body of literature. A systematic review extends beyond this. It attempts to determine the validity of individual studies and synthesize the results of these. The goal is to offer a thorough, yet condensed, view on the evidence in a particular area.

In business, social sciences and health industries, systematic reviews are increasingly used to inform policy and decision-making. Currently, it is most common in medicine, in particular, in studies using randomized control trials. But they are of value anywhere a rigorous assessment of validity within a particular area of study will aid decision-making.

Systematic reviews offer:

- a transparent, verifiable and replicable approach;
- minimization of bias and error;
- conclusions of higher validity and reliability;
- a comprehensive picture of a research area that can be quickly disseminated to researchers, practitioners and policy-makers;
- context for interpreting the results of a new study.

Approach

The basic steps of systematic review are:

1. *Formulate the research question* – Like any research process, a clear, unambiguous research question will help set the direction for your study: e.g., 'What type of health promotion campaigns have been most effective in reducing smoking rates of Australian teenagers'; *or* 'Does school leadership make a difference to educational standards?'.
2. *Develop and use an explicit, reproducible methodology* – Key to systematic reviews are that bias is minimized and that methods are transparent and reproducible.
3. *Develop and use clear inclusion/exclusion criteria* – The array of literature out there is vast. Determining clear selection criteria for inclusion is essential.
4. *Develop and use an explicit search strategy* – It is important to identify all studies that meet the eligibility criteria set in step 3. The search for studies should be extensive and draw on multiple databases.

5. *Critically assess the validity of the findings in included studies* – This is likely to involve critical appraisal guides and quality checklists that cover participant recruitment, data collection methods and modes of analysis. Assessment is often conducted by two or more reviewers who know both the topic area and commonly used methods.

6. *Analyze findings across the studies* – This can involve analysis, comparison and synthesis of results using methodological criteria. This is often the case for qualitative studies. Quantitative studies generally attempt to use statistical methods to explore differences between studies and combine their effects (see meta-analysis below). If divergences are found, the source of the divergence is analyzed.

7. *Synthesis and interpretation of results* – Synthesized results need to be interpreted in light of both the limitations of the review and the studies it contains. An example here might be the inclusion of only studies reported in English. This level of transparency allows readers to assess the review credibility and applicability of findings.

With all the methodological safeguards in place, systematic reviews should be bullet-proof. The reality of applied research, however, means that there are likely to be differing opinions on what constitutes quality; how to deal with results from various research traditions; limited resources; and varying levels of research skills and experience. It is worth remembering that systematic reviews are only as good as the ability of researchers to follow protocols. Nonetheless, systematic reviews constitute a good way to generate interesting and robust research results when studies abound. Box 5.8 highlights centers dedicated to advancing systematic reviews.

BOX 5.8

Centers dedicated to advancing systematic reviews

The Center for Evidence-Based Management (www.cebma.org)

'The Center for Evidence-Based Management is a non-profit member organization dedicated to promoting evidence-based practice in the field of management through systematic reviews. We provide support and resources to managers, consultants, organizations, teachers, academics and others interested in learning more about evidence-based management.'

The website includes online research databases, discussion forums, white papers, journal articles, training videos, statistical glossaries and sample size calculator.

(Continued)

(Continued)

The Cochrane Collaboration (www.cochrane.org/)

'The Cochrane Collaboration is an international network of more than 28,000 dedicated people from over 100 countries. We work together to help health care organizations, policy-makers, patients, their advocates and carers, make well-informed decisions about health care, by preparing, updating, and promoting the accessibility of Cochrane Reviews— over 5,000 so far, published online in the **Cochrane Database of Systematic Reviews.**'

Concentrating on the area of health care, the Cochrane Collaboration site offers systematic review training links, an extensive library and vast review resources, including the world's largest collection of randomized controlled trial records.

The EPPI Centre (eppi.ioe.ac.uk)

'The Evidence for Policy and Practice Information and Co-ordinating Centre (EPPI-Centre) is part of the University of London. Since 1993, we have been at the forefront of carrying out systematic reviews and developing review methods in public policy. We are dedicated to making reliable research findings accessible to the people who need them, whether they are making policy, practice or personal decisions.'

The EPPI Centre site offers a series of links to systematic review training, tools, methods and databases. It also has a library of over 165 reviews in education, and public health and participative research.

Meta-analysis

Meta-analysis is the statistical analysis and synthesis of the results of two or more primary studies that address the same hypothesis in the same way – common in systematic reviews.

What is the difference between a systematic review and a meta-analysis? A systematic review, as indicated above, locates, critically appraises and synthesizes the findings and results of credible studies by using transparent reproducible methods. Meta-analysis is simply one of those transparent reproducible methods. In fact, it is the gold medal standard of systematic review methods. And this is because it implies that studies under review are quantitative, are highly comparable and are treated statistically, thereby minimizing bias.

Meta-analysis, if carried out within a rigorous systematic review, should offer an unbiased synthesis of empirical data. The goal is a more statistically robust analysis than that which could be achieved with a single study with a single set of assumptions and conditions.

As compared to single studies, meta-analysis offers:

- more statistical power;
- more confidence in results;

- possible explanations of variance;
- greater ability to apply findings to general population.

On the downside, meta-analysis can:

- be costly as it can be a time-consuming challenge to find 'combinable' studies;
- require advanced statistical techniques;
- be tainted by publication bias (studies with results that fit a particular agenda are more likely to be published).

Approach

Since meta-analysis is a subset (but not a requirement) of systematic reviews, basic steps are similar. Therefore, only point 6 is expanded upon. For more on the other points, see systematic reviews above.

1. Formulate the research question.
2. Develop and use an explicit, reproducible methodology (this step was done when meta-analysis was originally decided upon).
3. Develop and use clear inclusion/exclusion criteria.
4. Develop and use an explicit search strategy.
5. Critically assess the validity of the findings in included studies.
6. Analyze findings across the studies – statistical analysis would involve decisions related to:

   a) the dependent and independent variables under review;
   b) how studies will be weighted according to sample size;
   c) how to conduct sensitivity analysis (the extent to which study results stay the same given different approaches to aggregating data).

7. Synthesis and interpretation of results.

Box 5.9 includes examples of business-relevant meta-analyses.

BOX 5.9

Examples of meta-analysis

It's quite easy to search databases for meta-analyses, since the term meta-analysis is often included in the article title. Here is a very brief summary of three studies that show diversity of topic and approach.

(Continued)

(Continued)

Schyns, B. and Schilling, J. (2013) 'How bad are the effects of bad leaders? A meta-analysis of destructive leadership and its outcomes', *The Leadership Quarterly*, 24(1): 138–58.

   This meta-analysis utilized 57 studies on leadership and organizational outcomes. Results indicated that negative or destructive leadership correlates positively with turnover intention, resistance and counterproductive work behavior.

Dorien, T.A., Kooij, M., Kanfer, R. and Dikkers, J. (2011) 'Age and work-related motives: results of a meta-analysis', *Journal of Organizational Behavior*, 32(2): 197–225.

   This meta-analysis examines 86 studies to determine whether work motivations change with age. The study found that intrinsic motivation correlates positively with age, and a strong negative relationship between age and strength of growth and extrinsic motives was revealed. The predicted positive relation between age and strength of social and security motives was found only in certain subgroups.

Orlitzky, M., Schmidt, F.L and Rynes, S.L. (2003) 'Corporate social and financial performance: a meta-analysis', *Organization Studies*, 24(3): 403–41.

   This meta-analysis utilizes 52 studies to examine whether corporate virtue in the form of social responsibility and, to a lesser extent, environmental responsibility pays off financially.

When timelines are short, as they are in small-scale applied workplace-based research projects, leveraging existing studies and data can be invaluable. They can provide evidence and background for your own research topic.

CHAPTER SUMMARY

- Existing data can be found in documents, databases and on the Internet – none of which was created by the researcher for their research purposes.
- Working with existing data can save time and resources as well as eliminate researcher bias. However, because this data has been collected for another purpose, it may lack relevance, currency or be tainted with methodological flaws.
- Unprecedented amounts of data exist online. This opens up the possibility to use the Internet as a library and an archive, as well as a source for user-generated big data.
- Research studies abound. You can take advantage of existing studies by understanding systemic reviews and meta-analysis.

GATHERING PRIMARY DATA

THE BENEFITS AND CHALLENGES OF PRIMARY DATA

Primary data is data collected by researchers expressly for their research purposes – it is data that does not exist independent of the research process. Primary data is current, it is wholly owned by the researcher, and most importantly, it is targeted at specific issues the researcher is exploring. It can be used to explore an emerging issue or update understanding of an existing one. It allows us to ask – what exactly is the root of the problem? How can we tackle this issue? What solutions have the greatest support?

When situations that were once understood evolve and novel problems arise, primary data may provide key information to aid responses, solutions and adaptations. It is, therefore, a critical resource for decision-making. In external environments, primary data can help make sense of changes and developments that impact organizations; in the internal environment, it can also drive improvements by applying new information to product and service design, enhancing offerings and improving the organizational process.

In his research on organizational success, Choo (1996) identifies 'intelligent learning organizations' as those most effective in managing informational needs, gathering and use. Primary data is the first step towards anticipating, adapting and responding to challenges.

It is worth noting that primary data is valued in so far as it helps to accomplish these goals. Only relevant and timely information is useful; irrelevant or confusing information merely exacerbates problems. For this reason, primary data collection must be targeted and appropriate:

- Targeted – information required must useful to the question, challenge or dilemma being explored.
- Appropriate – methods must be the best suited to obtaining the required information given constraints of time and access.

Primary data, unlike existing data, is collected first hand and does not rely on the efforts and interpretations of others. There is, therefore, a significant time investment in collecting primary data. Whether it be surveys, interviews or observation studies, designing your own research protocols is challenging. Survey instruments are notoriously difficult to get right. Getting through a series of interviews and thoughtfully analyzing them can be an exercise in frustration. But this is not meant to put you off – primary data can be instrumental. This is simply a cautionary note that challenges, such as getting enough respondents within your timeframe and racing around different locations to conduct interviews, need to be factored into the research design decision-making process.

Since small-scale applied workplace-based research projects operate under tight timeframes, it's important that you understand what methods are best suited to your study.

Primary data collection methods

Broadly speaking, there are three primary data collection methods in small-scale applied workplace-based research: interviewing, surveys and focus groups. Each of these comes with their own advantages and disadvantages regarding logistics, data volume, data depth and time investment (see Table 6.1). Depending on your research question, scope of the project and time constraints, one or more of these methods may be useful.

Interviews

Interviews are one of the most common methods of primary data collection. This method involves gathering information from individuals one at a time, through

Table 6.1   Table of primary data collection methods

Method	Participants (at a time)	Time investment	Data volume	Data depth
Interviews	1	High	Low	High
Surveys	10+	Low	High	Low
Focus groups	6–10	Medium	Medium	High

an extended and somewhat formalized conversation. Typically, interviewees are experts or insiders; however, they may also be customers, clients, employees or other individuals depending on the purpose of the research.

This data collection method is favored because it yields rich data. Some researchers use this interviewing in the first stages of their project, as an exploratory tool to narrow appropriate themes and lines of inquiry which may be tested through survey instruments in a larger population. Other researchers use interviews, particularly of elites, as the primary component of their project.

One considerable challenge of this method is that it is time-consuming for both researcher and participant. Gaining access to respondents, building rapport with interviewees and organizing logistics are essential if any worthwhile information is to be gathered. Moreover, the process of conducting an interview can be intimidating for both the interviewer and the interviewee, since the person on the other side of the table is likely to be someone senior or more experienced. Some of these concerns can be allayed through rigorous planning and relevant practice.

Focus groups

Focus groups offer a useful alternative to time-intensive one-on-one interviews. In this method, a group of people participate in a discussion about their perceptions, opinions, beliefs, attitudes towards a product, service, advertisement, idea or concept. The group discussion is moderated by a facilitator (generally you). Common uses for this method include consumer focus groups that provide feedback on current or proposed products, voter groups that may provide feedback on political campaigns, or a demographic sampling that tests the viability of new television series, etc. The first focus group was thought to have been used during the Second World War to examine the effectiveness of propaganda!

Focus groups are interactive. Participants talk with other group members as much as with the facilitator. For this reason, the size of a focus group is usually limited to 6–10 subjects. A larger group may limit the detail of responses as respondents share airtime, while a smaller group may struggle to offer enough cohesion and diversity of opinion. Since the facilitator is but one among five or more talkers, it is best that the burden of full note-taking not be added. Ideally, raw data should be preserved through audio recording.

Surveys

Surveys involve gathering information from a sample of the population by means of standardized questions. Surveys are one of the most popular methods of data collection for government, business and social institutions in need of critical information due to time and cost savings. Questionnaires can be submitted to larger audiences at one time, and the responses can be obtained more easily. Questionnaires require a relatively low time commitment from participants, and yield a high volume of data points. They are also extremely versatile, and may be conducted by telephone, on paper, in person or online.

But wait. Before you run out and plug your colleagues' email addresses into SurveyMonkey, there are a few caveats. First, what surveys and questionnaires save in data collection speed, they make up for in survey design time, as will be covered later in the chapter. Moreover, there are complications of response rates and representativeness, depending on the distribution of questionnaires. A pilot study is often necessary to iron out complications, but this is even more challenging given the limited timeframe of your small-scale applied workplace-based projects. The use of surveys yields a high volume of data points but must be carefully constructed in order for those data points to be useful for your research.

Are two methods better than one?

The methods detailed above are the most common for organization-based research. But can you use more than one? The answer is yes. Different data collection methods, primary and secondary included, can be used to complement one another. But it is a case of balancing the benefits of triangulation with the time constraints you are likely to face. In small-scale applied workplace-based research, the key criterion is the ability to (a) credibly answer your research question while (b) making deadlines. Box 6.1 gives a good example of a mixed-method approach.

BOX 6.1

Mixed methods at the museum: Loralei's story

I worked in a natural science museum and designed my research project around one of the priorities in the museum's Vision2020 document – boosting visitor numbers. The museum had a mission of public education and visitor numbers were seen as the indicator of whether they were meeting that goal. The museum already had lots of quantitative data about the number of tickets sold and the distribution between adult and child tickets, but I wanted to look deeper into the ages of kids that were coming. I had read some research that getting young children and their parents in the door is the best investment, because if done well, you're creating a visitor for life!

I knew it would be difficult to arrange formal interviews or focus groups for parents of young children so I decided to first try to talk to them in the museum. Obviously I didn't want to chase people around exhibits or block the exit by standing there with a clipboard. I noticed that the museum had an enclosed child's play area on the fourth floor where parents hung out without having to worry that their child was going to run amok through the legs of the Tyrannosaurus Rex exhibit. I set up shop there for a couple of hours throughout the week.

While their kids were preoccupied with playing, I was able to talk to the parents. In just a few minutes, I got their insights into why they came to the museum, what they thought could be improved, etc. It was really interesting actually. Since I'm not a parent myself, I had never noticed that some of the interactive screens for kids were just too high for young children; there wasn't even a water fountain low enough for them! I used their suggestions to develop a list of options for the museum to consider.

Then I set up a screen in the same play area where parents got to vote which option they liked best. It was a lot easier to get quick feedback when you give people a list of options, rather than an open-ended 'Comments' form. And it was great evidence to present to my manager about how the budget could be best utilized in attracting and keeping our younger visitors!

The first element of any study is to define who has the data you need and how to get it.

SEEKING RESPONDENTS

If the research process is all about getting your research question answered, then it is probably a good idea to think about who might hold the answer to your question. So let's think about this for a minute. Ask yourself whether answers rest with a broad segment of society. Do you need to know what the 'masses' do, think or feel? In this scenario surveys and quantitative data might be the way to go. In fact, one of the main reasons we work with quantitative data is because we want to reach such a broad sector of society that gathering qualitative data would not be feasible.

In 'qualitative' models of research, however, the opposite tends to be true. Because we want to preserve powerful text and rich narrative, what we tend to target are answers that are held by the 'few' rather than the 'many'. Yes, answers may still sit with a broad sector of society or within a population, but they might also be held by experts and insiders or even within the experiences of a particular individual. Equally, they might be held within the practices of a setting, say for example, a workplace.

No matter what the scenario, it is absolutely crucial to figure out who might hold the answer to your research question and how you will open up opportunities to gather information from those in the know. Respondent groups, however, can be quite diverse, so you may need to employ several strategies for finding those with the answers. Seeking broad societal representation (sampling a population), for example, may be most appropriate. But working with those in the know (by selecting key informants) might be better suited to some qualitative approaches.

There are, of course, plenty of challenges. Whether you decide to work with populations or key informants, locating and accessing respondents who are appropriate, representative, open, honest, knowledgeable, have good memories, are not afraid to expose themselves and do not feel a need to present themselves in any particular light might be more difficult than you would expect.

You may decide that what is most appropriate is a defined sampling strategy that can generate a representative sample. At other times, you will need to be strategic. You may decide to turn to where you know you have an 'in' with key individuals. Whether you decide to work with samples or informants, there will be plenty of issues and challenges you will need to work through.

Sampling for primary data collection

While it might be the goal, it is simply impractical to interview, observe and survey entire populations. There just isn't enough time or resources available. But, we can sample.

A sample is a subset of a population. Samples avoid the problem of assessing an entire and possibly 'infinite' group. The human population, for instance, is infinite in that its size is typically so vast that no single measurement (such as height) can be completed for all without the population size itself changing in the interim.

The goal is to select a sample that is: (1) broad enough to allow you to speak about a particular population; (2) large enough to allow you to conduct the desired analysis; and (3) small enough to be manageable. In studies with goals of generalizability, this will involve using the most practical procedures possible for gathering a sample that best 'represents' a larger population. At other times, however, the nature of the research question may find representativeness unable to be assessed or inappropriate. In these cases, researchers will still strategically select their samples, but in ways that best serve their stated research goals.

Meeting these goals will require you to think through a number of sampling issues, including the need to: define your population; construct a sample frame; determine appropriate sample size; and select a suitable sampling strategy.

Defining your population

It is important to have a clear and well-defined population in mind before you do any sampling. This means you will need to go into your study knowing the total class of 'elements' you want to be able to speak about. For example, say you want to present findings that will be representative of 13–18-year-olds in San Francisco. Your population here is made up of individuals with a particular set of defining characteristics, in this case both age (13–18) and geography (in San Francisco). Keep in mind that in a study of individuals you might have used other defining characteristics, such as gender, marital status, race, etc.

And, of course, populations don't always need to be made up of individuals. Depending on the nature of your question, 'elements' of your population might be households, workplaces, or even events. For example, your population might be board rooms across the United States. In this case, it is a particular type of organizational setting that makes up the population. Defining characteristics include both geography (across the US) and type of setting (board room). Other possibilities for defining 'organizations' might include number of employees, years of operation, public or private, etc. An example of a population made up of events might be professional soccer matches held in Barcelona in 2016. Defining characteristics here are type of activity (professional soccer matches), geography (Barcelona) and time period (2016).

Constructing a sample frame

A sample frame is a list that includes every member of the population from which a sample is to be taken, and is essential to all sampling processes. Now ideally, a sample frame would match your target population, but this is rarely the case. Being able to define your population does not guarantee you will have access to every element within it. There are plenty of times when you just cannot get the full 'list'. Listing all McDonald's customers in Chapel Hill, North Carolina, for example, would be impossible. That kind of list simply does not exist and cannot be generated with any accuracy.

The key here is to make strategic decisions that ensure your sampling frame is as close to the target population as possible, and to be ready to argue the relevance of your frame despite any discrepancies.

Determining sample size

Once you have come up with the best possible sampling frame, you will need to figure out how many elements from within that frame should be in your sample. And the answer to the question 'how many?' really is 'it depends'. There are no hard and fast rules. Sample size is highly dependent on the shape and form of the data you wish to collect, and the goals of your analysis.

Statistical analysis of quantitative data, for example, will require a minimum number. Statistics and the ability to work with probabilities rest on adequate and appropriate sample size. On the other hand, the in-depth nature of qualitative data will generally limit sample size; you simply cannot collect that type of data from thousands. But fortunately you don't have to. Qualitative data analysis strategies are not generally dependent on large numbers.

The following guidelines might help you work through the intricacies of determining appropriate sample size:

- *Working with quantitative data/analysis* – When working with quantified data, the basic rule of thumb is to attempt to get as large a sample as possible within time and expense constraints. The larger the sample, the more likely it is to be representative, hence generalizable. Minimum numbers are determined by the level of statistical analysis you wish to do:

  o Minimal statistical analysis: Because statistical analysis is based on probability, the most basic statistical analysis requires a minimum of about 30 respondents; anything smaller and it can be difficult to show statistical significance, particularly if findings are widely distributed. Keep in mind that, with small samples, you will need to argue representativeness.
  o Intermediate statistical analysis: As you move to more sophisticated analysis, the use of any 'subdivisions' will require approximately 25 cases in each category. For example, you may have a sample of 500 members of a particular community, but only 263 females. Out of this, there are

62 mothers with children under 18, and only 20 mothers with children under 5. Statistical analysis of mothers with children under 5 would be difficult. Similarly, if you want to show significance in multivariate analysis (the analysis of simultaneous relationships among several variables), you will need at least 10 cases for each variable you wish to explore.

○   Advanced statistical analysis: If you want to represent a known population with a defined level of confidence, you can actually calculate the required size using the following formula:

$$n = [(K \times S)/E]^2$$

○   in which K is the desired confidence level, S is the sample standard deviation and E is the required level of precision. Personally, I do not believe in working with formulae unless I have to, so I tend to use a 'sample size calculator' where the only things I need to know are: the population size; the confidence interval (the range you will accept above and below the mean, say ± 5%); and the confidence level (how sure you want to be that your findings are more than coincidental, generally 95% or 99%) (see Chapter 7). Table 6.2 was generated with a calculator from www.surveysystem.com/sscalc.htm and gives you some idea of the required sample size for more commonly used confidence levels. Note that as the population increases, shifts in sample size do not increase that dramatically. What does require a significantly increased sample size, however, is a desire for higher levels of confidence.

•   *Working with qualitative data* – Many researchers who collect qualitative data in order to understand populations are not looking for representativeness. Their goal is often rich understanding that may come from the few rather than the many. Such studies are reliant on the ability of the researcher to argue the 'relativeness' of any sample (even a single case) to a broader context. For

Table 6.2   Required sample size

Population	95% ± 5% CI	99% ± 5% CI	99% ± 1% CI
30	28	29	Insufficient
100	80	87	99
500	217	286	485
1,000	278	400	943
5,000	357	588	3,845
10,000	370	624	6,247
50,000	381	657	12,486
100,000	383	661	14,267
1,000,000	384	665	16,369

those who want to collect qualitative data from a sample that does represent a target population, the challenge is being able to do this in-depth collection from a large enough sample size. There are two strategies you can call on here. The first is to 'handpick' a limited sample using criteria chosen to assure representativeness. For example, selecting your sample based on a clearly defined population profile, i.e. individuals with the average age, income and education, of the population you are studying. Rather than relying on numbers, you will need to logically argue that your sample captures all the various elements/ characteristics of your population. The second strategy is to select a sample large enough to allow for minimal statistical analysis. This will give you the option of quantitatively summarizing some of your findings in order to make more mathematical generalization about your population.

- *Working with both quantitative and qualitative data* – If you are working with both data types, you will find that the nature of collecting qualitative data will limit your sample size. However, any planned statistical analysis will require a minimum number of cases. The best advice is to determine the minimum size necessary for any statistical analysis you wish to do (see Table 6.2), then consider the practicalities of collecting and analyzing qualitative data from this sample. Unless you have unlimited time and money, there will usually be some trade-off between the collection of rich, in-depth qualitative data and the level of statistical analysis that might be possible.

Keep in mind that all the advice above needs to be checked against the criterion of 'doability'. Yes, large samples are likely to mean less 'error', but they also mean more money and more time. But this does not mean you can simply cut sample size and forget about 'generalizability'. On the contrary, the credibility of your research needs to be paramount in all methodological considerations. What doability does highlight, however, is the need for credible research to be designed with practicalities firmly in mind.

Employing a sampling strategy

Once you have defined your population, constructed a sample frame and determined appropriate sample size, it is time to adopt a strategy for gathering your sample. There are two main ways to go about this. The first is to use a strategy for random selection. The second is to use a strategy that aims to strategically select your sample in a non-random fashion. The best method will depend on a number of factors, including the nature of your question, the make-up of your population, the type of data you wish to collect and your intended modes of analysis.

Random sampling

Random samples rely on random selection, or the process by which each element in a population has an equal chance of being selected for inclusion in a sample, e.g. names drawn out of a hat, or computer-generated random numbers. The idea here is that if you have an adequate sample frame and a large enough sample size, random selection will allow you to: control for researcher bias; represent a population; and generalize findings to that population. An example is Nielsen Ratings, which monitor a small percentage of TV viewers' habits but generalize back to the entire population. Random samples are therefore seen as the gold-medal standard in social science research.

At the technical end, the logic of random samples is based on the central limit theorem (CLT). CLT posits that a random sample of observations for any distribution with a finite mean and finite variance will have a mean that follows a normal distribution. This allows researchers to conduct quite sophisticated analysis in the form of inferential statistics (see Chapter 7). Random sampling, however, demands that (1) all elements of a population are known and accessible and that (2) all elements are equally likely to agree to be part of a sample.

If this is not the case, two types of error can occur:

1. *Coverage error* – This is when your sample frame is deficient and does not adequately represent your target population. For example, while every name in the hat has an equal chance of being drawn, if your name belongs in the hat but wasn't put in there, you have a coverage error. This was once a common problem in telephone surveys of households. It was not so long ago that many poorer homes did not have a phone, and of course there are still households where this is the case. Surveys reliant on e-mail addresses have a similar problem. Unless a population is defined by the fact that each individual within it has an e-mail address, coverage is likely to be lacking. It is therefore important to consider whether your sample frame is complete and how you can give a voice to any sector of the population that might miss inclusion.
2. *Non-response bias* – This is when those who agree to be in a sample are intrinsically different from those who decline. Non-response is not problematic if the characteristics of those who accept and those who decline are basically the same. But that is not often the case. For example, in customer satisfaction surveys, it might be that those who agree to participate have an axe to grind. Or you may want to offer an inducement that appeals to those with a particular need for, or interest in, what is being offered. In both cases your eventuating sample will not be representative of your population and you will need to come up with strategies that will ensure broad representation.

As demonstrated in Table 6.3, it is important to note that representativeness and generalizability are not interchangeable. Any findings generated from sampling cannot be generalized beyond that population. For example, a study on the spending habits of university students using a sample of Cambridge University students cannot easily be generalized to other universities. You would need to be careful about claiming that the findings represent the spending habits of all university students in the UK, or that Cambridge student spending is similar to that of Stanford. Of course timeliness is also important. A study from the 1990s may have

Table 6.3   Random sampling

Simple random sampling

- Involves identifying all elements of a population, listing those elements, and randomly selecting from the list
- All elements have an equal chance of inclusion
- Considered 'fair', and allows for generalization
- Rarely used in practice because the process of identifying, listing and randomly selecting elements is often unfeasible
- Resulting samples may not capture enough elements of particular subgroups you are interested in studying

Systematic sampling

- Involves selecting every nth case within a defined population. For example, selecting every 20th person on a list
- Easier to do than devising methods for random selection
- Offers a close approximation of random sampling as long as elements are not in a particular order, i.e. you would not have a random approximation if you were to go to every 10th house within a housing development, which just happened to always be a larger detached house on a corner

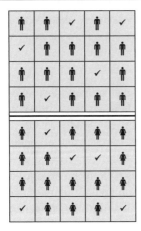

Stratified sampling

- Involves dividing your population into various subgroups and taking a random sample within each one
- Ensures your sample represents key subgroups of the population, i.e. males and females
- Representation of the subgroups can be *proportionate* or *disproportionate*, i.e. if you wanted to sample 100 nurses with a population of 80% females and 20% males, a proportionate stratified sample would be made up of 80 females and 20 males. In a disproportionate stratified sample you would use a ratio different from the population, e.g. 50 males and 50 females
- Stratification can be used in conjunction with systematic as well as random sampling

(Continued)

Table 6.3   (Continued)

	Cluster sampling
	• Involves surveying within whole clusters of the population • Clusters can include schools, hospitals, regions, etc. • Clusters are sampled so that individuals within them can be surveyed/interviewed. The thinking here is that the best way to find high school students is through high schools; the best way to find hospital patients is through hospitals • Often conducted in multiple stages, i.e. if your population is hospital patients in China you would use a random sampling strategy to select regions across China, then use a sampling strategy to select a number of hospitals within these regions, before employing another sampling strategy to select your final patients from these selected hospitals. Full population lists are not required, and eventuating samples can be geographically clustered

little relevance to how students spend their money in the twenty-first century. In this way, do not ask more of the data than it purports to measure. Your project is about insights, not building global theories.

These limitations are perfectly natural and expected, particularly in small-scale research. Be sure that when you write up your study, you note any limitations and guard against the temptation to be able to speak authoritatively about very large groups. Your results are relevant and useful for the task at hand without claiming more.

Non-random sampling

Non-random samples are just that – they are samples that are not drawn in a random fashion. Now there are some quantitative researchers who view non-random samples as inferior because they cannot be statistically assessed for representativeness. For these researchers, 'non-random' implies samples that are gathered through strategies seen as second best or last resort.

There is growing recognition, however, that there is no longer a need to 'apologize' for these types of samples. Researchers using non-random samples may be involved in studies that are not working towards representativeness or generalizability. They may be selecting their sample for other defined purposes common in 'qualitative' research. For example, they may be looking to include deviant, extreme, unique, unfamiliar, misunderstood, misrepresented, or unheard elements of a population. This is why non-random samples are sometimes called 'purposive' or 'theoretical' samples.

There is also growing recognition that non-random samples can credibly represent populations if (1) selection is done with the goal of representativeness in mind and (2) strategies are used to ensure samples match population characteristics. When working with populations that are hard to define and/or access, non-random strategies may be the best option. There is, however, an added burden of responsibility in ensuring that eventuating samples are not biased. Specifically, researchers who are after representativeness need to be aware of unwitting bias and erroneous assumptions.

- *Unwitting bias* – This is the tendency to unwittingly act in ways that confirm what you might already suspect, something that can be quite easy to do when you are handpicking your sample. For example, you may want to conduct a focus group that can help evaluate an initiative you have started in your workplace. Unless you make a conscious decision to do otherwise, it is just too easy to stack the deck in your favor.
- *Erroneous assumptions* – This refers to sample selection premised on incorrect assumptions. Say, for example, you want to study customer dissatisfaction and you select what you believe are extreme cases of dissatisfaction. If your assumptions are incorrect and what you see as extreme is actually quite average, the generalizations you make will not be valid.

Table 6.4 highlights a range of non-random sampling strategies. While they can be used to build representative samples, these strategies can also be called upon in studies that do not rely on representativeness; for example, when the goal is to build knowledge by working with cases and/or key informants.

Table 6.4 Non-random sampling

	**Handpicked sampling** • Involves the selection of a sample with a particular purpose in mind • Representativeness will depend on the researcher's ability to select cases that meet particular criteria including typicality, wide variance, 'expertise', etc. • Other options include the selection of critical, extreme, deviant or politically important cases. While not likely to be representative, the selection of such cases allows researchers to study intrinsically interesting cases, or enhance learning by exploring the limits or boundaries of a situation or phenomenon

(Continued)

Table 6.4   (Continued)

	**Snowball sampling** • Involves building a sample through referrals • Once an initial respondent is identified, you ask him or her to identify others who meet the study criteria. Each of those individuals is then asked for further recommendations • Often used when working with populations that are not easily identified or accessed, i.e. a population of homeless persons can be hard to identify, but by using referrals a sample can build quite quickly • Snowballing does not guarantee representativeness. An option here is to develop a population profile from the literature, and assess representativeness by comparing your sample with your profile
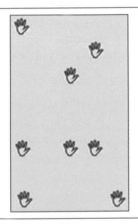	**Volunteer sampling** • Involves selecting a sample by asking for volunteers. For example, putting an ad in the newspaper or going to local organizations such as schools or community groups • While convenient, it is not likely to be representative. The characteristics of those who volunteer are likely to be quite distinct from those who do not • Arguments for representativeness will rely on strategies used to minimize the difference between volunteers and the rest of the population
	**A note on 'convenience' sampling** In the course of your reading, you may have come across something referred to as 'convenience' sampling: that is, selecting a sample in a manner convenient to the researcher. In fact, non-random sampling is sometimes referred to in this way. But keep in mind that convenience sampling has no place in credible research There needs to be more to a sampling strategy than just convenience. Limited time and resources may see convenience as one factor in sample selection. But convenience should not be the main criterion or descriptor of a sampling strategy. Regardless of type, all sampling strategies need to work towards the ultimate goal of research credibility

Key informants: working with experts and insiders

There is no doubt that research has a bias towards samples, particularly representative samples. Because we can make arguments about generalizability, we think this is where we need to go in order to gather credible data. But the goal in rigorous research is to determine the best possible means for credible data collection, and, depending on your question, this might just mean working with key informants rather than samples.

There is nothing like having an inside track or having an expert at your fingertips. In fact, key informants can be instrumental in giving you access to a world you might have otherwise tried to understand while being locked on the outside. The insights you can gather from one key informant can be instrumental not only to the data you collect, but also to how you process that data. Now this does not mean that all your data should come from key informants. Informants may end up being just one resource in your bid to build understandings – but they can do this in several ways. Key informants can:

- *Be instrumental to preliminary phases of an investigation* – Key informants can be called upon by researchers to build their own contextual knowledge. They might also be used to help generate relevant interview questions, or be called on to aid in the construction or review of a survey instrument.
- *Be used to triangulate or confirm the accuracy of gathered/generated data* – Data from interviews with key informants can be used for triangulation, to confirm the authenticity of other data sources such as data gathered by survey, observation, or document review. Key informants might also be called upon in a less formal way to overview data to confirm credibility, or to explore researcher interpretations for misunderstandings, misinterpretations, or unrecognized bias.
- *Be used to generate primary data* – In-depth interviews with key informants can also be a primary source of qualitative data in its own right.

Informant selection

There are six challenges you need to face before you can work with key informants. The first is to identify the type of informant you are after. Now it is important to recognize that key informants do not need to be experts. There are a number of characteristics that might make someone useful to your research processes. For example, the office manager or administrator has more experience in the organization/industry than the CEO. It's the people who serve in these (often underappreciated) roles that really know where the bodies are buried! This is the case in almost any institution, organization or group you might want to explore. There tend to be people 'in the know'. Depending on your research question and context, any or all of the following might have something to offer:

- *Experts* – the well-respected who sit at the top of their field.
- *Insiders* – those who sit on the inside of an organization, culture, or community and who are willing to share the realities of that environment.

- *The highly experienced* – perhaps not deemed as expert, but those with a rich depth of experience related to what you are exploring.
- *Leaders* – this might be at a formal or informal level.
- *The observant* – individuals in an organization or community who have a reputation for knowing who's who and what's what.
- *The gossips* – similar to the observant, but these individuals enjoy passing on observations (and sometimes rumors); it will pay to make sure your information here is accurate.
- *Those with secondary experience* – for example, if exploring the problem of youth suicide, in addition to youth you might look to certain counsellors, teachers or parents to provide relevant insights.
- *The ex* – this might include someone who is disenfranchised, alienated, recovered, converted, retrenched, fired or retired.

The second challenge is to identify individuals who have the characteristics associated with that type. It makes sense to ask around or try a *snowball technique* in which you generate a list of informants through a referral process. One person in the know is likely to lead you to a host of others. A snowball method allows participants to recommend other individuals. This means you can start with a small group of interviewees, and build your list after each interview.

The snowball method also serves as a potentially less awkward introduction. It's a much easier phone call or email to say, 'Hi, I'm Darrell and I was given your contact information through our mutual friend/colleague, David' than to cold-call a random individual in the department and try to explain your purpose before they assume you're a telemarketer and hang up.

The third challenge is to confirm the status of those identified. Do they really have the expertise, experiences or insider knowledge that will inform your study in a credible way? The advice here is to seek confirmation by looking for things like a long record of involvement, direct personal experiences, and detailed comments from potential informants that show internal consistency. You are after more than just broad generalizations.

The fourth challenge is related to your ability to gather open and honest information from your informants. Key informants must be accessible and willing to share information. If they have the knowledge you are after, but are not willing to share it, they will not be of any use to your study. Building trust will be essential.

The fifth challenge is to look for and recognize informant subjectivities. All respondents will have a particular worldview and some will have a real agenda operating. Some may want to be listened to, some may have an axe to grind, some may like the sound of their own voice, some think they know a lot more than they do, and some think their particular take on an experience is how the world should or does respond to the same experience (sounds like a family reunion!). You will need to develop and build a level of trust with your key informants, not only so they can open up to you, but so you are in a position to know how to best treat the data they provide.

The sixth challenge is related to ethics. If you look at the list of informant types above and think about their motivation, it should be pretty obvious that ethics and integrity need to come into play when selecting and working with key informants. In addition to the challenge of managing bias (both yours and theirs), you will need to think about your power as a researcher. You have to remember that key informants can be put, and can put themselves, in very vulnerable positions. It is your responsibility to respect their needs at all times.

Working with cases

When it comes to respondents, how many is really enough: 100, 200, 1,500? Well, these are the kinds of numbers we have in mind when we think of samples/respondents. Even in 'qualitative' research we are looking at 10, 20, 30 interviews. But what about one or two? Can one or two ever be enough? Can such research ever be more than thin?

A case study is all about depth; it requires you to dig, and to dig deep. You need to delve into detail, dig into context, and really get a handle on the rich experiences of the individual, event, community group or organization you want to explore. The goal is to get underneath what is generally possible in, for example, large-scale survey research.

If you think the answer to your research question might require this type of in-depth exploration, then legitimate, valid and worthwhile answers might just be held by or within a particular 'case' or in a 'case study'.

The use of cases in organizational research is more common than you might realize. Researchers often limit their methodological design to a particular context in a bid to maximize both relevance and practicality. At the practical end, cases are often located in one site, which means travel is minimized, access is enhanced and costs are reduced.

If you decide to tackle a case study, you may come across an individual who just won't give the time of day to any study not deemed to be representative or generalizable. But if you can clearly articulate your goals and show how your study contributes to a particular body of knowledge, you are more likely to establish credibility and worth.

Case selection

After determining the appropriate number of cases to be explored, the selection of any particular case or cases is generally done through a strategic process with researchers often handpicking cases with a particular purpose in mind. Factors that will influence case selection include:

- *Pragmatics* – There is nothing wrong with being practical. Pragmatics can involve commitments such as being commissioned/sponsored to study a particular case. They might also involve timely opportunities that see you take advantage of current events and work at being in the right place at the right time, e.g. studying a community recovering from a flood event, or exploring a recent sports-related riot. Pragmatics can also involve accessibility where you take advantage of access that might normally be hard to get, e.g. exploring a case that has connections to your own workplace, or delving into a case involving an individual with whom you have an existing relationship based on mutual trust and respect.

- *Purposiveness* – Researchers will often select cases they hope will enable them to make particular arguments. For example, if the purpose is to argue representativeness, you may select a case considered 'typical'. 'Extreme' or 'atypical' instances may be chosen in order to debunk a theory or highlight deviations from the norm, while wide variance in cases might be used to build new understandings and generate theory. The section on non-random sampling at the beginning of this chapter provides strategies that can be used in purposive case selection.
- *Intrinsic interest* – Researchers might also select a particular case because it is interesting in its own right. It might be relevant, unique, unfamiliar, misunderstood, misrepresented, marginalized, unheard, politically hot, or the focus of current media attention. In this situation, the challenge is to argue the inherent worth and value of a particular case.

It is worth keeping in mind that a prerequisite to all case selection should be access. It is absolutely essential that researchers who wish to delve into cases will be able to reach required people and data. When working with individuals, your ability to generate rich data will depend on building high levels of trust and rapport. In an organizational setting, you may need to gain high-level access to relevant records and documents or be allowed broad access to an array of individuals associated with a case. In fact, organizational case studies may require you to seek respondents from within the case itself. This can see you searching for both key informants and samples as discussed earlier in the chapter. No matter what the situation, the holistic understanding and rich detail demanded in case studies will require you to have access to what is going on 'inside'.

COLLECTING SURVEY DATA

No matter what primary data collection method you use, there will be trade-offs between opportunities and challenges, and this is certainly true when thinking about conducting a survey. While surveys can offer much to the production of knowledge, their reputation for being a relatively simple, straightforward and inexpensive approach is not really deserved – they can actually be a somewhat thorny and exasperating process, particularly if done well.

Now, on the plus side, surveys can:

- reach a large number of respondents;
- represent an even larger population;

- allow for comparisons;
- generate standardized, quantifiable, empirical data;
- generate qualitative data through the use of open-ended questions;
- be confidential and even anonymous.

They do, however, have their downside. Constructing and administering a survey that has the potential to generate credible and generalizable data is a truly difficult task. It is not something you can do off the top of your head. Challenges associated with surveying include:

- capturing the quantifiable data you require;
- gathering in-depth data;
- getting a representative sample to respond;
- getting anyone at all to respond!;
- needing proficiency in statistical analysis;
- only getting answers to the questions you've thought to ask;
- going back to your respondents if more data is required.

Surveys require quite a lot of advance planning. While questions can be adjusted in the middle of the interview, survey environments offer no such flexibility. Since a poorly done survey will likely not be very useful for your results, it's worthwhile to invest the time in doing it well. It all starts with planning.

Planning

Survey construction is one of the most laborious and underestimated time-sinks in research. And that's not just by students – professional researchers can also have a hard time getting this right. Yet it is essential, because the data that even a poor survey generates can be used in all kinds of decision-making processes. The best advice is to take it in steps and get lots of feedback from your peers and other researchers. You'll also need to have a trial run. Piloting might be important in all data collection methods – but in surveying, this is absolutely crucial. It is almost impossible to get a questionnaire just right the first time around.

Without a doubt, the success of your survey will hinge on the forethought you put into your planning processes. A good survey does not just happen. It is planned. From knowing your target population and how your sampling approach will represent that population, through to issues of access and ethics, consideration of who you are in terms of both biases and skills, and of course being clear about the data you seek and how you will prepare for the unexpected, are crucial considerations necessary before you even begin the task of survey construction. Table 6.5 can help you sort through some common considerations.

Table 6.5   Considerations for your survey

Do you plan to sample or ask everyone in your population?

Census: A survey that does not rely on a sample. In other words, a survey that covers every single person in a defined population

The US Census is a good example. A smaller scale census might be all the customers in a particular store

Cross-sectional surveys: Surveys that use a sample or cross-section of respondents. The goal is to be able to represent your target population and generalize findings back to that population

Most surveys fall under this category, e.g. a community survey that targets only 1 in 10 households but aims to represent the entire community

---

Will your survey simply describe or attempt to explain?

Descriptive surveys: The goal is to get a snapshot or to describe your respondents by gathering: demographic information, i.e. age, socioeconomic status and gender; personal information/behaviors, i.e. voting patterns or use of illegal drugs; and attitudinal information, i.e. attitudes towards multinational corporations, abortion or healthcare costs

A classic example here is political polling, which attempts to describe voters and voter intentions

An Australian newspaper recently conducted a survey that collected data describing attitudes towards the new trade deal, the TransPacific Partnership, as well as data used to establish what might shape and form those attitudes, e.g. personal experience, familial attitudes, and political leanings

Explanatory surveys: The goal is to build complex understandings that go beyond description or even correlation. The aim is to figure out why things might be the way they are; in other words, determine cause and effect

---

Will you survey over a period of time and, if so, do you want to explore changing times or changing people?

Trend surveys: A trend survey asks the same cross-section (similar groups of respondents) the same questions at two or more points in time. The goal here is to see whether classifications of individuals change over time

An example here is a three-phase survey conducted over a 20-year period (1989, 1999, 2009) that asks university students about their support of high income tax. The goal is to assess whether attitudes of university students now are the same as attitudes of the population in the late 1980s and 1990s

Panel study: A panel study involves asking the same (not similar) sample of respondents the same questions at two or more points in time. The goal here is to see whether individuals themselves change over time

Using the example above, if you had surveyed individuals in 1989, you would survey these same individuals in 1999 (10 years later) and again in 2009 in order to assess attitudinal shifts as individuals get older

---

How do you plan to administer your survey?

Face-to-face surveys

Pros: Good response rate, allows rapport and trust to be established, can motivate respondents, allows for clarification, prompting, probing, and the reading of non-verbal cues

Cons: Can be lengthy and expensive, limits geographical range, does not assure anonymity or confidentiality, and requires surveyor training

One example here is the mall or supermarket survey where you are stopped by someone with a clipboard ready to ask you a series of questions

Telephone surveys

Pros: Relatively inexpensive, allows wide geographic coverage, offers some assurance of anonymity and confidentiality, and allows for some clarification, prompting, probing

Cons: Response rate can be low, it is easy to catch people at a bad time, respondents can hang up on you if they have had enough, and you are limited to surveying only those with a telephone

In market research the telephone tends to be the mode of choice – but as more and more individuals get annoyed by this, it becomes harder for social science researchers to get individuals to participate over the phone

Self-administered mail/email/online surveys

Pros: Can offer confidentiality/anonymity, allows wide geographic coverage, and gives respondents the opportunity to answer in their own time

Cons: Response rates can be very low, does not allow for clarification, and the snail mail version can end up being costly

These can include snail mail, e-mail and online surveys. Online/e-mail can save you thousands in printing and postage costs, but you are limited to surveying within online populations. Additionally, the proliferation of spam mail means that unless your respondents know you, your survey may not even get looked at

---

Questionnaire development

Surveying is not easy. As it turns out, human beings are sensitive to not only what is being asked, but in what order relative to other questions. This can produce what is known as sequencing effects. Further, people respond differently to the same question framed in a different way (known as framing effects). As part of 'acquiescence bias', people tend to agree with positively phrased questions regardless of the actual question. For example, research by Schuman and Presser (1981) demonstrated that 10–20% of respondents tend to agree with both a statement and its opposite when the direction of the agreement is reversed. Finally, research demonstrates that respondents try to anticipate and mirror what researchers want to hear.

In particular, respondents conform to expectations of social desirability even when answering anonymous questionnaires. When formulating questions and response categories then, it's helpful to guard against these. See Box 6.2 for the types of bias to be aware of when constructing your own survey instrument.

BOX 6.2

Types of biases and effects

- *Telescope bias* – Respondents usually recall an event in the distant past as happening more recently. Longitudinal survey data from the United States shows that most people who claim to have used firearms to protect themselves within the last six months are really referring to incidents that happened much earlier than that, leading to severe overestimation of self-defensive gun use over time (Hemenway, 1997).
- *Social desirability response bias* – People like to present themselves in a favorable light, so they will be reluctant to admit in a survey to unsavory attitudes (such as racism) or politically incorrect opinions. This may also include other topics that are sensitive to social desirability, such as personal income and earnings (which are often inflated when low and deflated when high), indicators of charity (often inflated) and illegal acts (often denied).
- *Acquiescence bias* – People tend to agree with positively phrased questions regardless of the actual question. This effect was documented extensively by Schuman and Presser (1981).
- *Fundamental attribution error* – Also known as self-serving bias, this is the tendency of people to attribute positive outcomes or successes to internal factors (such as their own effort, commitment or worthiness), and negative outcomes/failures to external factors beyond their control. For example, being hired for a job is attributed to personal factors, whereas failure to obtain a job is attributed to external factors. Psychologist Tony Greenwald's *American Psychologist* article on this topic cited some very amusing examples of the self-serving bias, taken from insurance claimants; for example the explanations drivers gave to their insurers after an accident, such as 'The telephone pole was approaching. I was attempting to swerve out of its way when it struck my front end.'
- *Non-response bias* – Also called participation bias, this results when respondents differ in meaningful ways from non-respondents. Example: if parents of severely obese children declined to participate in a survey studying childhood health the results would be skewed as a result of a particular group opting out (as happened in a 2006 UK study). This is also a concern in online polling where evidence suggests that only people who feel strongly about the topic bother to participate. You will need to keep this in mind as you seek to develop and deliver your survey instrument.

Don't let the complexity of the human mind throw you off questionnaires, just be aware that survey instruments must be carefully phrased. A pilot will allow you to make necessary adjustments before rolling it out.

As discussed more fully below, developing a questionnaire will entail: (1) formulating your questions; (2) deciding on response categories; (3) providing background information and clear instructions; (4) making determinations about organization and length; (5) working on aesthetically pleasing layout and design; and finally (6) administrating the survey. Which, of course, all needs to be done in conjunction with several stages of seeking feedback, piloting and redevelopment.

Formulating questions

Formulating questions requires careful consideration of what you are trying to measure. You will need to operationalize concepts; this means going from abstract concepts to variables that can be measured. Then you will need to draft questions and decide on response categories. There are quite a few minefields to avoid here. The literature on questionnaire design is littered with spectacular failures.

An early consideration is the number of questions in your survey. You want to ensure that the volume does not deter respondents. Ideally, a questionnaire should take between 10 and 30 minutes to complete. After that, response fatigue may set in, which may cause respondents to choose uniform or inaccurate answers. This is an important effect to be aware of as it can ruin all your hard work in overcoming the other biases noted above!

As you construct questions, think about the ease of comparison between respondents. Closed responses are usually the easiest to compare across respondents, so binary and scaled questions are quite appropriate for this primary data collection tool. The psychometric Likert scale is popular for this reason: it allows respondents to rate agreement and satisfaction on a scale of −5 (strongly dissatisfied/strongly disagree) to +5 (strongly satisfied/strongly agree).

Careful phrasing and scaling is paramount to ensure that responses are meaningful, valid and useful. Box 6.3 lists some questions to avoid. While in a live interview you can adapt and reword questions as you go, questionnaires offer no such flexibility once they have been distributed (particularly in hard or soft copy). It is thus extremely important that phrasing, framing, sequencing and question selection are polished before it is distributed. For this reason, most researchers choose a pilot structure first – releasing the questionnaire to a smaller group and soliciting revisions of wording, etc. before proceeding to the larger sample size.

BOX 6.3

Questions to avoid

Good questions should be unambiguous, inoffensive and unbiased. But this is actually easier said than done. It's not difficult to fall into the trap of constructing poor questions. This includes questions that are poorly worded, biased, leading or problematic to answer.

(Continued)

(Continued)

Poorly worded

Complex terms and language – Big words can offend and confuse. If they aren't necessary, don't use them. This is my favorite example: 'Polysyllabic linguistic terminology can act to obscure connotations', vs. 'Big words can be confusing.'

Ambiguous questions – Frames of reference can be highly divergent, so writing an ambiguous question is easy to do. Take, for example, the question 'Do you use the Internet before you get out of bed?'. 'Internet' is actually an ambiguous term. Some respondents will only consider the World Wide Web, while others may include corporate email on their smartphones. Others might use a frame of reference of any online application, such as games, social media, etc.

Double negatives – Most people have trouble with double negatives. Take the following Yes/No question: 'Do you disapprove of the government's new policy to increase the retirement age?'. To state that you do approve, you'd have to choose 'No', which can be quite confusing.

Double-barrelled questions – This is when you ask for only one response to a question with more than one issue. For example, 'Do you consider CEOs to be honest and effective leaders?'. Respondents may think yes, effective – but definitely not honest.

Biased, leading or loaded

'Ring true' statements – These are statements that are easy to agree with simply because they tend to 'ring true'. Some good examples here are agree/disagree statements, like 'You really can't rely on people these days', or 'Times may be tough, but there are generally people around you can count on'. Both of these somewhat opposite statements are likely to get a high percentage of 'agrees' because they tend to sound reasonable.

Hard to disagree with statements – These are statements where your respondents are likely to think 'Yes that's true, BUT …' They are not, however, given a chance to elaborate and are forced to either agree or disagree. For example, 'It is good for young children if their mothers can stay at home through the week.'

Leading questions – Leading respondents in a particular direction can be done unintentionally, or can be done intentionally for political purposes. Consider how the wording of these agree/disagree statements might affect responses: 'Protecting defenceless endangered species from inhumane slaughter is something the government should take seriously', vs. 'The protection of biodiversity should be a government priority.'

Problematic for the respondent

Recall-dependent questions – These are questions that rely on memory. For example, 'How many jobs have you had?' Without descriptive boundaries such as level (full-time/

part-time), wage compensation (does a full-time unpaid internship count?) or time-frame, this question can be easy to answer inaccurately.

Offensive/sensitive questions – If respondents take offence to a question or a series of questions, not only are they likely to skip them, they may just throw out the entire survey. Offensive questions can range from 'What do you think you did that caused you to gain so much weight?' to 'How much money do you earn?'.

Questions with assumed knowledge – Try not to assume that your respondents know about, or are familiar with, the same things as you. Take for example the agree/disagree statement 'Marxist theory has no place in 21st century politics'. You shouldn't be surprised to find out that a common response here is, 'What kind of academic crap is this!' – followed by a quick trip to the bin with your questionnaire.

Questions with unwarranted assumptions – Respondents are likely to be at a loss when it comes to answering a question that contains an assumption they do not agree with. For example the question to recent guests 'What was the most enjoyable part of your hotel stay?' assumes that the respondent enjoyed something about their hotel!

Questions with socially desirable responses – This is more likely to be an issue in face-to-face surveying. For example, a respondent may be uncomfortable disagreeing with the statement 'Do you think women serving in the armed forces should have the same rights and responsibilities as their male colleagues?'

Response categories

As if getting your questions as precise and non-problematic as possible wasn't enough, a good survey, and good survey data, are equally dependent on the response categories you decide to use. And there is a lot to consider here. For one thing, response categories will influence the data you collect. For example, if you add an 'I'm not sure' option to a controversial Yes/No question, it will affect your findings. Secondly, different types of response categories generate data with different types of measurement scale; and data with different measurement scales demand quite distinct statistical treatment. In fact, understanding the difference between nominal, ordinal, interval and ratio data (as discussed in Chapter 7) will definitely facilitate the process of survey construction, particularly determining response categories. But until you actually have some data to play with, understanding the relationship between data types and survey construction is quite abstract.

This makes conducting your first survey a real challenge. So again, we emphasize the need for a good pilot study. Not only will a pilot study allow you to assess your questions and response categories from the perspective of your respondents, it will also allow you to generate a mini data set that you can enter into a database and work with statistically. This really is the best way to see how your data collection protocols, including response category determination, will impact on your analysis.

So what are the options when it comes to response categories? As highlighted in Box 6.4, there are quite a few.

BOX 6.4

Response categories

Open responses

Respondents are asked to provide answers using their own words. They can offer any information/express any opinion they wish, although the amount of space provided for an answer will generally limit the response. The data provided can be rich and candid, but can also be difficult to code and analyze.

Closed responses

Respondents are asked to choose from a range of predetermined responses. The data here are generally easy to code and analyze statistically. Closed response categories come in many forms, each with their associated issues.

Yes/No – Agree/Disagree

Do you think student loans should be interest free?   Yes/No

Do you think PhD tuition should be free?   Agree/Disagree

While it can be easy to work with 'binomial' data (or data with only two potential responses), you need to consider whether respondents will be comfortable with only two choices. For example, in the first question, a respondent might be thinking 'Does only two or three times a year count?', or for the second question, 'It depends on how much you're talking about'. A potential strategy is to offer a Don't know/No opinion option – but this allows for a lot of 'fence sitting'.

Fill in the blank

How much do you earn?   _____

Even a simple question like this (assuming your respondents know the answer and are willing to tell you) can lead to messy data. Will respondents tell you their annual salary (or monthly wage) or all earnings including investment and rental property?

Choosing from a list

As an aviation employee, whom do you enjoy working with the most?

Pilots   Ground Crew   Customers   TSA

There is an assumption here that there will not be any 'ties'; you need to consider what you will do if more than one option is circled. You also need to make sure all options are covered (are collectively exhaustive) and don't overlap (are mutually exclusive). A potential strategy is to offer an 'Other' or 'Other:_____' option.

Ordering options

Please rank the following according to how you think corporate bonuses should be dispensed:

Cash   Extra vacation time   Donated to charity   Travel voucher

These questions tend to be quite difficult for respondents, particularly if lists are long and unclear. It's worth remembering that if respondents get frustrated trying to answer, they are likely to leave the question blank, leave it half finished, or just write anything at all.

Likert-type scaling

It is acceptable for private sports teams to demand public money to build sports stadiums.

Likert scales offer a range of responses, generally ranging from something like 'Strongly disagree' to 'Strongly agree'. In Likert scales, the items must be statements not questions.

Private sports teams should receive public money to build stadiums

1	2	3	4	5
Strongly disagree	Disagree	Unsure	Agree	Strongly agree

Information and instructions

A survey instrument is not complete without some level of background information. This information is included (1) to give credibility to the study and (2) to make your respondents feel like they're a part of something. In your background information it's a good idea to include: the sponsoring organization/university; the survey's purpose; assurances of anonymity/confidentiality; return information, including deadlines and return address; and a 'thank you' for time/assistance. This information can be included at the start of the survey, or as a cover letter.

Also crucial are your instructions. What might be self-evident to you may not be so obvious to your respondents. Instructions should introduce each section of the survey; give clear and specific instructions for each question type; provide examples; and be easy to distinguish from actual survey questions. You may want to use a distinct font – try changing the style, size, boldness, italics, underlining etc. It may take a couple of drafts to get your instructions as clear and helpful as possible. Be sure you seek advice and feedback from other researchers, peers and your pilot group.

Organization and length

Once you are comfortable with all the various elements of your survey, you will need to put it together in a logical format that is neither too long nor too short. Too short – and you won't get all the data you need. Too long – and your survey might be tossed away, returned incomplete, or filled in at random. People might not mind spending a few minutes answering your questions, but ask for much more and they may not be bothered to help you out. Appropriate length is another aspect of your survey you can assess in your pilot run. Be sure to ask your trial respondents what they thought of the overall length and the time it took to complete the survey.

In terms of logical organization, there are a few schools of thought. Some suggest that you start with demographics in order to 'warm up' your respondents. Others, however, suggest that you start with your topical questions and finish off with questions related to demographic information. What's right for your survey will depend a lot on the nature of both your questions and your respondents. In fact, you may want to pilot two different versions of your questionnaire if you are unsure how it should be laid out.

There is one consistent piece of advice, however, and that is to avoid starting your survey with questions that might be considered threatening, awkward, insulting, difficult etc. It's really important to ease your respondents into your survey and save sensitive questions for near the end.

Layout and design

All done! Well almost. You've written clear and unambiguous questions with appropriate, well-thought-out response categories that are accompanied by clear instruction and organized into a sensitive, logical and manageable form. And you've done this by going through multiple iterations taking into account as much feedback as possible. There's only one thing left – aesthetics.

Aesthetics is important. Your survey needs to look professional – no poor quality photocopying, faint printing, messy and uninteresting layout, etc. Respondents are more likely to complete a survey that is professionally presented. It is also worth keeping in mind that the potential for mistakes increases dramatically if surveys are cluttered, cramped or messy. So the effort here is well worthwhile.

Piloting and modification

Good planning and development is essential – but not sufficient. The only way really to know if something is going to work is to give it a try.

- *Have a run-through* – Pilot your process with a group of respondents whose background is similar to those in your 'sample'.
- *Reflect* – Reflect on the piloting process and note any difficulties you encounter. Also review your data and note any difficulties in making sense of your completed surveys.
- *Seek feedback* – Get feedback from the pilot group in relation to the effectiveness of the cover letter, the overall layout and design, the usefulness of the instructions, the question wording, and the length of time it took to complete the questionnaire.
- *Trial your stats package* – Attempt to create variables, code the pilot responses and then enter them into a statistical program to see whether you are likely to encounter any issues when you input your main data.
- *Make modifications* – This will be based on your reflections, the feedback from your pilot group, as well as the quality of the data generated.
- *Back to the start?* – If the need for modification is substantial, you may need to revisit your planning, development and piloting process.

As you can see, survey data typically yields a high volume of data but the quality of that data is dependent on the time and effort you invest in it. In survey research, much of that effort is front-loaded. For interviews and focus groups, the situation is a little different. The next part of the chapter examines the planning, formulating and collection of interview data.

Conducting the survey

Survey construction complete! You can now get down to the business of administering your questionnaire, collecting your data and making sense of it all. And yes, whether face-to-face, snail mail, email or online, it is time to get your survey out to your respondent group.

To execute your survey you will need to:

1. Distribute your questionnaires, by mail, email, telephone, door to door or face to face.
2. Collect your completed questionnaires.
3. Send out reminder letters if response rates are low.
4. Put a low response rate plan into action if not enough data has been gathered by your deadline.
5. Record and manage responses so they are ready for analysis.

One note of caution: Given the short timeframes inherent in small-scale workplace-based research projects, you might want to consider conducting your surveys in person and with a 'captive audience'. For instance, if you are distributing question-naires to individuals inside your organization, you might ask permission to arrange a brief meeting with them and *sit there with them* while they fill it out. Yes, it seems less annoying to allow people the flexibility to fill it out at their leisure at their desk, but the odds are your colleagues don't have leisure time and the survey will languish unfinished on those desks. In-person surveys are the most efficient means of ensuring they are completed fully (and respondents can ask you if they have specific questions about certain elements of the questionnaire). Otherwise, you may have to exert twice the effort to chase up paperwork. Remember, without complete responses, all your preparation and hard work will have been wasted.

Should you decide that in-person surveys aren't practical (you don't have access to the respondents or they are geographically scattered), online surveys may be the way to go. Box 6.5 details their use.

BOX 6.5

Using online surveys

It is easy to understand the popularity of online surveys. They offer terrific flexibility for both the researcher and respondent. As pictured in Photo 6.1, they have low adminis-tration costs – no printing or postage – and can be completed at the convenience of the respondent. Moreover, data is automatically captured in a database – no manual data entry required. Together these are great tremendous advantages.

Photo 6.1   Online surveys offer benefits to both researcher & respondent

But it is absolutely essential to consider whether your targeted response group has the ability to respond to your online survey. For example, does your population have Internet access? Is all of your population online? If not, who is missing and do you/how do you attempt to capture them? And even if you're happy that your online sample does indeed capture your intended population, have you considered whether or not they could be bothered to fill in your questionnaire? Response rates in online surveys can be notoriously low, and with the proliferation of spam, this is a trend not likely to abate.

It is important to remember that online surveying will only work if all segments of your population are online AND you are able to reach out to your sample and convince them to respond. Without a representative sample and adequate response rate, you're likely to come face to face with non-response bias, where those who participate in your survey are qualitatively different from those who don't, thereby leaving you with results that cannot be generalized back to your population.

If you believe, however, that your research question warrants an online approach and you have worked through the challenges of adequate and representative response, there are some fantastic survey development and administration tools online. Most have limited free versions – with more sophisticated elements reserved for those willing to pay. A few choices worth a look include:

SurveyMonkey (www.surveymonkey.com)

Wufoo (www.wufoo.com)

SurveyGizmo (www.surveygizmo.com)

Zoomerang (www.zoomerang.com)

Qualtrics (www.qualtrics.com)

PollDaddy (www.polldaddy.com)

QuestionPro (www.questionpro.com)

LimeSurvey (www.limesurvey.org)

Things to look for in a good program include the ability to:

- manipulate the look and feel of the survey – for high flexibility and customization;
- use skip logic – those who answer 'no' to question 9 should be able to skip to question 13;
- pipe – this pulls answers from one part of the survey into one another – so if your respondent says she worked at Google, that name is inserted into future relevant questions such as 'How long did you work at Google?';
- randomize – randomizes question order within selected sections;

(Continued)

(Continued)

- integrate with an existing website – allows for having your survey on its own page or integrated into an existing site;
- analyze data – most offer simple summary descriptive statistics, but others offer complex inferential tools.

Keep in mind, however, that programs come and go, so it is worth checking to see what the latest and greatest might be.

COLLECTING INTERVIEW DATA

> If we were meant to talk more than listen, we would have two mouths and one ear.
>
> Mark Twain

Interviewing: is it the 'art of asking' or the 'art of listening'? Well, both are crucial to the interview process – but while we tend to spend plenty of time discussing the questioning side, most of us don't spend nearly enough time on the listening end of things (see Box 6.6). Unfortunately, there are too many researchers and interviewers out there who would rather talk than listen. Remember, your job is to talk only enough to facilitate someone else's ability to answer. It is your interviewee's voice that you are seeking, and it is their voice that needs to be drawn out.

BOX 6.6

On listening

> Speaking opens up our mouths. Listening opens up our minds.
>
> Muhammed Haider

> Most people do not listen with the intent to understand, they listen with the intent to reply.
>
> Stephen R. Covey

> It [research] demands the open-mindedness with which one must look and listen, record in astonishment and wonder that which one would not have been able to guess.
>
> Margaret Mead

What could be better than getting out there and actually talking to real people, asking them what they really think, finding out first-hand how they genuinely feel? Well, interviews allow all of this, but like any other data collection method, its opportunities are balanced by a series of challenges. Interviews:

- allow you to develop rapport and trust;
- provide you with rich, in-depth qualitative data;
- allow for non-verbal as well as verbal data;
- are flexible enough to allow you to explore tangents;
- are structured enough to generate standardized, quantifiable data.

Now many of these 'pros' are the result of the human element in interviewing – but so too are the 'cons'. The closer you become to your respondents and the closer they become to you, the bigger the challenge you will face in managing the process. Such challenges include:

- gaining access to interviewees in an ethical manner (see Table 6.6);
- a lack of respondent anonymity;
- resisting the urge to lead your respondents;
- making a good impression that will keep doors open.

Access is typically one of the most difficult parts of the interview method. Once you have selected your respondent sample, you need to find a way to contact these individuals and convince them to give up 20–50 minutes of their life. Keep in

Table 6.6   Gaining access to interviewees in an ethical manner

Using power	Abusing power
✓ Using official channels and protocols	✗ Avoiding and skirting around official channels and protocols
✓ Establishing points of contact	✗ Going around or above the appropriate person's head
✓ Using gatekeepers and insiders	✗ Asking gatekeepers and insiders to act unethically or to go behind management's back
✓ Building rapport	✗ Ingratiating yourself to the point of becoming sycophantic
✓ Leaving doors open	✗ Becoming a nuisance
✓ Offering something back	✗ Making promises you cannot or do not intend to keep

mind that for some people, granting an interview is extremely nerve-wracking. How will their comments be used? What is on/off the record? You will need to carefully consider these issues and have a considered answer ready when posed by potential interviewees.

Planning

So exactly how much planning needs to go into an interview? Once access issues are taken care of, don't you just show up and ask a few questions? If only it were that easy. Box 6.7 takes you through some of the planning considerations of the interview method.

BOX 6.7

Planning your interview

The success of your interview will hinge upon the forethought you have put into the planning process. You will need to consider the following:

1. *Population and sample/respondent/participants* – who you plan to speak about (population) and gather data from (sample) (see Chapter 7).
2. *Access* – The first step in an interview is access. If this research takes place within an organization, can you coordinate access with your manager and other department heads? If not, how can you gain access and introductions to relevant groups?
3. *Your role* – How will you present yourself? How will you strike a balance between formality and rapport? Is your interview style/research goal better suited to officiousness or informality? What tone of voice will you use? Will you joke around? Also consider body language. Reading non-verbal cues (while your interviewee is reading yours) is worth thinking about. Are you both making eye contact, looking down, looking around, picking your nails, coming across aggressively, looking relaxed?
4. *Your biases* – recognizing and controlling for subjectivities in ways that can best ensure the credibility of any survey instrument you use.
5. *Ethics/ethics approval* – being mindful of 'doing no harm'; consider whether there are any ethical dilemmas inherent in your project.
6. *Data* – exactly what it is you want to elicit from your respondents, i.e. memories, descriptions, feelings, thoughts, opinions, etc.
7. *Details* – appointments, timing (travel time, interview time, wait-around time), location, recording methods, etc.
8. *Potential cultural/language barriers* – familiarizing yourself with, and planning for, any potential language and/or cultural issues. Find and trial a good translator if necessary.
9. *Contingencies* – the unexpected, the unplanned and the unfortunate. This means developing a contingency plan in case key interviews fall through.

You also need to consider the type of interview that would be most useful for your research question. Would you prefer a strict interview question list that will make it easier to compare answers? Or do you want to explore the topic and allow time for unanticipated avenues to be explored? These considerations will be dependent on you or your respondents and the research question you're trying to answer. Interview types are included in Table 6.7.

Table 6.7   Types of interviews

Will you conduct your interview in a formal manner or will it be more relaxed?	
Formal: The interviewer attempts to be somewhat removed from the interviewee, and maintains distance and neutrality/objectivity. This is often done within a formal setting	This is the classic job interview. While formality can allow interviewers a high level of control it can limit interviewee comfort, and possibly the free flow of information
Informal: Bends or ignores rules and roles associated with formal interviewing in order to establish rapport, gain trust and open up lines of communication. The style is casual and relaxed in order to minimize any gulf between the interviewer and the interviewee	Settings are not limited to an office and might occur over a beer at a bar, or while having a cup of coffee at the local preschool. The idea is to do what you can to get your interviewee chatting comfortably

Will your interviews be highly structured or more free flowing?	
Structured: Use of pre-established questions, in a predetermined order, with a standard mode of delivery. Interviewers often call on a formal style to help them stay on track	Best suited for interviews where standardized data is a goal. Inexperienced interviewers generally feel most comfortable with this high level of structure
Semi-structured: Use of a flexible structure. Interviewers can start with a defined questioning plan, but will shift in order to follow the natural flow of conversation. Interviewers may deviate from the plan to pursue interesting tangents	The advantage here is being able to come away with all the data you intended but also interesting and unexpected data that emerges. This style of interviewing can take a bit of practice
Unstructured: Attempts to draw out information, attitudes, opinions and beliefs around particular themes, ideas and issues without predetermined questions. The goal is to draw out rich and informative conversation. Often used in conjunction with an informal structure	Most interviewees enjoy this type of interview because it allows them to talk and really express their ideas in a way not dictated by the interviewer. Interviewer challenges here are to avoid leading the conversation and to keep it focused enough to get the data needed

(Continued)

Table 6.7   (Continued)

Will you interview one person at a time or will you attempt to tackle a group?	
One-on-one: An interaction between an interviewer and a single interviewee. It is thought that one-on-one allows the researcher control over the process and the interviewee the freedom to express their thoughts. One-on-one can also involve an additional person such as a translator or note-taker	One-on-one interviews are generally conducted face-to-face, but can also be done over the telephone in order to increase geographical range or capture a difficult to get hold of respondent. The lack of non-verbal cues in telephone interviews, however, can be a challenge
Group: Interviewing more than one person at a time. Can be done in a formal structured way, or may involve a more open process where the researcher acts as a moderator or facilitator. In this less structured approach, interviewees are often referred to as a focus group	Not only can a group interview save time and money, it can really get people talking. Some, however, might feel unheard or marginalized. Group interviews can be difficult to follow, so most interviewers attempt to preserve raw data by tape recording
Will you conduct your interviews face-to-face or remotely?	
Face-to-face: Sitting down with your interviewee	This is generally preferred. It is easier to build rapport, gauge reactions and adjust according to non-verbal cues
Online: Using real-time video such as Skype	Real-time video preserves some of the elements of physical presence, but as with all things Internet, it can be prone to technical curveballs. Poor sound quality, dropped connections and a time delay between the picture and sound can be unnerving and frustrating for both interviewee and interviewer
Phone: Making a call	This approach creates distance, making it a less preferable option. Some, however, find this buffer makes it easier to conceal nerves (no one can hear the paper shuffling)

Formulating questions

As you can see from Table 6.7, interviews are typically divided into structured or unstructured. Structured interviews draw from the same inventory of questions, while unstructured interviews may start with similar questions but branch off into lines of spontaneous inquiry in keeping with previous responses.

So, which is better? Think about what data you are trying to collect and who you are trying to collect it from. Are you seeking their expertise on a particular issue (as an expert), or are you gathering their experience in a particular setting (perhaps as a customer)? This will impact your choice. A good strategy here is to consider what you believe will facilitate an interviewee's ability to talk with authenticity. Often this leads to a less-structured approach. The same is true with formality. Who you interview is paramount. A good rule of thumb is to interview in ways that lessen the power distance between you and the researched.

Regardless of formality or structure, start with easier questions first and then build up from there. It is common to begin with questions about the individuals themselves first to verify their inclusion in the study and then move on from there.

Preparing the interview schedule

You will then need to prepare questions and/or themes. For a structured interview, this will involve drafting and redrafting your questions, and making sure that you have not included questions that will be confusing, leading, offensive or problematic for your interviewees. For a less structured interview, you will need to think about the themes you want to cover and whether you will put any boundaries on potential conversation. You may not get this absolutely right on your first attempt. After all, 'Research is a process of going up alleys to see if they are blind' (Marston Bates). So it is essential to conduct a pilot before you construct your final draft.

As with surveying, conducting a 'good' interview is a process that requires a lot more steps than you may realize. Before you get to ask a question, you need to plan for all contingencies, prepare an interview schedule and data recording system, run a trial and modify the process as appropriate. As shown in Box 6.8, you also need to think about how you will facilitate a productive conversation.

BOX 6.8

Facilitating a good interview

Do your homework

- *Be prepared to talk about your research* – The ability to clearly articulate the rationale, aims, objectives and methods of your project can be instrumental in getting the right doors opened.
- *Prepare a brief outline of your project* – Certain individuals or organizations may want to have a document they can consider and/or present to 'gatekeepers'.
- *Have a letter of introduction* – A letter of introduction from your supervisor can professionally answer questions like 'So who are you and where are you from?'
- *Find out about appropriate protocols* – Sometimes the contacts that are most willing to help do not have the authority to authorize access. Finding out about appropriate protocols can help avoid awkward situations.

(Continued)

(Continued)

Be professional

- *Be respectful* – Choose the right time for your approach, be prompt, dress appropriately, and be modest in your initial requests.
- *Plan for the unexpected* – Very rarely does the research process run smoothly, especially when you are dealing with individuals; be prepared for glitches.
- *Leave doors open* – Many researchers swear they have collected all the data they are going to need, but later wish they could go back and ask just a few more questions.

Offer something back

- *Don't disappear* – Let your contacts know how things are progressing and/or send a note of thanks.
- *Make results available* – It is quite natural to have a sense of curiosity about studies of which you are a part; the results of your study can be quite valued by those who have facilitated your research.
- *Facilitate honest and open responses* even though your interviewees may want to impress, be liked or maintain privacy.

Remember that interviews are a means of data collection. However, they may also provide a strategic means to meet decision-makers, managers, experts and other insider groups. If you have a project for which their contribution is valuable, interviews may be an excellent way to network in a new organization and gain support for your recommendations down the track. One business student utilized this strategy to meet key personnel across the organization (see Box 6.9).

BOX 6.9

Networking through interviews: Suzanne's story

My research involved gauging the effectiveness of a new tool that was being rolled out across the organization. The goal was to determine who was using it, and who wasn't and why. First, I identified key individuals and managers in each department. I was quite intimidated to approach people I didn't know and ask them to take time out of their busy day to do an interview.

In the end, only one person said 'no', so that was fine. I realized that most people were very nice and genuinely wanted to help me. Plus I met lots of decision-makers without awkward networking approaches.

Piloting

Interviewing is a skill that takes practice, and giving your process a run-through can be invaluable. You can then review and refine until you are comfortable with the process and data collected. Steps in a good pilot include:

1. *Having a run-through* – A mock interview can boost confidence and highlight potential issues.
2. *Reflecting* – Note any difficulties you encountered, i.e. access, time taken, question clarity, structure, introductory information, instructions, prompts, pacing, comfort zones, recording/note-taking, roles, objectivity, conversational flow, ambiguities, cultural issues, etc.
3. *Seeking feedback* – Get feedback from the interviewees on the issues above and anything else they wish to discuss.
4. *Reviewing notes/transcribing data* – Make sure you can make sense of notes and that transcription (if a goal) is doable. You may be surprised at how labour-/time-intensive transcription tends to be.
5. *Making modifications* – This will be based on your own reflections, feedback from your interviewee, as well as the quality of the data generated.
6. *Going back to the start* – If the need for modification is substantial, you may need to revisit your planning, development and piloting process. This may involve a return to the ethics committee.

Conducting the interview

Interviews can be intimidating, regardless of which side of the desk you're sitting. No matter how well prepared you are, you're still likely to feel nervous at the beginning and wish you had done some things differently at the end. The task can seem complex. In addition to questioning, prompting and probing in ways that help you gather the richest possible data, you also need to actively listen to, and make sense of, what your interviewee is saying – while at the same time managing the overall process so that you know how much time has passed, how much time is left, how much you still need to cover and how you might move it all forward.

Practice makes perfect. If you are aware of the key steps and can walk through them a few times with a friend, relative or peer, you'll feel much more at ease. In order to conduct a good interview, you will need to do the following:

1. *Take care of preliminaries* – Quite a few things need to come together before you are in a position to ask the first question. You will need to make appointments (allowing for travel time, interview time and wait-around time), be on time, and make sure you are prepared with any note-taking, recording or other essentials beforehand.
2. *Establish rapport* – This includes introductions, small talk and expression of appreciation. It's also the part where you introduce the study, its purpose, why

their involvement is important and how long the interview will take. Do not waste time going into the minutiae of the study. Rather, concentrate on their contribution to it. Preclude any anxieties they might have by discussing issues of confidentiality, the right to decline any particular questions and the right to end the interview upon request.

3. *Ease your respondents into the interview* – Finally you can get down to business. As with surveying, it is important to ease your way into main questions and themes. If you start off with a 'sensitive' question or one that might be considered threatening, you may find yourself facing an uphill battle for the remainder of the interview. In fact, it can be easy to get an interviewee off-side, so it's well worth considering how you might handle such a situation.

4. *Ask questions that facilitate meaningful answers* – Try to ask questions that open up conversations and draw out rich responses. Questions should create possibilities, open up options, dig below the surface and lower defences.

5. *Keep it flowing* – Moving the interview forward might involve the use of prompts, i.e. giving the interviewee some ideas that might jog a response, and probes, which are comments and questions that help you dig for more, i.e. 'tell me more', 'really?', or 'why?'. Sometimes probes can be an inquisitive look or a few moments of silence.

6. *Keep on track/explore tangents* – If you are conducting a structured interview and have a limited amount of time, you will want to make sure you are keeping your interviewee on track and moving at a good pace. If your interview is less structured, you may find yourself wanting to explore interesting tangents as they develop. The trick here is to be mindful of the time, and be sure you end the interview with the full range of data you aimed to gather.

7. *Wind down/close* – Winding down involves questions that 'round off' an interview and asking respondents if there is anything else they would like to cover, contribute or clarify. The interview then ends by thanking your interviewee for their contribution and their time, and asking them if it might be possible to contact them again if you need to ask any further questions, or need to clarify any points. It's also good practice to offer something back, for example a copy of your completed report. Depending on which stage of the interview process you are at, you may also wish to ask if there is anyone else the interviewee would recommend that you speak to about this issue. This 'chain-referral' or 'snowball method' interviewing can provide useful leads and introductions, and has proven extremely useful to the authors in their own research projects.

What about recording?

One important consideration is how you record responses. Recording responses can be done in a number of ways; you may need to trial a couple of recording methods in order to assess what is best for you and your research process. You might also consider professional transcripts, as discussed in Box 6.11 at the end of this section.

- *Note-taking* – This can range from highly structured to open and interpretative. Highly structured note-taking often utilizes a form that can be filled in as the interviewee speaks. It may even include a list of codes for common responses (this can allow for statistical analysis if enough interviews are conducted). At the other end of the spectrum is unstructured note-taking that may take the form of a concept map or involve jotting down interpretative ideas during or even after an interview. Remember that if you are going to take notes during an interview, be sure you practice talking, listening and note-taking simultaneously – and that you can read your own writing. You also need to keep in mind that note-taking is actually a preliminary form of analysis (you are making decisions about what to record). You may want to consider taking notes in conjunction with audio/video recording.

  In most situations you will be responsible for both conducting an interview and capturing responses, but under some circumstances you may use a note-taker. Using a person to take notes or record your interview can allow you to focus and engage more fully in listening and directing your interview. But as well as considering resource implications, you need to carefully consider whether a third party is likely to have an effect on the respondent and the interview process. Once the interviewee/respondent is outnumbered, it can feel a bit less like a comfortable chat.

- *Digital audio recording* – This allows you to preserve raw data for review at a later date. Interviewers are therefore free to focus on the question/answer process at hand. Disadvantages, however, include the unease it can cause for the interviewee, an inability to capture non-verbal cues, potential equipment failure and the cost of data transcription. Audio recording can be done on dedicated recorders, your smartphone or other devices. Box 6.10 explores the use of smartpens for digital audio recording.

BOX 6.10

Audio recording with smartpens

There are some interesting tools available for interview recording, including digital pens, sometimes called 'smartpens' (Figure 6.1). These pens have ink, but they also come with internal flash drive and microphone. Unlike a regular digital recorder, they digitize notes and synchronize them with the audio. This means you can point to a line on your page of notes and the pen will automatically play the audio from that timeframe. Smartpens must be paired with smart paper for this feature, but could be worth the investment if you are conducting several interviews.

(Continued)

(Continued)

Figure 6.1   Smartpen and dot paper smart notebook (Livescribe)

- *Video taping* – Offers the added bonus of being able to record visual cues, but is more intrusive, is prone to more technical difficulties and can generate data that is difficult to analyze. Also be aware that being filmed may cause people to change their behavior. One of the earliest business studies detailed the Hawthorne effect, a type of reactivity whereby people modify their behavior when they know they are being watched (author George Orwell used this phenomenon in his classic dystopia *1984*, to explore how people become more complicit and conforming when their behavior is constantly monitored). To counteract this effect, try to set up the video equipment to the side so that the interviewee does not feel they are being closely scrutinized or interrogated.

For both audio and video recording, you'll need to be aware of the extra time required to procure the appropriate technology and become very comfortable with its use before your first interview.

- *Post-interview data dump* – This very useful method involves dumping your thoughts and impressions into a digital recorder straight after an interview. It is a great supplement to note-taking and can be helpful even after a recorded interview. Your impressions of an interview can be a valuable source of data in their own right. And while you think you might remember your insights, it is easy to lose them a few interviews later.

BOX 6.11

Transcription

Transcription can be extremely valuable – having your interview or focus group data typed out can dramatically ease the analysis process. But it is a slow and expensive process. A 30-minute interview can yield up to 30 pages of script. An option here is to use a professional transcription service.

Transcription services are increasingly affordable, usually about $1US per minute. Once the interviews have been transcribed, remember you may need to look through and correct small errors (usually the result of group members talking over one another).

Collecting focus group data

Focus groups are a form of group interview, but one that needs to be managed in distinct ways. They are quite common in a range of organizational research. Focus groups can test new products or services, or act as a sounding board for proposed advertising campaigns. They can also be used when a diverse group of people might work together to arrive at potential solutions, i.e. how to best tackle the challenge of an ageing workforce.

Focus groups are logistically more complex than one-on-one interviews. You need to secure the agreement of people to participate in your study. Planning also involves picking an appropriate venue. A lecture space with a lectern and rows of stadium seating are not conducive to discussion. Moreover, a public venue may not have the sound quality or privacy required. Aim for a room (perhaps a board room, local hotel space, or the like) with good acoustics, whereby chairs can be arranged together. With focus groups, the emphasis is less on Q and A and more on facilitating discussion *between* participants.

Remember that not all issues are conducive to focus groups. Sensitive issues may produce a room full of awkward silence, whereby a discussion of highly political issues may end in a shouting match. Madriz (2000) cautions against the use of focus groups for the discussion of intimate/private details, when participants may not be comfortable in each other's presence (e.g. bringing together people in a hierarchical relationship to each other, such as employees and managers) and when participants are likely to profoundly disagree with each other.

During the focus group interviews, you will need to manage this group discussion. For instance, if one or two participants begin to dominate discussion, you may need to ensure that other views are heard. Box 6.12 discusses issues you will need to consider before running a focus group.

BOX 6.12

Issues to consider for your focus group

- Have you designed a clear introduction to the topic of the research to participants?
- Have you secured a room or space conducive to group discussion (beware of echoes, drafts or noisy environments)?
- Have you thoroughly tested your recording equipment?
- Do questions encourage group interaction and discussion?
- Have you allowed enough time for discussion?
- Do you have a strategy if the group strays too far from the topic?
- Do you have a strategy to encourage equitable participation from all members?
- Have you devised a strategy to encourage those reluctant to speak?
- Have you practiced using any aids you will be presenting to the group (film clips, visual aids, etc.)?
- Have you considered strategies for conflict resolution?

One more consideration: given the number of participants (6–10), it is important to record these sessions. It will be problematic to try to take notes and facilitate a group discussion at the same time, much less try to keep accurate records of specific quotes.

MANAGING THE WORKLOAD

It's probably clear by now that primary data collection is labour-intensive. Now you know why it's so valuable! Balancing your research project, your work responsibilities and some semblance of a social/family life can stretch even the most astute time management skills. It may also require some negotiation around other responsibilities – this is why it is important to align your research project with organizational/department goals. It will be difficult to carve out the time and resources required to collect data for your research project if your manager is not sold on its value to the organization.

Aside from alignment and negotiation, you also need to consider the scope of the research collection method as you proceed. Perhaps you designed a mixed-method project whereby intensive interviews would be followed up with surveys. As you begin the data collection process, you may find that the limited timeframes of small-scale applied workplace-based research mean this is impractical.

The worst thing you can do is to proceed with an impractical scope while trying to uphold all other workload responsibilities as well. This will need to be carefully negotiated with your manager and may be contingent on the particular industry in which you are situated – for instance, high-profile financial or consulting services are known for long hours and high turnover (see Box 6.13).

BOX 6.13

Managing your small-scale research project: Is your work–life balance working?

We live in a world whereby 'busyness' in all areas of life has become a competitive sport. Finding a balance between your professional responsibilities, small-scale research project and personal commitments will be challenging. However, you must find a balance. Why is this so important?

Consider two recent headlines. When a 21-year-old German intern working '15-hour days' at Merrill Lynch in London was found dead after working through a string of all-nighters, overwork was assumed to have contributed to his death (Malik and Quinn, 2013). In 2015, a US-based intern in one of Goldman Sachs' most prestigious investment banking divisions died after telling his father of the stress he was experiencing from overwork (Moore, 2015). Thus far the financial and consulting industries have borne the brunt of criticism from previous interns and HR managers. Their horror stories describe a toxic environment in which 6½-day workweeks and all-nighters are expected. The extent of the problem was laid bare when Goldman Sachs publicly introduced a rule that interns must 'go home at midnight' and junior bankers must take Saturdays off! One wonders if there was actual progress on the front without a commensurate decrease in workload, i.e. client expectations.

The tragic deaths of these workers points to a dangerous corporate trend whereby overwork has become common and accepted. The current competition for jobs combined with this corporate practice have created unintended but not unforeseeable consequences. According to Chris Roebuck, a visiting professor at Cass Business School who has held senior HR roles at international banks, 'For reasons related to an individual's ambition or the current employment market, people are desperate to get jobs,' he said. 'Some employers are exploiting that fact, pushing people past the point where it makes sense for their health or from a business perspective' (Malik and Quinn, 2013).

Though there are calls for government intervention to address the problem, such regulation appears to be a long way away. Until then, the onus is on the workers themselves to establish workload boundaries. This involves carving out and defending your non-work time. As Nigel Marsh outlines in his TEDx talk in Sydney,

> If you don't design your life, someone else will design it for you, and you may not like their idea of balance. Never put the quality of your life in the hands of a commercial corporation ... Because commercial companies are inherently designed to get as much out of you [as] they can get away with ... We have to be responsible for setting and enforcing the boundaries that we want in our life. (Marsh, 2010)

(Continued)

(Continued)

This may sound radical, but it's common sense in other parts of the world. In Denmark, for instance, employees who work more than 40 hours a week are considered inefficient and are at risk of being fired. It is expected that without a healthy balance, your work will also ultimately suffer. So look to the rest of the world for moral support! And remember, if you don't set these boundaries, no one else will.

If you find that you haven't been able to negotiate the space for your project or find yourself feeling overwhelmed and falling further and further behind, it's worth having a chat to your manager and your academic supervisor. Conducting small-scale workplace-based research should be a challenge, but not one that knocks you over.

CHAPTER SUMMARY

- There are no easy answers when it comes to primary data collection. Each method comes with its own challenges and benefits that must be balanced with the timeframe, scope and purpose of the project.
- Finding appropriate respondents is fundamental to meaningful research results. Using the 'wrong' sample or informant can damage the credibility of your study.
- Whether you are conducting surveys or interviews, you need thorough planning and reflexive consideration. A pilot study is incredibly helpful in ironing out the kinks.
- Managing the workload is paramount for your study, your work and your health. Don't proceed with an untenable scope if you find the methods are unsustainable. When conditions change, change your plan!

ANALYZING YOUR DATA

Chapter preview

From raw data to meaningful understanding

Analyzing qualitative data

Analyzing quantitative data

Presenting findings

Drawing conclusions and formulating recommendations

FROM RAW DATA TO MEANINGFUL UNDERSTANDING

Congratulations, you have data! It may not be much to look at right now, but it's yours, and it shall be used for great things … just as soon as you figure out what it means. A common mistake of new researchers is to underestimate this task, both in terms of time and mental load. After all, it's tempting, after collecting the data, to think that you've conquered the hardest part of your research project. And yes, gathering credible data is certainly a challenge; but so too is making sense of it. Interpretation, the action of ascribing meaning, is your job as a researcher. So how do you go about doing it?

Diving in

> The middle of every successful project looks like a disaster.
>
> Rosabeth Moss Cantor

In streamlined diagrams labeled the 'research process', research proceeds linearly and logically through discrete stages. These simple flowcharts present an elegant process whereby the researcher moves from data collection to analysis to conclusions (which naturally and effortlessly follow), much as a person moves effortlessly from room to room in her own home. Oh, such beautiful lies!

In reality, research is much messier. This is particularly true when it comes to translating raw data into something useful. Analysis may begin before full data collection is complete (especially for pilot programs), unexpected analysis findings may result in a more careful look at research data collection methods (and possible errors) and collection started again. Analysis itself is often exhausting and confusing. New skills in software may have to be acquired (usually at the last minute). Raw data may not have a clear trend, pattern or insight … at least at first. Seeing the pattern may take some time, and these epiphanies may happen at an unexpected time (often in the shower!).

Then, there's the presentation of results. How to bundle days, weeks, months of work into a compelling narrative (including visuals!)? This is not to discourage, but to allay concerns that any obstacles you face at this point are unprecedented. At this point in your research journey it's important to remember that everything you're going through is completely normal. Yes, this includes a bit of chaos. The key is just to get started with your next step. Dive in. Approach uncertainty with gusto. As Albert Einstein said, 'If we knew what we were doing, it wouldn't be called research.'

Analysis is part art and part science. There is a level of creativity involved: can you spot trends, themes, anomalies? But there is a method to the madness. If you break the process of analysis down into a number of defined tasks, it's a challenge that can be conquered.

Here are five tasks that need to be managed when conducting analysis:

1. *Keeping your eye on the main game* – This means not getting lost in the pile of numbers and words in a way that causes you to lose a sense of what you're trying to accomplish. It's easy to get lost in the process. On the plus side this means being engaged and immersed and really getting a handle on what's going on. But getting lost can also mean getting lost in the tasks; that is, handing control to analysis programs and losing touch with the overall aim (see Box 7.1).
2. *Managing your data so that it's ready for your intended mode(s) of analysis* – Data can build pretty quickly. You might be surprised by the sheer amount you have managed to collect. Learning how to manage, sift, prioritize, code and utilize data is a crucial skill, and one that is usually built on painful experience. The key is employing a rigorous and systematic approach to data management that will allow you to build or create a data set that can be managed and utilized throughout the process of analysis.
3. *Engaging in the actual process of analysis* – For quantified data, this will involve statistical analysis, while working with words and images will require you to call on qualitative data analysis strategies. More on this later in the chapter.
4. *Presenting data in ways that capture understandings,* and being able to offer those understandings to others in the clearest possible fashion. Visualizing

and communicating data is part of connecting with your audience (including decision-makers). This means your data should be presented in a way that is compelling, accurate and easy to understand.

5. *Drawing meaningful and logical conclusions* that flow from your data and address key issues.

In addition to a summary and recommendations, you can also consider sharing your findings, insights and ideas in the form of an original framework or model. Such devices not only add clarity to your reporting, but also help you establish your credibility as a researcher able to make original contributions.

BOX 7.1

Questions for keeping the bigger picture in mind

Questions related to your own expectations

- What do I expect to find, i.e. how do I think my research question or hypothesis bears out?
- What don't I expect to find, and how can I look for it?
- Can my findings be interpreted in alternative ways? What are the implications?

Questions related to research question, aims and objectives

- How should I treat my data in order to best address my research questions?
- How do my findings relate to my research questions, aims and objectives?

Questions related to theory, frameworks and models

- Are my findings consistent with previous studies or theories? How? Why? Why not?
- Does a particular theory, framework or model inform/help to explain my findings? In what ways?

Questions related to methods

- Have my methods of data collection and/or analysis colored my results? If so, in what ways?
- Were there any problems related to methods that may have affected my findings?

The goal of most workplace-based research is to anticipate or explain trends, solve a problem or offer a new direction that informs decision-making. Whether you are working with qualitative or quantitative data, the main game of any form of analysis is to move from raw data to meaningful understanding. In quantitative methods, this is done through statistical tests of coded data that assess the significance of findings; coding the data is preliminary to any analyses and interpretation. In qualitative analysis, understandings are built by a more tangled and creative process of uncovering and discovering themes that run through the raw data, and by interpreting the implication of those themes in relation to your research questions. As you proceed through the analysis, be aware that many researchers find this the most cognitively taxing part. Gathering data requires effort, but analysis requires thinking, concentration.

ANALYZING QUALITATIVE DATA

In the world of qualitative analysis, raw data can be extremely messy. You might be facing a host of digital recordings, a mound of interview transcripts, a research journal (which can range from highly organized to highly disorganized), scribbled notes, highlighted documents, photographs, videos, mind maps – in fact the array is almost endless. And there is no doubt that a mound of messy data is extremely intimidating, especially if you are new to qualitative analysis.

As highlighted in Box 7.2, the best advice is to be systematic. No matter how reflexive and iterative you intend your analysis to be, you still need to approach the management of your data with methodical rigor.

BOX 7.2

Qualitative data management

While managing qualitative data is essential, it is worth noting that it is almost impossible to 'manage' qualitative data without engaging in some level of analysis. The process of organizing your data, e.g. deciding how you will group it, will see you engaging with your data and making decisions that will have an effect on analysis. This should therefore be recognized as a part of analysis.

The data management process
Step 1: Familiarize yourself with appropriate software

As discussed in the next section, it may not be necessary for all students to use specialist software for qualitative data analysis (QDA), but it is certainly worth becoming familiar with available tools. Programs worth exploring include:

- NVIVO, MAXqda, The Ethnograph – used for indexing, searching and theorizing text.
- ATLAS.ti – can be used for images as well as words.
- CONCORDANCE, HAMLET, DICTION – popular for content analysis.
- CLAN – popular for conversation analysis.

(Information on all of the above is available at www.textanalysis.info)

As with quantitative software, most universities have licenses that allow students access to certain qualitative programs. Universities may also provide relevant short courses.

Step 2: Log in your data

It is rare that qualitative data all comes in at the same time, or in the same form; it can end up being a lot messier than a pile of questionnaires, so it is wise to keep track of your qualitative data as it is collected. It is well worth noting the respondents/source, data collection procedures, collection dates and any commonly used shorthand.

Step 3: Organize your data sources

This involves grouping like sources, making any necessary copies and conducting an initial cull of any notes, observations, etc., not relevant to the analysis. As well as organizing, this process allows you to screen your data. If done early, you can uncover potential problems not picked up in your pilot, and make improvements to any ongoing data collection protocols.

Step 4: Read through and take overarching notes

It is extremely important to get a feel for qualitative data. This means reading through your data as it comes in and taking a variety of notes that will help you decide on the best way to sort and categorize the data you have collected. This is where the boundary between data management and data analysis becomes highly blurred, since any notes related to emerging themes are analysis.

Step 5: Prepare data for analysis/transcription

If using a specialist QDA program, you will need to transcribe/scan your data so that it is ready to be entered into the relevant program. If you plan on manually analyzing your qualitative data, you still need to go through this step so that you can print out your interviews, photographs, etc. You need to be able to actually put your hands on your data.

Step 6: Enter data/get analysis tool prepared

If you are using QDA software, you will need to enter your electronic data into the program. If you are manually handling your data, you won't need to 'enter' your data, but you will need to arm yourself with qualitative analysis tools such as index cards, whiteboards, sticky notes and highlighters. In both cases analysis tends to be ongoing and often begins before all the data has been collected/entered.

Steps in qualitative analysis for organization-based research

When it comes to QDA, the most important thing to recognize is the pressing need for ongoing rich engagement with the documents, transcripts, images and texts that make up your raw data. This will involve lots of reading and re-reading that needs to start at the point of data collection and continue through processes of data management, data analysis and even the drawing of conclusions. As articulated more fully below and drawn out further in Box 7.3, analysis then involves: (1) identifying biases and noting overall impressions; (2) reducing (an evil word, but an essential step in moving from messy raw data to rich understanding), organizing and coding your data; (3) searching for patterns and interconnections; (4) mapping and building themes; (5) building and verifying theories; and (6) drawing conclusions.

There are two important things to note here. The first is that while the goal is to move from raw data to rich theoretical understanding, this process is far from linear. Qualitative data demands cycles of iterative analysis. The discovery of anything interesting will take you back to an earlier step including re-reading, reviewing and re-engaging. The second thing to note is related to the notion of reduction. Students can get worried when they learn that part of the process is 'reducing'; they think this is antithetical to QDA's goal of preserving richness.

Richness is indeed important, but qualitative analysis involves more than just preserving richness. Good qualitative analysis actually requires you to build it. Put it this way: raw data may be rich, but it is also messy and not publishable. If publishing in a journal, for example, you need to move from up to 1,000 or more pages of raw data to a 10-page article, and this necessarily involves processes of reduction that make the data manageable and understandable. But you will also want to make the data meaningful. So after processes of reduction, you will want to find interconnections, develop themes and build theories. As shown in Figure 7.1, getting to the point of meaningful understanding means abstracting your data back outwards so that it tells a full and powerful story that is rich in dialogue with theory.

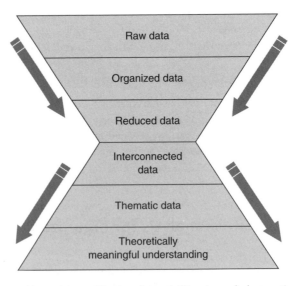

Figure 7.1   Working with qualitative data: drilling in and abstracting out

Now some of you are probably thinking, is all this necessary? I only have six interviews and three documents – can't I just report on what they said and what I found? Well, unfortunately, this happens all the time. There can be a tendency to skip analysis altogether and simply summarize the data from memory. But this does not work. If you do not rigorously analyze qualitative data, you are very likely to report on findings from interviews and documents in a discrete fashion. You are likely to miss the unexpected and not develop the rich themes and findings that come from interconnecting your data. Yes, there are several steps in qualitative analysis, but they are essential if you are after insightful interpretations and meaningful understanding.

Identifying biases/noting impressions

Because it is difficult to completely separate the process of data collection from analysis (you simply do not have the ability to constrain all thinking processes while engaged in listening to people's stories), you tend to analyze as you go. But this can be hazardous, since interpretations are always entwined with a researcher's biases, prejudices, worldviews and paradigms – both recognized and unrecognized, conscious and subconscious. Because of these biases, a good way to start your analysis is to list as many of your assumptions and preconceived notions as possible. A good technique here is to (1) list everything you expect to find; (2) list everything you do not expect to find; and (3) leave a blank column for things completely out of the blue. Doing this will prepare you for the unexpected.

The second step is to engage in careful reading of all collected data, with 'general impression' notes recorded throughout the reading process. The objective here is to get an overall feel for the data and begin a process of holistically looking at disparate sources of data as an overarching story. As well as various topics, this might involve identifying feelings and emotions. If you were exploring experiences of divorce, for example, anger, frustration and hurt would be as important as division of property or custody arrangements.

Reducing and coding into themes

The next stage of analysis is to undertake a thorough examination of all data sources. This involves systematic drilling of the raw data in order to build up categories of understanding. The idea is to reduce your data and sort it into various themes. If you are doing your analysis manually, a good approach is to make multiple copies of transcripts that you can highlight, cut and stack into relevant piles and play around with as your analysis progresses. If you are using QDA software, your program will allow you to undertake a comparable process, electronically.

As discussed above, this can be highly disconcerting. Suddenly your rich data is sorted and stacked into what may seem like superficial heaps. But remind yourself that this is just one stage in your analysis – and that this is a stage that you can revisit as your insights grow.

Now what you are looking for in this exploration are categories and themes, but this might be alluded to in several ways: that is, through the words that are used, the concepts that are discussed and the non-verbal cues noted by the researcher:

- *Exploring words* – Words can be explored through their repetition, or through exploration of their context and usage (sometimes called key words in context). Specific cultural connotations of particular words can also be important. Patton (2014) refers to this as 'indigenous categories', while Corbin and Strauss (2007) refer to it as 'in vivo' coding. When working with words, researchers often systematically search a text to find all instances of a particular word (or phrase), making note of its context/meaning. Several software packages such as DICTION or CONCORDANCE can quickly and efficiently identify and tally the use of particular words and even present such findings in a quantitative manner.
- *Exploring concepts* – To explore concepts, researchers generally engage in line-by-line or paragraph-by-paragraph reading of transcripts, engaging in what grounded theory proponents refer to as 'constant comparison'. In other words, concepts and meaning are explored in each text and then compared with previously analyzed texts to draw out both similarities and disparities. The concepts you explore can arise from the literature, your research question, intuition or prior experiences. To find these you read through your text and deductively uncover the themes. The other option is to look for concepts to emerge inductively from your data without any preconceived notions (the practice of grounded theory). With predetermined categories, researchers need to be wary of 'fitting' their data to their expectations, and not being able to see alternative explanations. However, purely inductive methods are also subject to bias since unacknowledged subjectivities can impact on the themes that emerge from the data.
- *Exploring non-verbal cues* – One of the difficulties in moving from raw data to rich meaning is what is lost in the process. And certainly the tendency in qualitative data collection and analysis is to concentrate on words rather than the tone and emotive feeling behind the words, the body language that accompanies the words, or even words not spoken. Yet this world of the non-verbal can be central to thematic exploration. If your raw data, notes or transcripts contain non-verbal cues, it can lend significant meaning to content and themes: exploration of tone, volume, pitch and pace of speech; the tendency for hearty or nervous laughter; the range of facial expressions and body language; and shifts in any or all of these can be central in a bid for meaningful understanding.

Looking for patterns and interconnections

Once your texts have been explored for relevant themes, the quest for meaningful understanding moves to an exploration of the relationship between and among various themes. For example, you may look to see whether the use of certain words and/or concepts is correlated with the use of other words and/or concepts. Or you may explore whether certain words/concepts are associated with a particular range of non-verbal cues or emotive states. You may also look to see whether there is a connection between the use of particular metaphors and non-verbal cues. And, of course, you may want to explore how individuals with particular characteristics vary on any of these dimensions.

Interconnectivities are assumed to be both diverse and complex, and can point to the relationship between conditions and consequences, or how the experiences of the individual relate to broader themes.

Mapping and building themes

As your range of patterns and interconnections grows, it is worth 'mapping' your data.

Technically, when deductively uncovering data related to 'a priori' themes, the map would be predetermined. However, when inductively discovering themes using a grounded theory approach, the map would be built as you work through your data. In practice, however, the distinction is unlikely to be that clear, and you will probably rely on both strategies to build the richest map possible.

Figure 7.2 offers a basic map exploring process improvement. This can be expanded with nodules off of each bubble. It is worth noting that this type of map can be easily converted to a 'tree structure' that forms the basis of analysis in many QDA software programs (see Figure 7.3).

Figure 7.2   Simple idea mapping

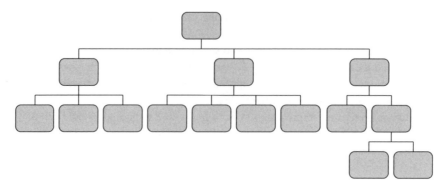

Figure 7.3 Qualitative data analysis 'tree' structure

This then moves your data from piles sorted under simple categories of reduction to understandings that sit under much more meaningful themes. Mapping becomes an exercise that involves engaging themes in a dialogue and juxtaposing the themes (as well as the tensions among the themes) with relevant research and theoretically-oriented literature. Reductive processes have thus expanded back out at a much more sophisticated level.

Developing theory

While your analysis may culminate with thematic mapping, the conceptualization and abstraction involved can become quite advanced and can go from model building to theory building. In other words, rich mapping is likely to spurn new ideas – that 'Hey, you know what might be going here' moment. It is quite exciting when you suddenly realize you are not just taking from the literature, but that you are ready to contribute back.

Drawing conclusions

Writing, to me, is thinking through my fingers.

Isaac Asimov

Drawing conclusions is your opportunity to pull together all the significant/ important findings of your study and consider why and how they are significant/ important. It is about clearly summarizing what your data reveals and linking this back to your project's main questions, aims and objectives. Your findings will need to be considered in relation to your study's aim and methodological constraints, and should clearly point to your overarching arguments. Remember: clarity is important, but do not force-fit your findings to portray a world without ambiguity and complexity.

Box 7.3 gives an example of studies using QDA and thematic analysis.

BOX 7.3

Stepping your way through effective QDA

How might the steps outlined above unfold in practice? Let's look at children's toys. For the purpose of this exercise, imagine you work for a toy company and you want to undertake a study that explores how toys are marketed to children through commercials (or perhaps even online apps). You select commercials for a certain product (Lego sets) and find 15 examples over several years using YouTube. Analysis might unfold as follows.

Step 1: Identifying biases/noting overall impressions

We all have biases. You might, for example, think that toy companies over-commercialize childhood (think of children who spend more time playing with the box the toy came in, rather than the toy itself) or that certain toys such as i-Pads and games shouldn't be marketed to toddlers. Doing this step fully is extremely important. If you do not acknowledge preconceived notions and actively work to neutralize them, you are likely to find exactly what you expect to find!

The next step is to watch all 15 commercials and take notes of overall impressions, perhaps related to content, emotions, colors, participants, style (these categories may derive from your own interests, insights or the literature).

Step 2: Reducing and coding into themes

This involves watching each commercial in turn and noting everything you possibly can related to the categories you noted/generated in step 1 as well as any other categories you inductively uncover along the way. When it comes to participants for Commercial 1, for example, you might find themes of problem-solving, creativity and teamwork. In this way, you build both categories and subcategories that are likely to expand as you work your way through each commercial.

Step 3: Searching for patterns and interconnections

You are likely to have overlapping themes across your 15 commercials – so this step asks you to search for commonalities and divergences. For example, you may find that the commercial marketing to older children tends to focus on one gender (all-boy, or all-girl groups), or that Lego sets marketed for girls tend to focus on fantasy themes (princesses, unicorns, etc.) while sets marketed for boys focus on science themes (such as space exploration).

Step 4: Mapping and building themes

One small section of a preliminary map or word cloud might be as seen in Figure 7.4. These clouds use different type sizes and fonts to give prominence to words that appear most

(Continued)

(Continued)

often in your text. (Wordle.net has a fantastic program for creating 'clouds'.) From here you would: (1) continue mapping all the main themes (genre, gender, etc.); (2) create even more subcategories as appropriate; and (3) map various interconnections.

Figure 7.4   Word cloud

Now if you did not have clear boundaries on your study at the onset, you will probably come to realize that doing qualitative analysis of all aspects of toy advertising is a huge task that may not be manageable – so you may decide to narrow in on one or two particular interesting areas, say, for example, gender. Remember: it is much better to do a really rigorous job on a smaller scale than a mediocre job on a bigger scale.

Step 5: Building and verifying theories

This is your 'Hey, you know what might be going on here' moment, which will hopefully dawn on you as you watch the commercials for the twentieth time and play around with your maps for the tenth time. Who knows? You may come up with a mind-blowing insight that sets the toy industry on fire.

Step 6: Drawing conclusions

You are likely to find out much more through the processes than you could possibly share, so you will need to decide what is most significant/important and link this back to your project's main questions, aims and objectives in the most compelling and credible way.

ANALYZING QUANTITATIVE DATA

It wasn't long ago that 'doing' statistics meant working with mathematical formulae. No more! Statistics in the twenty-first century is more about your ability to use statistical software than your ability to calculate means, modes, medians and standard deviations – and look up p-values. To say otherwise is to suggest that you can't ride a bike unless you know how to build one. What you really need to do is to learn how to ride, or in this case learn how to run a stats program (see Box 7.4).

Admittedly, these programs do assume and demand a basic understanding of the logic and the language of statistics. This means you need to have a basic understanding of: (1) the nature of variables; (2) the role and function of both descriptive and inferential statistics; (3) appropriate use of statistical tests; and (4) effective data presentation. If you can do this, effective statistical analysis is well within your grasp.

Note that while this chapter will familiarize you with the basic logic and essential 'lingo' of statistics, it really is best if your reading is done in conjunction with some hands-on practice (even if this is simply playing with the mock data sets provided in stats programs, or following along on a YouTube class). For this type of knowledge 'to stick', it needs to be applied.

BOX 7.4

Useful software

Most universities have licences that allow students certain software access, and many universities provide relevant short courses. Programs themselves generally contain comprehensive tutorials complete with mock data sets. Programs you are likely to come across include:

- SPSS – sophisticated and user-friendly (www.spss.com).
- SAS – often an institutional standard, but some feel it is not as user-friendly as SPSS (www.sas.com).
- Minitab – more introductory, good for learners/small data sets (www.mini tab.com).
- Excel – while not a dedicated stats program, it can handle the basics and is readily available on most PCs (Microsoft Office product). There is also an add-on to perform statistical analysis in Excel (available from www.real-statistics.com or XLstat.com).
- R – free software environment for statistical computing and graphics (www.r-project.org).

Disclaimer: You need to remember that while algorithms might be able to do the 'tasks', it is the researcher who needs to work strategically, creatively and intuitively to get a 'feel' for the data; to cycle between data and existing theory; and to follow the hunches that can lead to sometimes unexpected yet significant findings for yourself and the organization.

Understanding variables

Understanding the nature of variables is essential to statistical analysis. A key way to differentiate variables is through cause and effect. This means being able to clearly identify and distinguish your dependent and independent variables. Now while understanding the theoretical difference is not too difficult, being able to readily identify each type comes with practice.

- *Dependent variables* – These are the things you are trying to study or what you are trying to measure. For example, you might be interested in knowing what factors are related to high levels of stress, a strong income stream or levels of achievement in secondary school – stress, income and achievement would all be dependent variables.
- *Independent variables* – These are the things that might be causing an effect on the things you are trying to understand. For example, conditions of employment might be affecting stress levels; gender may have a role in determining income; while parental influence may impact on levels of achievement. The independent variables here are employment conditions, gender and parental influence.
- One way of identifying dependent and independent variables is simply to ask what *depends* on what. Stress *depends* on work conditions or income *depends* on gender. If you think about it, it doesn't make sense to say gender depends on income unless you happen to be saving for a sex-change operation!

Using measurement scales

Measurement scales refer to the nature of the differences you are trying to capture in relation to a particular variable. There are four basic measurement scales that become respectively more precise: nominal, ordinal, interval and ratio (see Table 7.1). The precision of each type is directly related to the statistical tests that can be performed upon them. The more precise the scale, the more sophisticated the statistical analysis you can do.

- *Nominal* – Numbers are arbitrarily assigned to represent categories. These numbers are simply a coding scheme and have no numerical significance (and therefore cannot be used to perform mathematical calculations). For example, in the case of gender you would use one number for female, say 1, and another for male, 2. In an example used later in this chapter, the variable 'plans after graduation' is also nominal with numerical values arbitrarily assigned as 1 = vocational/technical training, 2 = university, 3 = workforce, 4 = travel abroad, 5 = undecided and 6 = other. In nominal measurement, codes should not overlap (they should be mutually exclusive) and together should cover all possibilities (be collectively exhaustive). The main function of nominal data is to allow researchers to tally respondents in order to understand population distributions.

- *Ordinal* – This scale rank orders categories in some meaningful way – there is an order to the coding. Magnitudes of difference, however, are not indicated. Take, for example, socioeconomic status (lower, middle or upper class). Lower class may denote less status than the other two classes but the amount of the difference is not defined. Other examples include air travel (economy, business, first class), or items where respondents are asked to rank order selected choices (biggest environmental challenges facing developed countries). Likert-type scales, in which respondents are asked to select a response on a point scale (for example, 'I enjoy going to work': 1 = strongly disagree, 2 = disagree, 3 = neutral, 4 = agree, 5 = strongly agree), are ordinal since a precise difference in magnitude cannot be determined. Many researchers, however, treat Likert scales as interval because it allows them to perform more precise statistical tests. In most small-scale studies this is not generally viewed as problematic.
- *Interval* – In addition to ordering their data, this scale uses equidistant units to measure difference. This scale does not, however, have an absolute zero. An example here is date – the year 2017 occurs 41 years after the year 1976 but time did not begin in AD1. IQ is also considered an interval scale even though there is some debate over the equidistant nature between points.
- *Ratio* – Not only is each point on a ratio scale equidistant, there is also an absolute zero. Examples of ratio data include income, age, height and distance. Because ratio data are 'real' numbers, all basic mathematical operations can be performed.

Descriptive statistics

Descriptive statistics are used to describe the basic features of a data set and are key to summarizing variables. The goal is to present quantitative descriptions in a manageable and intelligible form. Descriptive statistics provide measures of central tendency, dispersion and distribution shape. Such measures vary by data type (nominal, ordinal, interval, ratio) and are standard calculations in statistical programs.

Measuring central tendency

One of the most basic questions you can ask of your data focuses on central tendency. For example, what was the average score on a test? Do most people lean left or right on the issue of environmental regulations on businesses? Or what do

Table 7.1   Measurement scales

	Nominal	Ordinal	Interval	Ratio
Classifies	✓	✓	✓	✓
Orders		✓	✓	✓
Equidistant units			✓	✓
Absolute zero				✓

Table 7.2   Central tendency for age of customers

Data related to age of customers for a particular product	
Raw data	12, 12, 10, 9, 12, 15, 11, 12, 11, 11, 15, 16, 17, 12, 13, 13, 14, 11, 10, 9, 9, 8, 13, 14, 12, 14, 15, 13, 13, 10, 9, 13, 14, 13, 9
n (no. of cases)	35
Mean (average)	12.11
Median (midpoint)	12
Mode (most common value)	13

most people think is the main problem with our tax system? In statistics, there are three ways to measure central tendency: mean, median and mode – and the example questions above respectively relate to these three measures.

- *Mean* – The mathematical average. To calculate the mean, you add the values for each case and then divide by the number of cases. Because the mean is a mathematical calculation, it is used to measure central tendency for interval and ratio data, and cannot be used for nominal or ordinal data where numbers are used as 'codes'. For example, it makes no sense to average the 1s, 2s and 3s that might be assigned to public-sector workers, private (for-profit) workers and Private (non-profit) workers.
- *Median* – The mid-point of a range. To find the median you simply arrange values in ascending (or descending) order and find the middle value. This measure is generally used in ordinal data, and has the advantage of negating the impact of extreme values or outliers, e.g. one extreme salary at $3 million will push up the mean income level, but it will not affect the median. Of course, this can also be a limitation given that outliers can be significant to a study.
- *Mode* – The most common value or values noted for a variable. Since nominal data is categorical and cannot be manipulated mathematically, it relies on mode as its measure of central tendency.

Table 7.2 illustrates central tendency within a data set related to the age of customers for a particular product.

BOX 7.5

A plea to save the outliers

An outlier is an observation or case that is abnormal, that is far from the average of other observations. In statistical analysis it is common to toss out the outliers as measurement errors or unrepresentative results. In a notably fun TEDtalk, positive psychologist Shawn Anchor notes that 'One of the first things that we teach people in statistics in business, in psychology, is how do we in a statistically valid way, eliminate the outliers' (Anchor, 2012). Yes, outliers, according to statisticians, are not your friends and should be exterminated as quickly and painlessly as possible.

However, if we always systematically disregard results that fall outside the average, we may never explore interesting cases. For example, star athletes, thinkers, performers or students are outliers. The study of them was popularized in the Malcolm Gladwell book *Outliers: The Study of Success* (2008). Similarly, Shawn Anchor (2012) argues that automatically deleting outliers may close off valuable lines of enquiry.

Do you have any outliers in your results? Perhaps instead of deleting them, you may wish to consider what we can learn from them. By identifying why or how these outliers exist, we may be able to glean useful insights.

Measuring dispersion

While measures of central tendency are a standard and highly useful form of data description and simplification, they need to be complemented with information on response variability. For example, say you had a group of employers with IQs of 100, 100, 95 and 105, and another group of employees with IQs of 60, 140, 65 and 135, the central tendency, in this case the mean, of both groups would be 100. Dispersion around the mean, however, will require you to design training materials and engage learning with each group quite differently. There are several ways to understand dispersion, which are appropriate for different variable types. As with central tendency, statistics programs will automatically generate these figures on request (see Table 7.3).

- *Range* – This is the simplest way to calculate dispersion, and is simply the highest minus the lowest value. For example, if your respondents ranged in age from 8 to 17, the range would be 9 years. While this measure is easy to calculate, it is dependent on extreme values alone, and ignores intermediate values.
- *Quartiles* –This involves subdividing your range into four equal parts or 'quartiles' and is a commonly used measure of dispersion for ordinal data, or data whose central tendency is measured by a median. It allows researchers to compare the various quarters or present the inner 50% as a dispersion measure. This is known as the inner-quartile range.
- *Variance* – This measure uses all values to calculate the spread around the mean, and is actually the 'average squared deviation from the mean'. It needs to be calculated from interval and ratio data and gives a good indication of dispersion. It's much more common, however, for researchers to use and present the square root of the variance, which is known as the standard deviation.

Standard deviation

This is the square root of the variance, and is the basis of many commonly used statistical tests for interval and ratio data. As explained below, its power comes to the fore with data that sits under a normal curve.

Table 7.3 Dispersion for age of customers

Data related to age of customers for a particular product	
Raw data	12, 12, 10, 9, 12, 15, 11, 12, 11, 11, 15, 16, 17, 12, 13, 13, 14, 11, 10, 9, 9, 8, 13, 14, 12, 14, 15, 13, 13, 10, 9, 13, 14, 13, 9
n (no. of cases)	35
Range (spread of the data)	8–17 = 9
Inner quartile range (spread between 25th and 75th %)	10–14 = 4
Variance (spread around the mean)	4.93
Standard deviation (square root of variance)	2.22

Measuring the shape of the data

To fully understand a data set, central tendency and dispersion need to be considered in light of the shape of the data, or how the data is distributed. As shown in Figure 7.5, a normal curve is 'bell-shaped'; the distribution of the data is symmetrical, with the mean, median and mode all converged at the highest point in the curve. If the distribution of the data is not symmetrical, it is considered skewed. In skewed data the mean, median and mode fall at different points.

Kurtosis characterizes how peaked or flat a distribution is compared to 'normal'. Positive kurtosis indicates a relatively peaked distribution, while negative kurtosis indicates a flatter distribution.

The significance in understanding the shape of a distribution is in the statistical inferences that can be drawn. As shown in Figure 7.6, a normal distribution is subject to a particular set of rules regarding the significance of a standard deviation (s.d.). Namely that:

- 68.3% of cases will fall within one standard deviation of the mean.
- 95.4% of cases will fall within two standard deviations of the mean.
- 99.7% of cases will fall within three standard deviations of the mean.

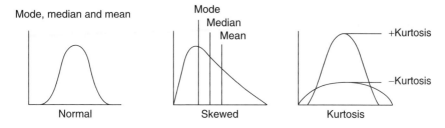

Figure 7.5   Shape of the data

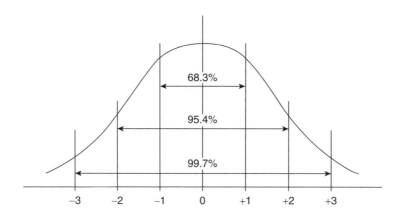

Figure 7.6   Areas under the normal curve

So if we had a normal curve for the sample data relating to 'age of customers' (mean = 12.11, s.d. = 2.22 – see Tables 7.2 and 7.3), 68.3% of participants would fall between the ages of 9.89 and 14.33 (12.11–2.22 and 12.11 + 2.22). Table 7.4 shows the actual curve, skewness and kurtosis of our sample data set.

These rules of the normal curve allow for the use of quite powerful statistical tests and are generally used with interval and ratio data (sometimes called parametric tests). For data that does not follow the assumptions of a normal curve (nominal and ordinal data), the researcher needs to call on non-parametric statistical tests in making inferences.

Inferential statistics

While the goal of descriptive statistics is to describe and summarize, the goal of inferential statistics is to draw conclusions that extend beyond immediate data. For example, inferential statistics can be used to estimate characteristics of a population from sample data, or to test various hypotheses about the relationship between different variables. Inferential statistics allow you to assess the probability that an observed difference is not just a fluke or chance finding. In other words, inferential statistics is about drawing conclusions that are statistically significant.

Statistical significance

Statistical significance refers to a measure, or '*p*-value', which assesses the actual 'probability' that your findings are more than coincidental. Conventional *p*-values are 0.05, 0.01 and 0.001, which tells you that the probability your findings have occurred by chance is 5/100, 1/100, or 1/1,000 respectively. Basically, the lower the *p*-value, the more confident researchers can be that findings are genuine. Keep in mind that researchers do not usually accept findings that have a *p*-value greater than 0.05 because the probability that findings are coincidental or caused by sampling error is too great.

Questions suitable to inferential statistics

It's easy enough to tell students and new researchers that they need to interrogate their data, but it doesn't tell them what they should be asking. Box 7.6 offers some common questions which, while not exhaustive, should give you some ideas for interrogating real-world data using inferential statistics.

BOX 7.6

Questions for interrogating quantitative data using inferential statistics

- How do participants in my study compare to a larger population?
  These types of question compare a sample with a population. For example, say you are conducting a study of patients in a particular coronary care ward. You might ask whether the percentage of males or females in your sample, or their average age, or their ailments are statistically similar to coronary care patients across the country. To answer such questions you will need access to population data for this larger range of patients.

- Are there differences between two or more groups of respondents?
  Questions that compare two or more groups are very common and are often referred to as 'between subject'. I'll stick with a medical theme here ... For example, you might ask whether male and female patients are likely to have similar ailments; or whether patients of different ethnic backgrounds have distinct care needs; or whether patients who have undergone different procedures have different recovery times.

- Have my respondents changed over time?
  These types of question involve before and after data with either the same group of respondents or respondents who are matched by similar characteristics. They are often referred to as 'within subject'. An example of this type of question might be 'Have patients' dietary habits changed since undergoing bypass surgery?'

- Is there a relationship between two or more variables?
  These types of question can look for either correlations (simply an association) or cause and effect. Examples of correlation questions might be, 'Is there an association between time spent in hospital and satisfaction with nursing staff?' or 'Is there a correlation between patient's age and the medical procedure they have undergone?'. Questions looking for cause and effect differentiate dependent and independent variables. For example, 'Does satisfaction depend on length of stay?' or 'Does stress depend on adequacy of medical insurance?'. Cause and effect relationships can also look to more than one independent variable to explain variation in the dependent variable. For example, 'Does satisfaction with nursing staff depend on a combination of length of stay, age and severity of medical condition?'.

(While all of these examples are drawn from the medical or nursing fields, their application to other respondent groups is pretty straightforward. In fact, a good exercise here is to try to come up with similar types of question for alternative respondent groups.)

Selecting the right statistical test

There is a baffling array of statistical tests out there that can help you answer the types of question highlighted in Box 7.6. Programs like SAS and SPSS are capable of running such tests without you needing to know the technicalities of their mathematical operations. The challenge, however, is determining which test is right for your particular application. Luckily, you can turn to a number of test selectors now available on the Internet (see Bill Trochim's test selector at www.socialresearchmethods.net/selstat/ssstart.htm) and through programs such as SPSS.

But even with the aid of such selectors (including the tabular one given below), you still need to know the nature of your variables (independent/dependent); scales of measurement (nominal, ordinal, interval, ratio); distribution shape (normal or skewed); the types of questions you want to ask; and the types of conclusions you are trying to draw. Box 7.7 explains the distinction between univariate (one variable), bivariate (two variables) and multivariate (three or more variable) analysis and Table 7.4 will help you visualize the appropriate uses of various statistical methods.

BOX 7.7

Univariate, bivariate and multivariate analysis

Univariate analysis

The goal of univariate analysis is to provide a clear picture of the data through examination of one variable at a time. It is a cornerstone of a descriptive study and consists of measures of central tendency, dispersion and distribution as discussed under descriptive statistics. While univariate analysis does not look at correlation, cause and effect, or modeling, it is an essential preliminary stage in all types and levels of statistical analysis.

Bivariate analysis

The goal of bivariate analysis is to assess the relationship between two variables; for example, whether there is a relationship between education level and television viewing habits, or gender and income. As covered in Table 7.5, the range of tests that are used to explore such relationships is quite extensive and varies by variable type. The most common tests are cross-tabulations (chi-squared) (used for two nominal variables), ANOVA (used for one nominal and one ratio variable) and correlations (used for two ratio variables).

Multivariate analysis

The goal of multivariate analysis is to explore relationships among three or more variables. This allows for a level of sophistication that offers researchers the opportunity to explore cause and effect, as well as test theories and build/test models. With multivariate analysis not only can researchers explore whether a dependent variable is dependent on two or more independent variables (i.e. income is dependent on both gender and educational attainment), but also it allows them to acknowledge the relationship between the dependent variables (i.e. the relationship between gender and educational attainment). Some of the methods used in multivariate analysis are factor analysis, elaboration, structural equation modeling, MANOVA, multiple regression, canonical correlation and path analysis. It is worth noting that statistics specialists are often called upon at this level of analysis.

Table 7.4 goes into much more depth and covers the most common tests for univariate (one variable), bivariate (two variable) and multivariate (three or more variable) data. The table can be read down the first column for univariate data (the column provides an example of the data type, its measure of central tendency, dispersion and appropriate tests for comparing this type of variable to a population). It can also be read as a grid for exploring the relationship between two or more variables. Once you know what tests to conduct, your statistical software will be able to run the analysis and assess statistical significance.

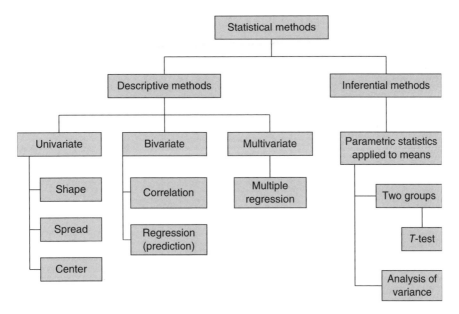

Figure 7.7   Flowchart of statistical methods

At this point in the research project, your head is probably swimming. Perhaps it would be easier to take a break and tackle something doable – like your inbox. Don't give up! But do try to employ some strategies to assist you at this difficult stage. Try a free online class in statistics (e.g. through MIT OpenCourseWare); learn on your own through YouTube or self-guided texts. Of course you can always also ask more senior members of the team or your academic supervisor for help.

PRESENTING FINDINGS

Your analysis is likely to yield rich results. But how should you present them to decision-makers? In deciding how to present findings, there can be a tendency to do so by either (1) methods or (2) questions (the process). Presenting findings by methods means that they are presented according to interview, survey or existing data results. Presented this way, findings are separate, not integrated. Presenting them by question means proceeding through questions and sub-questions. This may get the job done but, again, it's not sophisticated. Decision-makers are interested in the use of your data, rather than its mere existence. The methods and process are infinitely less interesting than the results. It is, therefore, more helpful to present findings according to themes or insights of results. Integrate findings into the discussion and use visuals where useful to convey data in a concise and compelling way.

Table 7.4   Data related to age of customers for a particular product

Data related to age of participants in a local youth group

Raw data	12, 12, 10, 9, 12, 15, 11, 12, 11, 11, 15, 16, 17, 12, 13, 13, 14, 11, 10, 9, 9, 8, 13, 14, 12, 14, 15, 13, 13, 10, 9, 13, 14, 13, 9
N (no. of cases)	35

Histogram (distribution)	

Std Dev. = 2.22
Mean = 12.1
N = 35.00

Skewness (symmetrically)	0.070
Kurtosis (flatness)	−0.562

* Figures and histogram generated with SPSS.

Table 7.5   Selecting statistical tests

Univariate		Bi-/multivariate	
	Nominal	Ordinal	Interval/ratio (assumption of normality – if not normal use ordinal tests)
Nominal			
2-point scale, e.g. gender: 1 = female, 2 = male	Compare two or more groups: chi-squared	Compare two groups: **Mann-Whitney** Three or more groups: **Kruskal-Wallis**	Compare two or more groups: **ANOVA followed by t-test**

Univariate		Bi-/multivariate	
3-point scale, e.g. religion: 1 = Catholic, 2 = Protestant, 3 = Jewish Central tendency: **mode** Dispersion: **frequency**	Compare within same group over time: 2 pts: **McNemar's test** 3+ pts: **Cochran'SQ**	Compare within same group over two times: 2 pts: **Wilcoxon signed-rank test** 3+ pts: **Cochran's Q** Three or more times (2+ pts): **Friedman's test**	Compare within same group over times (2+ pts): **ANOVA followed by t-test**
Compare sample with population: **chi-squared**	Relationship with other variables: yes/no: **chi-squared** Relationship strength: 2 pts: **phi** 3+ pts: **lambda**	Relationship with other variables: yes/no: **chi-squared** Relationship strength: 2+ pts: **lambda**	Relationship with other variables: Yes/no: **Pearson's product moment correlation** Relationship strength: **F-test** With two or more independent and one dependent variables: **MANOVA** 2+ dependent variables and 3+ groups: **multiple regression** or **path analysis**

Ordinal			
TV viewing, order of preference: 1 = sitcoms, 2 = dramas, 3 = movies, 4 = news, 5 = reality TV or Likert scale: 1 = strongly disagree, 2 = disagree, 3 = neutral, etc. Central tendency: **median** Dispersion: **inter-quartile range**		Small sample, <10: **Kendall's tau** Larger sample: **Spearman's rho**	**Jaspen's coefficient of multi serial correlation** With the interval/ratio variable as dependent: **ANOVA**
Compare sample with population: **Kolmogorov -Smirnov**		With one variable as dependent: **Somer's d**	

Interval/ratio			
Interval, e.g. IQ score Ratio, e.g. real numbers, age, height, weight Central tendency: **mean** Dispersion: **standard deviation** Compare sample with population: **t-test**			Relationship with other variables – no dependent/independent distinction: **Pearson's product moment correlation** With one independent and one dependent variable: **Pearson's linear correlation** With two or more independent and one dependent variables: **multiple regression** With two or more independent and two or more dependent variables: **canonical correlation**

Presenting qualitative data

Not many books adequately cover the presentation of qualitative data, but they should. Students often struggle with the task and end up falling back on what they are most familiar with, or what they can find in their methods books (which are often quantitatively biased). So while students working on a qualitative project may only have three cases, five documents or eight interviews, they can end up with some pseudo-quantitative analysis and presentation that includes pie charts, bar graphs and percentages. For example, they may say 50% feel … and 25% think … when they are talking about a total of only four people.

This simply isn't where the power of qualitative data lies. The power of qualitative data is in the actual words and images themselves – so use them. If the goal is the rich use of words, then avoid inappropriate quantification and preserve/capitalize on language.

One way to do this is through storytelling. What you need here is a clear message, strong argument and compelling storyline. The aim is to selectively use your words and/or images in a way that gives weight to that story. The qualitative data you present should be pointed and powerful enough to draw your readers in.

Figure 7.8 was generated by pasting all the text on qualitative data analysis from this chapter and putting it into Wordle to create a word cloud with font size depending on the prevalence of words. Wordle is not only a terrific qualitative analysis tool, it is also a very effective way to present qualitative data.

Remember, what we actually want to accomplish through small-scale applied workplace-based research is to contribute to evidence-based decision-making. To do this we must influence others. And while good research should stand on its own merit, we still need to make it punchy in order to sell it. We need to share stories, challenges and passions. This is the power of qualitative data. It is the power to share data in ways that simply cannot happen with statistical analysis

Figure 7.8   Qualitative data analysis word cloud

of quantified experiences. So if you've collected it, use it, share it, and be true to the experiences you have captured. You may be surprised at how powerful your 'reporting' can become.

Presenting quantitative data

> A heavy bank of figures is grievously wearisome to the eye, and the popular mind is as incapable of drawing any useful lessons from it as of extracting sunbeams from cucumbers.
>
> Arthur Briggs Farquhar and Henry Farquhar (1891)

You've probably been confronted with rows and rows of numbers only to feel your eyeballs glaze over. The human mind is designed to see and interpret patterns; without these cues, details quickly blur and are forgotten. Visualizations of your data allow others to see the patterns and trends you've identified. In this way data visualizations can (and should) help your audience process and retain complex information.

Now when it comes to *how* your data should be presented, there is one golden rule: it should not be hard work for the reader. Your challenge is to graphically and verbally present your data so that meanings are clear. Graphs and charts should require only simple interpretation. So while you need to include adequate information, you don't want to go into information overload. Resist the temptation to offer graphs, charts and tables for every single variable and result in your study. The key to effective data presentation is to carefully determine what is most important in your work. Your findings need to tell a story related to your aims, objectives and research questions, and the overall utility to the organization.

Finally, data visualizations should match the purpose and scope of your data. Think about the types of information you might need to convey and what is the most aesthetically pleasing way to convey it. These visuals should be concise enough that they don't confuse the audience. They should also be compelling enough that they don't make you reach for the nearest smartphone distraction during the meeting.

There is no shortage of options. You are probably most familiar with traditional line graphs, flow charts, org (organization) charts, bar charts and pie charts, but what about area charts, bubble charts, candlestick charts, donut charts, gauge charts, histograms, scatter charts, Sankey diagrams, tree maps, motion charts, heat maps and infographics? Well, they are worth exploring, particularly in workplace-based research where reports are designed not only to inform, but to persuade.

Bar charts and pie charts

Bar charts and pie charts are widely used visualizations in organizational research. They present data cleanly and neatly (assuming that scales are consistent). The charts shown in Figures 7.9 and 7.10 were both produced in Excel, and while these are printed in black and white, the use of color makes these visualizations much more engaging.

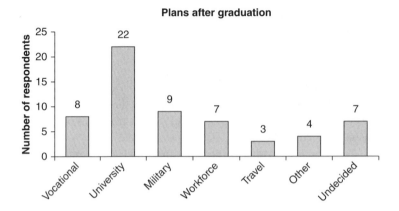

Figure 7.9   Bar chart

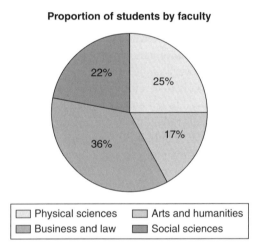

Figure 7.10   Pie chart

Some statisticians loathe pie charts. Personally, we think they are useful. The key is to ensure the data is appropriate for it. For instance, for more than about eight categories, the slices may be too small to distinguish. Moreover, if the sum total does not add up to 100%, a pie chart is *not* the right tool.

Aside from traditional bar charts, line graphs and pie charts, there are several other tools you can consider that may be useful to present your data.

Figure 7.11 Tree map of Benin's export portfolio 2012 (*source*: UN Comtrade data)

Tree maps

Tree maps are one of our favorites. They allow you to present a lot of information in a small space, and color coding helps identify patterns. Figure 7.11 shows a visualization of a country's export portfolio in a given year with each export color-coded to the key at the bottom. The style of example shown started out as a student project at the Massachusetts Institute of Technology (MIT), and more of these full-color visualizations can be found at the MIT Observatory of Economic Complexity website at https://atlas.media.mit.edu.

Motion chart

A motion chart displays longitudinal data (that is data across different time periods) through the use of a moving bubble. In this way, motion charts provide a dynamic way to facilitate understanding of large and multivariate data. Examples of motion charts include Gapminder, Many-Eyes, and Google Motion Charts and SOCR. The last two mentioned are open-source and so may be quite useful for mapping your own data.

Gapminder is one of the handiest tools around to navigate data sets. Its creator, Hans Rosling, a Swedish medical statistician, bemoaned the fact that decades of data collected by international organizations are scattered across the Web, hidden

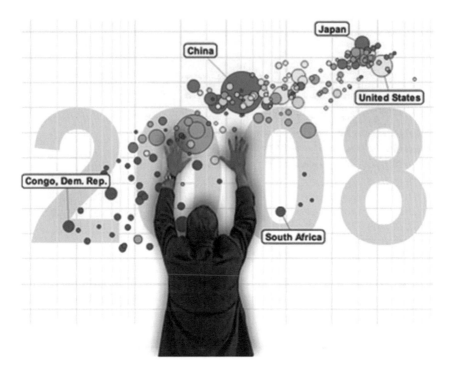

Figure 7.12   Interactive graphics using Gapminder

behind non-user-friendly interfaces and locked within paywalls. He developed software to convert statistics into moving, interactive graphics.

In the example in Figure 7.12, each bubble represents a different country (color-coded by region) in which the diameter of the circle is proportional to its population (large bubble equals large population). This software allows you to identify trends within a country over time or between countries. It can also allow you to 'see' business statistics trends – the growth of purchasing power in particular populations, the level of Internet and mobile phone penetration within a society, education levels of the workforce, etc. This information could be used to help identify new markets for products and services, locations for offshore labor partnership and other joint venture or capital investment project opportunities.

For an engaging (and hilarious) demonstration of its uses, see the creator himself in his widely acclaimed TED Talk, 'The Best Stats You've Ever Seen' (Rosling, 2006), which is available on YouTube.

Stack area graphs

Another popular tool is stack area graphs. Stack area graphs are great for visualizing segmentation. In the example in Figure 7.13, global data was used to identify the shifts and growth in energy consumption.

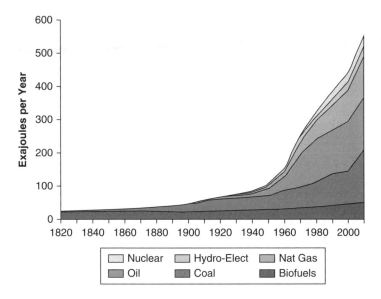

Figure 7.13 World energy consumption 1880–2010. (source: Gail Tverberg OurFiniteWorld.com 2012)

With a stack graph it becomes easy to see the trend. For example, from Figure 7.13 we can see that that energy consumption has grown exponentially over the last 100 years, and includes a more diverse mix of fuels.

Geographic maps

Geographic maps are another incredibly useful and versatile tool for presenting information. You could plot locations (or retail shops) for your organization, identify which states/locations have the highest number of customers, or identify relevant population characteristics of new markets. Figure 7.14 demonstrates the growth of electric car charging stations across the United States. Notice how the map provides more detail than a simple bar chart of the number of charging stations. You can see the colour version at www.slideshare.net/leannekroll/info graphic-the-rise-of-electric-car-charging.

The great thing about map-based data is that it can be used for more than its original purpose. For instance, in the example in Figure 7.14 these locations could be useful for other organizations beyond electric car sellers. Given the high upfront cost of these vehicles, these dots may represent affluent economic areas, or population clusters that are more environmentally conscious and thus willing to pay the premium. If your organization sells sustainability products, or encapsulates those principles in its mission, these areas of growth could identify emerging markets.

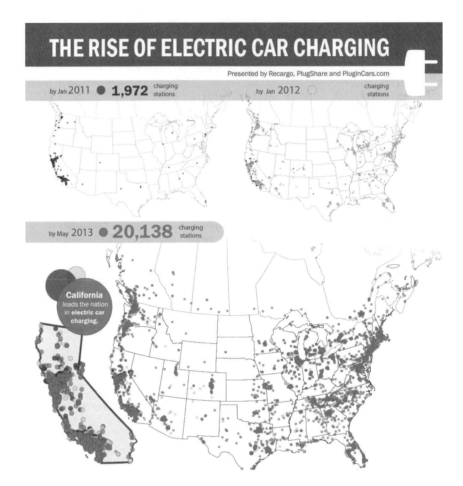

Figure 7.14   Electric car charging stations in the United States (© Leanne Kroll, 2013)

Infographics and pictographs

Technically, all graph charts are infographics, that is 'information graphics', but the term is more commonly used to refer to creative and information-packed visuals. These may be poster-sized, or just an interesting take on traditional data presentation. For instance, we think of bar charts as displaying data as exactly that – bars, but other visual objects can be substituted as well. For example the pictograph in Figure 7.15 was created using the 'Piles of Money' tool in Google.

Pictographs and infographics are eye-catching and considered more innovative than 'boring' line and bar charts. However, keep in mind that as these

Figure 7.15 Revenues by country

visualizations become more popular, they are not always intuitive for the audience. Three-dimensional shapes may not be to scale, or may make it difficult to accurately ascertain proportions. For instance, in Figure 7.15, the viewer's perspective of the money piles means that the bar width is not uniform and distorts the total proportions. If the purpose of visualizations is to accurately communicate information, the meaning should be easily ascertained by the audience. The key, then, is that visualizations must be clear, compelling and suited to the task. They must also be used sparingly for maximum effectiveness. If you throw chart after chart into your report (or presentation), your audience may suffer 'graph fatigue' and all your hard work creating visualizations may be for naught.

Generating visualizations

It is not difficult to generate the data visualizations above, but you will need to dedicate some time to learning the ropes. So, where to start? Well there are two ways to do this and both involve sitting in front of a computer (and a healthy dose of self-motivation). The first is to have someone in the know show you what to do and then practice it. The second is to sit down by yourself and have a go with various software (YouTube has some great training videos). While reading can give you familiarity, the best way to learn this kind of stuff is by doing. Highly recommended is Google Tools (pictured in Figure 7.16), which provides a great selection of chart tools available for free.

We have selected just a few of the exciting possibilities for data visualization. Becoming familiar with these and embedding them in your research is a great way to make you and your work stand out. A Princeton polymath, John Tukey (1915–2000), said, 'the greatest value of a picture is when it forces us to notice what we never expected to see'. With practice and a bit of time, your data can help the organization see opportunities in a new way.

For inspiration and help along the way, a list of resources is provided in Box 7.8.

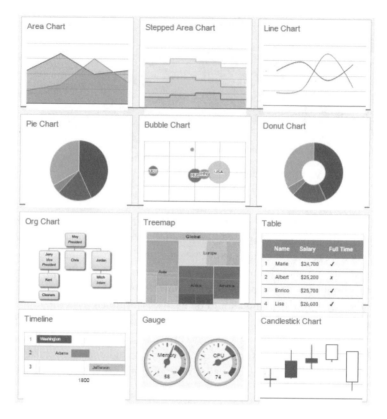

Figure 7.16   Chart tools in Google

BOX 7.8

Data visualization resources

Data visualization has evolved to a high art-form, necessitating its own full-time position at news behemoths such as *The Economist*. Given the increasing availability of data, the ability to translate this information into meaningful visual forms is a skill high in demand. Check out these free resources for translating raw data into interesting visualizations:

www.visualizingeconomics.com

www.informationisbeautiful.net

www.flowingdata.com

http://www.everydayanalytics.ca/

http://bost.ocks.org/mike/

www.visual.ly

www.tableau.com

www.piktochart.com

DRAWING CONCLUSIONS AND FORMULATING RECOMMENDATIONS

Drawing conclusions

You'd think that sound findings powerfully presented would be enough – but you need to draw it all together to conclude. Drawing conclusions is all about clearly summarizing what your data reveals and then linking this back to your project's main questions, aims and objectives. If you really get in there and engage with your data (whether it's quantitative or qualitative) you are likely to discover that your findings and conclusions follow on quite naturally and logically from your analysis. All of your findings should arise from your data and should be pointing you (and when you present it, your readers) to your overarching arguments and final conclusion (the concluding remarks in Box 7.9 below serve as a short example).

To draw appropriate, relevant and significant conclusions you will need to:

- consider your findings in light of current research 'literature';
- consider your findings in light of the limitations and methodological constraints of your study;
- pull together all the significant/important findings of your study and consider why and how they are significant/important;
- search for clarity, but don't force-fit your findings to portray a world without ambiguity and complexity;
- clearly link your findings to your research question, aims and objectives, and relevant theory.

As you draw together your conclusions, you may find that you have begun to conceptualize a bigger picture in a fairly sophisticated manner, and that sharing these thoughts, insights and ideas might be best communicated in the form of an original framework or model. In fact, while many studies into workplace-based problems culminate in recommendations, it's not unusual to see conclusions come together as a potentially useful new model for understanding and/or action.

One word of caution: it is important that there are no curve balls or surprise endings in your conclusion. It is not the place for new information. What you think is a novel twist, could be a wrench in the works. At the very least, it's distracting and is particularly confusing when a research project designed entirely on objective protocols draws conclusions not supported by evidence. Uphold the credibility and utility of your research project by drawing on the work you have done.

Formulating recommendations

Most likely, your small-scale applied workplace-based research project is formulated around solving a problem, addressing an issue and providing information on what the organization needs to do, which means recommendations. Recommendations are options, next steps, and strategies for the way forward. But effective recommendations not only highlight what should be done, but how it might happen.

Ironically, one of the most useful professional outputs, recommendation, is rarely discussed in undergraduate education. This means that recommendation formulation can be a daunting task. Start at the beginning. Remember that recommendations should flow logically from your findings and conclusions.

BOX 7.9

Problem definition: Stephanie's story

As an intern at the Department of Road and Maritime Services in Auckland, New Zealand, I conducted a research project that identified reasons for high accident roads on a particular stretch of road. I interviewed several police officers at the nearest precinct who cover traffic accidents to ascertain why accidents are so prevalent there.

Responses varied from people not driving to the conditions (going or exceeding the speed limit even though conditions aren't optimal), poor visibility in the area, and lack of awareness that this is a dangerous section requiring caution. Each represented a different problem definition with different solutions. The first was assumed to be human error (in which case the solution could be traffic law enforcement, or the installation of traffic cameras), the second an infrastructure issue (in which the solution is install lighting, cat eyes between lanes, rumble strips on the shoulder, or even just refresh the road paint), the third a problem of ignorance (in which the solution could be to post caution signage or a tally of fatalities). Of course there are other solutions as well that do not neatly fall into categories. Perhaps those speeding when it rains are unaware that the most dangerous time to be on the road is right as it starts to rain because the water mixes with the oil leaks on the road to create a thin slick. Incorporating this information into driver education programs could lead to better judgement in rainy situations.

I prepared the report outlining the different solutions, with associated costs and anticipated outcomes. As financial outlay was the most important consideration for management given recent budget cuts, I performed a cost–benefit analysis and recommends three relatively low-cost actions, one for each of the three problem areas: human error, visibility, and awareness: installing a second speed limit sign on the same post that lowers the speed limit during rain, refreshing the paint in that section to increase visibility, and adding a question on the driver's exam about when the most dangerous time to drive on the road (at the start of rain, in the middle of the rain shower, or at its conclusion) with associated information in the online driver education materials. Together these solutions targeted the problem and worked proactively in prevention.

For an example of how New Zealand approached this problem with another novel solution, see the 'Bleeding Billboard' (2009) https://www.youtube.com/watch?v=FlS yieFqql4.

Think carefully about implementation. What kinds of recommendations are most likely to be implemented? One strategy here is to recommend incremental change. Another is to offer a cost–benefit analysis for each of your recommendations. If you can prove that your solution is cheaper or easier than the scale of the problem if unaddressed, you're likely to have a very interested audience.

Given that the goal of recommendation is actual implementation, recommendations should never be a wish list! Instead, offer practical and incremental steps. You may consider formulating recommendations on increasing levels of cost or timeframes – i.e. the immediate response to the problem would be step 1, then later on steps 2 and 3 down the track. The first step, in particular, should be immediately actionable with relative ease. If the first step isn't doable, you can toss the rest of plan out of the window!

CHAPTER SUMMARY

- Whether you are working with qualitative or quantitative data, the main game of any form of analysis is to move from raw data to meaningful understanding.
- Quantitative and qualitative analysis is about drawing out meaning and making sense of your data. Good analysis will identify and anticipate trends, explain problems and organize data for decision-making.

- When it comes to how your data should be presented, there is one golden rule: it should not be hard work for the reader. Your challenge is to graphically and verbally present your data so that meanings are clear and compelling.
- Conclusions should summarize what your data reveals and link back to the project's questions, aims and objectives, while recommendations should offer clear guidelines for further action.

PRODUCING EFFECTIVE DELIVERABLES

Chapter preview

Delivering the deliverables

Writing for varied audiences

Preparing persuasive presentations

A note on employability

DELIVERING THE DELIVERABLES

Deliverables are the product and outcome of data gathering and analysis. These outputs represent a condensed form of your hard work and insight, and can take many forms, including essays, reports, policy papers and presentations. Deliverables vary by type, use and audience, but can be broadly divided between academic and professional outputs.

Academic outputs are written in 'journal' style. They vary greatly in terms of length (from 3,000 words for a journal article or edited book chapter to 150,000 words for a monograph/book). However, they all present a central thesis (argument or hypothesis) regarding a gap in knowledge for a small audience. This audience is generally assumed to be well-versed in the discipline.

Professional outputs tend to be presented in 'report' form and center around recommendations and actions to meet a particular problem or challenge. These deliverables have shorter, more standardized templates, that can be quite distinct from academic expectations.

Indeed, entire sections that are of paramount importance in academic outputs (such as the methods section) may be relegated to the appendix in a professional report. Other sections, such as action plans and implementation, may not be included in academic essays. The audience of professional reports is usually not a small group of experts, but a wider audience of generalists and stakeholders. Table 8.1 summarizes some of the important distinctions:

Table 8.1   Differences between academic and professional outputs

	Academic essay	Professional report
Main point	Thesis Argument	Recommendation Action plans
Purpose	Inform	Persuade
Content	Theory generation Theory testing	Problem-solving Action-oriented
Audience	Experts	Generalists
Dissemination	Publishing	Circulation
Readership	Limited	Typically larger (including general public)

Of course there are some deliverables that bridge the gap. Consultancy work is often produced by academic researchers commissioned by government agencies and private industry. These outputs tend to follow a report-based structure, while drawing heavily on academic rigor and research conventions. Other forms of research dissemination such as op-eds or community presentations may take a hybrid form of informing, illuminating and recommending certain courses of action.

Regardless of template, we would argue that small-scale applied workplace-based research should be:

1. *Problem-focused* – Policy reports tend to be problem-focused, exploring the dimensions and impact of a particular issue. The scope is limited and practical.
2. *Analysis-driven* – Possible solutions for any given problem are diverse and involve trade-offs. Policy papers analyze different options, taking into account the impact and feasibility of alternative policies by looking at the potential costs, benefits and impacts for different stakeholder groups.
3. *Evidence-based* – To convince decision-makers, ideas must be demonstrably well founded. Evidence could involve primary data, case comparisons and/or effects of inactions or policies taken in other contexts/environments on this issue.
4. *Offers viable recommendations* – Policy papers are action-oriented. The goal of a policy paper is to persuade a decision-maker to address a specific issue and implement the recommendation devised. To be practical and actionable, recommendations should also demonstrate contextual awareness, and link to win–win outcomes.

That said, deliverables must address the needs and expectations of the audience. This means you may need to produce both a research report for your academic institution and a professional report for your organization. This chapter detangles the differences, so you leverage your research project to produce both academic and professional outputs.

WRITING FOR VARIED AUDIENCES

The first rule of writing is to *know your audience*. For academic work, that is generally your professors and your supervisor. These individuals are intimately familiar with your topic and its importance. This means you have a well-informed and enthusiastic audience of approximately one!

For small-scale applied workplace-based research in government or industry, the audience is completely different, and larger. Decision-makers, managers and directors, as well as colleagues and junior staff in your department, may all be part of your audience. Some of these individuals may have expertise in your area of research but most will be generalists. You will have to convince them of the merits of your topic and the findings related to it. This task becomes even more challenging when you consider that these findings may be widely circulated to other individuals or departments (such as IT or accounting) depending on the problem and/or recommendations. For this reason, your report needs to transcend department boundaries and broach the concerns of time, money and resources for all those likely to be involved in approving and implementing your recommendations. Suddenly the small academic audience that you've been writing for has ballooned to a dozen people, all with different expertise, priorities and agendas!

The second rule is to *begin with the outcome in mind*. For academic audiences, problem identification and research process may be the most valuable part of the project. This is why the methods section is typically quite long in academic/scientific reports. However, professional audiences have different priorities. You may be consumed with the problem, but your audience is more interested in the recommendation. Articulate how your solution will solve or alleviate a particular problem, and the benefits thereof. Is there a cost saving, or time saving, associated with your solution? If so, share it.

Finally, *write concisely*. You may have a word count for academic deliverables (which are designed to help you cultivate an appropriate scope), but that will likely not be the case for a professional report. Why? Because no one cares how short it is, as long as it gets the job done. Overall, professional writing tends to be more concise and stylistically less cluttered than academic prose. This is not to say that all academic writing is intentionally impenetrable. However, as mentioned in Chapter 4 it is written by academics for academics. An intimate understanding of the context and vocabulary is assumed to be understood. By contrast, professional/generalist audiences appreciate clear, unambiguous language with key terminology defined.

One factor that contributes to sentence complexity is length. For business and government reports, try to rein in sentences that run over three lines. Reading professional trade journals or practitioner journals (which cater to academic and professional audiences) will help you get a sense of the style and formatting. Your manager can help direct you to appropriate source material, including recent in-house reports. Box 8.1 offers tips for writing up your report in a professional style.

BOX 8.1

Tips for writing a professional report

1. Read examples of professional reports. Consulting firms such as McKinsey and Co, Deloitte and Boston Consulting Group offer plentiful high quality examples.
2. Leave enough time for writing up. Reports, while short, still take time to produce.
3. Favor short and punchy sentences over extremely complex sentence structures.
4. Shelve theories. Organizations generally care little about theories; they are more likely to care about reality. If a business framework or theoretical framework is useful, by all means use it. But don't expect managers to be impressed with a theory without substantiating evidence.
5. Ruthlessly edit for conciseness. A short report is a good report.
6. Make the document easy to read and navigate. Leave spaces between paragraphs and sections, use high-quality visuals, and do not minimize margins. Insert page numbers (and a table of contents).
7. Have a colleague or manager read for revision. You may have polished it three times already, but still call it a 'draft' for the purposes of getting 'feedback'. Someone else is bound to suggest an improvement, plus you are getting buy-in from whoever reads it in its early stages.

The logic of research reports and professional reports

When drafting your report, it may help to think of your report as a conversation. This conversation will have a slightly different focus depending on whether you are talking to a professional or academic audience (see Table 8.2). As demonstrated by Table 8.2, the four main differences between academic research reports and professional reports are abstracts and executive summaries, the literature review, the methods section and recommendations.

Abstracts vs. executive summaries

First, an academic research report includes an abstract while a professional report has an executive summary. The difference is more than semantics. An abstract is a brief summary (200 words or so) of the report/article stating the research topic and question, the methods employed and also a brief teaser related to findings.

The executive summary has a different purpose. Aside from a specialist or generalist audience, findings and recommendations are foremost. In fact, the recommendations take center stage. In this way, the problem is closely linked to the recommendation with just a brief overview of anything else. Second, the executive summary tends to be longer, 500–750 words, compared to an abstract, which is normally no more than 200.

Table 8.2 The standard conversation

The questions	The answers that structure the sections of the report
So tell me what your research is about?	Title Executive summary (for professional reports) OR Abstract (for academic reports)
And why did you choose this particular topic/question?	Introduction • rationale
What do you hope to achieve?	Introduction • aims and objectives
I really don't know much about this, can you fill me in?	Background • context • literature review (this will likely be more detailed in an academic report)
How exactly did you go about doing your research?	Research design/approach (this will likely be more detailed in an academic report) • methods (techniques/procedures) • limitations
And what did you find out?	Analysis/findings • text, tables, graphs, charts, themes, quotes, etc. Discussion • interpretation and meaning of findings
What do we do now?	Conclusion and recommendations • implications • significance • action plans (professional report)

Literature review

After dedicating a whole section of the book to lit reviews and their importance in academic work, it saddens me to say they are not so valued in professional writing. In academia, you aim to publish works where you will be unknown to your audience – it is therefore important to establish your credibility and that of your research process. A strong lit review can do this. In small-scale applied workplace-based research, credibility is more tangible and is based more on who you are and what you've done. Reviewing literature may be essential to the conduct of good research, but the formal lit review is not required or even appreciated.

Methods section

For academic audiences, the method section is rigorously detailed because the process is just as important as the findings, perhaps even more so. For me, academics know that findings are inextricably linked to research design. Methods need to be carefully described and scrutinized to ensure findings are valid. Second, methods can be used across different research areas, so it's important that methods be documented and promulgated for further use.

Professional audiences are no doubt interested in the credibility of your findings, but they are infinitely less interested in a play by play of question formulation and concept operationalization. They want the result, the trend, the pattern and the insight. A laborious methods section can delay the receipt of that insight. But that does not mean that you should bypass the methods section. It is important, just keep it concise.

You might say something like, 'To answer the research question, I conducted X number of surveys across five different departments last month. The results were analyzed using specialized software and the results triangulated with employment data from the company's annual report'. You can always expand from there, but the last thing you want to do is proceed with a chronological account of your research journey, a sort of 'creation story': 'In the beginning … I had a thought about why this problem exists. So I sat down and did some reading. And I decided to do a survey, but this took many drafts to get all 42 questions ready. For instance, Question 1 …' Instead of an inner monologue, provide only the information necessary to assure your audience of the robustness of your research work. Then prioritize elements of the report that are most important to your audience, that is the conclusion and recommendations.

Recommendations

This is really what sets academic and professional deliverables apart. Academic research reports conclude with their findings, significance and implications for further research. Typically, the only recommendation is to conduct more research on the topic!

In professional deliverables, recommendations are THE point of the research and the end goal in 'applied' research. In fact, we would venture to say that the rest of the report is just an extended justification of the recommendations. Recommendations should be situated carefully into the resource scope and political landscape of the organization. The point is to make a series of scaffolded steps that make implementation seem practical and necessary.

Anatomy of an academic report

Academic reports have a very standard structure with many subheadings. The list below is quite expansive and should give you a good sense of academic expectations related to research accounts.

- *Title* – Go for clear, concise and unambiguous.
- *Summary/abstract* – Abstracts are so condensed that they are hard to get right. But they are extremely informative to your processes. Make sure it represents your work from aims and objectives through to methods, findings, discussion and conclusions.
- *Research question/hypothesis* – This is your last chance to really nail the articulation of what you attempted to find out.

- *Introduction/rationale* – The main job of this section is to introduce your topic and convince readers that the problem you want to address is significant and worth exploring (which is why a few existing stats related to the extent/depth of the problem can be effective). This section should give some context to the problem, and lead your readers to a 'therefore' conclusion that sets up your aims and objectives. The trick is to write purposefully.
- *Aims/objectives* – There should be a goodness-of-fit between what you set out to do and what you eventually did.
- *Literature review* – The goal here is to review past research in order to show a place for your own research processes. Depending on the nature of your project, as well as covering past research, your literature review may have a section that situates your study in a conceptual or theoretical framework.
- *Background* – This is a fairly straightforward chapter/section that offers the reader contextual information about your research setting, culture, political arena, etc. For example, if your study were on the threats of tourism to the traditional culture of Palau, you would need to offer your readers context regarding Palau's geography, tourism potential, history and culture, as well as tourism trends. Remember to include only what a reader needs in order to work through your thesis. If it is not essential, don't include it.
- *Methods* – All research design sections include methods comprising information on how you found respondents, i.e. population and sample/sampling procedures; data collection methods, i.e. surveying, interviewing and document analysis; and methods of analysis, i.e. statistical or thematic analysis.
- *Limitations/delimitations* – You will need to clearly articulate all factors that have had an impact on your research processes/results. While it is crucial that you offer full disclosure here, try to avoid being overly apologetic. You need to offer strong justification for what you did and why your data is credible in spite of any constraints.
- *Ethical considerations/approval procedures* – You will need to review the processes you adopted in order to ensure the emotional, physical and intellectual well-being of your study participants; and the approval processes you may have gone through.
- *Findings* – Findings are the presentation of the answers you have found to your key questions. They are neither raw data nor the full abstraction of your data back to theory. Rather, this is a summative description of data that you find most significant. It is therefore important to resist the temptation to summarize the answer to every question you asked in your research processes. What you need to present is what is most key, interesting, educative, informative and best makes the case regarding your research question/hypothesis.
- *Discussion* – This is where you get to make something of your data. The structure here is almost always thematic and tied to the storylines that have emerged from your data. It is your opportunity to take what you discovered in your findings and argue their implications/significance. So while the findings section

may be fairly straightforward reporting, the discussion section/chapter is made up of purposeful arguments, arguments that emerge from your findings and show that you have met your aims and objectives. Discussion sections are not always present in qualitative research.

- *Conclusions* – Drawing conclusions is all about clearly summarizing what your research processes have revealed and linking this back to your project's main questions, aims and objectives in the most compelling and credible way. This is generally a tight section/chapter (and should be, given the work your 'discussion' has done). You do not tend to introduce new material in the conclusion other than the possibility of an original framework or model.

- *Recommendations* – In social science research, recommendations are often limited to 'recommendations for future research' – made on the basis of need for further verification due to the limitations and delimitations of the study, the next logical step in understanding an issue, or the identification of an existing gap in the literature. Such recommendations are generally included in the conclusion. In applied science research, however, recommendations are an essential part of the back end of a report and often warrant their own section. Such recommendations should be clearly linked to findings, highly applied and practicable. Consider grouping these by ease of implementation, i.e., timeframe, cost, difficulty and stakeholder involvement.

- *References* – Perfection! Nothing less is expected or accepted. Take the time to do this right – it's a good time to be obsessive about detail.

Anatomy of a professional report

The most widely used professional deliverable is a report. This is good news because there is one template, and many examples are available in the public and private sectors. Everything from business reports to policy briefs tends to follow roughly the same formula of six sections (though sometimes one or two are combined):

1. Executive summary.
2. Introduction and background.
3. Research design and analysis.
4. Recommendation and outcomes.
5. Conclusion.
6. References/Appendix.

Avoid the temptation to tinker with this model of efficiency. Your audience is very comfortable with this consistent, reliable and useful format; anything else is an unnecessary cognitive load or distraction. At the very least, your manager may assume that severe deviations from this model are proof of your inexperience in the art of report writing.

- *Executive summary* – This is the most important part of the report, named for the busy manager who has no time to read pages 2–59. The executive summary should be a microcosm of your entire report. It's interesting, it's informative, it's useful and most of all, it is highly concentrated. Just add water and it will expand to fill your bathtub! Sounds straightforward, right? Unfortunately executive summaries are also the most misunderstood and abused sections of the professional report.

  Let's clear up the confusion by considering what an executive summary is *not*. As mentioned, an executive summary is not an abstract, it is not a teaser, nor a film trailer. It is not a mystery novel with a surprise ending. The busy professional will not bother to hunt for your point. Reports are generally not read, they are scanned. Assume your reader is too busy even to turn the page. This means you should get the important points on the first page, in the first paragraph. And what's the most important point? Recommendations.

  Relinquish your recommendations. Yes, up front – and yes, it can be uncomfortable. You may think, 'Where's the chronology and context? Where's the nuance?'. It will be in the second paragraph. The most effective executive summaries tend to work backwards from the recommendation. For this reason, the executive summary should be written last, when you are well-practiced with the material and can articulate and condense it most concisely. Since it needs to be concise, clear and readable to a generalist, it is a good idea to have at least two other people outside the organization read it and provide feedback. For more tips, an example of an effective executive summary is included later in this chapter.

- *Background information* – This section provides valuable context. What is the issue? How did it come to be an issue (very briefly)? What will happen if we do not address this problem? Typically this section involves a lot of data. Facts, figures, quotes, visuals (but don't overload your readers). The point is to convey the scale of the issue and its urgency. This is not to say that the origin story need be evil; it might be a good issue. For example, strong growth of the company (a good thing) may mean that processes created for a smaller company may have become inefficient in the changing environment. The point is to demonstrate that this situation is unsustainable and costing valuable resources in the interim.

- *Research design and analysis* – The analysis evaluates several possible solutions to the problem identified in the background section. Remember that all problems have multiple solutions depending on how they are defined. These solutions will likely have different costs, benefits and angles. Feel free to include an analytic framework such as a cost–benefit analysis, or decision matrix.

  This section may also utilize primary data such as data collected from surveys or focus groups (68% of those surveyed favored solution C) to assist the decision-making process. Notice that this does not require a lengthy description of methods. Only the briefest of overviews is necessary about the origin of this data, i.e. 'a total of 56 individuals were interviewed across three departments' rather than a laborious recount. Similarly, lengthy rows of raw data or transcribed interviews are not generally preserved. Quotes and snapshots are acceptable, but if you think a complete data set is important for credibility purposes, include it as an appendix.

- *Recommendations* – This section should pluck the best solutions from the analysis section and sell them! Remember to link to all your hard work in the previous section. A sample segway could be: 'Based on the analysis in the previous section, it is recommended that the solution of X be implemented. It is anticipated that the following outcomes of implementing this recommendation will be …'

  Once the benefits have dazzled your audience, it's time for a peek behind the curtain. Outline costs and timelines. Remember initial and maintenance costs of both time and money. Yes, no matter how glorious your solution and its benefits may be, the job is incomplete if the accounting department remains unconvinced. Help guide them through the skepticism with a 'pilot program'. Roll out your solution in one team, one location, or one group of customers. This is cheaper (which pleases the accountants) and less risky (which pleases whoever has to sign off), and means you can scale up the project later with the benefit of feedback.

- *Conclusion* – Wrap up with a call to action. Remember that problem you identified in the background section? It isn't going away. Even as we speak, time, money, lives could be saved! Insert a strong statistic about the scale of the problem and its compounding awfulness/inefficiency. Then cut to your recommendation (one sentence). Keep it concise (two paragraphs should do it). Your audience has hung in through charts, graphs and laborious costing and they are tired now. Leave them on a high note and then bow gracefully into the reference section.

- *Referencing* – Credible, recent sources bolster the strength and persuasiveness of the report. Let the experts at the International Monetary Fund (etc.) convince your boss. Good references also reflect well on you as a professional. They demonstrate your skills as a critical consumer of information, selecting only the finest quality cuts.

- *Appendix* (optional) – Assume that this section will be read only by the rarest of souls. Cost calculation worksheets and detailed schedules may find an audience in those who are held responsible for implementation, but mostly accounting and finance will peruse this section. Think people who enjoy doing their taxes. For this reason, never put vital information here that is found nowhere else. Readers will not flip to page 49A in the middle of the report to find whatever gem you have hidden there. Instead state the information (even if it's an estimate) and follow with 'for more details, see the Appendix, page 49A'.

Creating an effective executive summary

An executive summary is a first date, first impression and panel job interview all at once. Done poorly you can lose the audience's confidence and even the audience itself. By contrast, a well-articulated and polished executive summary puts the reader at ease and builds respect.

Clearly the stakes are high. But don't panic. Even seasoned professionals have problems producing an effective executive summary. The good news is that poor executive summaries are usually not the result of bad writing, but of a failure to understand the purpose and components of the section (See Box 8.2).

- *Purpose of the executive summary* – The executive summary is a concise, compelling synthesis of the report highlights. It must be informative, persuasive and capable of standing alone.
- *Components of an executive summary* – The two most important elements of the executive summary are: the problem and the solution (your recommended course of action).
- *Problem identification* – You may choose to identify trends that have been building towards a particular problem that now requires resolution. Another approach is to detail the scale of the problem (statistics and hooks work well here – remember to include a citation). The problem should have some urgency, otherwise there is no impetus to correct it.
- *Craft an actionable scope* – Inspire action by breaking the problem into a smaller, actionable scope. You cannot fix a large looming public deficit with a single executive summary, but you can make a grounded argument to the Minister of the Economy to phase out petrol subsidies to all but the poorest segments of society over a 3-year period; and use part of the savings to fund vulnerable portfolios, such as public health.
- *Recommendation* – The proposed solution should solve the problem identified and give some indication of outcomes. 'This report advocates that the organization pursue the following course of action, X, given the importance/problem of Y and anticipated outcomes of Z.'

BOX 8.2

Common mistakes in the executive summary

The most common mistake made in executive summaries is to focus on the parts of the report rather than the content. This presents itself innocuously as informing the reader of the sequence of the report, i.e. 'The first section details the background while sections

(Continued)

(Continued)

two and three offer analysis and debate for the recommendation in section four ...' (and then proceeds to go through each section in turn).

This is not an executive summary. It is a glorified table of contents, and just as dull to read. To make the situation compelling enough for the reader to act to remedy it, get to the point as quickly and concisely as possible (preferably within one page, single spaced). Perhaps the best way to learn how to write an executive summary is to dissect an example or two.

Executive Summary 1

Bowel surgeon Andrew Wakefield was the lead author of a 1998 study published in the medical journal *The Lancet* that purported to establish a link between the Measles–Mumps–Rubella vaccine (MMR) and autism in children. Wakefield's media splash induced paranoia in some parents, leading to a critical drop in the number of children vaccinated with MMR, particularly in the UK, US and Australia. Immunization rates were particularly low among educated, high-income families.

Suspicion of Wakefield began to mount, however, as other scientists were unable to reproduce Wakefield's results. An investigation published in *The Sunday Times* questioned the methodology and medical ethics behind Wakefield's study, as well as exposing Wakefield's commercial interest in discrediting MMR – he had filed a patent on a vaccine to replace it. As a result, 10 of the paper's original 13 authors withdrew their findings, and *The Lancet* formally retracted the paper. The UK General Medical Council opened an inquiry and pronounced their verdict: Wakefield had acted dishonestly, having misled the public by fixing the data to suit his case. Wakefield was barred from the practice of medicine in the UK in 2010 for scientific misconduct.

Mumps is now on the rise as unvaccinated populations enter university. It is imperative that educational facilities work to combat its spread. This paper details how this can be accomplished.

Word count: 253

Executive Summary 2

Universities should require eligible students to obtain an MMR (measles–mumps–rubella) vaccine before commencing their studies on campus. This recommendation follows the recent explosion in mumps, a highly contagious, air-borne virus that can cause sterility and, in some cases, death.

Mumps is entirely preventable and was considered eradicated in developed countries until 1998, when Dr Andrew Wakefield claimed to have found a link between the vaccine and autism. Take-up of the vaccine has fallen by 70% in some areas of the US, UK and Australia leading to outbreaks years after Wakefield was disbarred from medical practice when his work was found to have been an 'elaborate fraud' (Cohen and Falco, 2011).

As of 2009, mumps cases had risen exponentially from 70 in 2001 to over 1,300 in the UK alone (WHO, 2010). The most susceptible populations are those currently in university, as their cohort has one of the lowest rates of immunization.

As university presents an environment conducive to outbreaks (large gathering of people, communal living, etc.), and educational facilities have a duty of care to their students, universities would be negligent if they did not require that all eligible students meet the minimum requirements of vaccination in order to commence on-campus studies. It is anticipated that this effort will help to secure the health of all students (including immune-compromised students who can't be vaccinated) as well as to help educate the next generation of parents and thus finally overturn the campaign of misinformation promulgated through Wakefield's study.

Word count: 246

Which is the better executive summary? Most would agree that it is Executive Summary 2. The recommendation (in bold) is stated clearly from the outset. Moreover it is linked clearly to an urgent problem, and is tied to a specific organization to act in its own and the public's best interests. Rather than following a chronology of events, Executive Summary 2 focuses on the recommendation, and then works backwards to cover the main problem and its potential scale if left untreated.

As you construct your own executive summary remember to start with the outcome in mind and prioritize the recommendation. If your manager can't find it, can't see its relevance, or remembers it 10 seconds later, your recommendation stands a poor chance of being implemented.

From first to final draft

What is written without effort is in general read without pleasure.

Samuel Johnson

Photo 8.1 The challenge of writing up

Regardless of the nature of the deliverable, you still need to write it, and writing up can be one of the most challenging parts of your research project. Even when you have data, visuals and an interesting narrative, putting it all together is hard work. As pictured in Photo 8.1, writing can be exhausting, and revision even more so. The good news is, you are not alone (see Box 8.3).

BOX 8.3

On writing

Writing is easy. You just sit down at the typewriter, open up a vein and bleed it out drop by drop.

Walter 'Red' Smith

The road to hell is paved with works-in-progress.

Philip Roth

No pen, no ink, no table, no room, no time, no quiet, no inclination.

James Joyce

I am irritated by my own writing. I am like a violinist whose ear is true, but whose fingers refuse to reproduce precisely the sound he hears within.

Gustave Flaubert

I was working on the proof of one of my poems all the morning, and took out a comma. In the afternoon I put it back again.

Oscar Wilde

Writing ... a combination of ditch-digging, mountain-climbing, treadmill and childbirth.

Edna Ferber

Being a good writer is 3% talent, 97% not being distracted by the Internet.

Anonymous

It is essential that your report is polished and sharp. Your authority can be enhanced or destroyed not only by the quality of your research but also by its presentation. So be prepared to seek and take advice, and draft, redraft and redraft again.

Drafting and redrafting

There is no doubt that the journey from first draft to submission can be long and challenging. In fact, contrary to the desire of just about every fibre in your body, you may find that your final document does not retain much from that first draft. The irony is of course that you can't get to that final draft without all the drafts in between!

While it may seem somewhat tedious, almost all good writers do go through some variation of this process. Box 8.4 offers a number of checklists for helping you get to a quality end product.

BOX 8.4

Checklist for the redrafting process

Reworking the first draft

It would be nice if your first draft were it. But it rarely works that way. When you step back and take stock, you are likely to find that the process of writing itself has evolved your ideas, and that your thoughts have moved beyond what you initially managed to capture on paper. As you work through your first draft, ask yourself:

- Is this making sense? Does the logic flow between sections?
- Is the 'voice' I am using professional and polished?
- Do I need to incorporate more material/ideas – or are sections really repetitive?
- Is each section complete?
- Have I sought and responded to feedback?

Reworking the second draft

Once you are happy with the overall ideas, arguments, logic and structure, it is time to fine-tune your arguments and strive for coherence and consistency. In doing this, ask yourself:

- How can I make my points and arguments clearer? Do I 'waffle on' at any point? Am I using lots of jargon and acronyms? Should I incorporate some/more examples?
- Do I want to include some/more diagrams, photos, maps, etc.?
- Are there clear and logical links between sections?
- Is the length and format on target?
- Have I sought and responded to feedback?

Moving towards the penultimate draft

Being ready to move towards a penultimate draft implies that you are reasonably happy with the construction and logic of the arguments running throughout and within your document. Attention can now be turned to fluency, clarity and overall readability. Ask yourself:

- Are there ways I can further increase clarity? Are my terms used consistently? Have I got rid of unnecessary jargon?
- Are there ways I can make this read more fluently? Can I break up my longer sentences? Can I rework my one-sentence paragraphs?

(Continued)

(Continued)

- Are there ways I can make this more engaging? Can I limit the use of passive voice? Are my arguments strong and convincing?
- Am I sure I have protected the confidentiality of my respondents/participants?
- Have I guarded against any potential accusations of plagiarism? Have I checked and double-checked my sources, both in the text and in the references or bibliography?
- Have I written and edited any preliminary and end pages, namely title page, table of contents, list of figures, appendices and references?
- Have I thoroughly checked my spelling and grammar?
- Have I done a word count?
- Have I sought and responded to feedback?

Producing the final draft

You would think that if you did all the above, your final document would be done. Not quite; you now need to do a final edit. If it is a large work and you can fund it, you might want to consider using a copy editor. It is amazing what editorial slip-ups someone with specialist skills can find, even after you have combed through your own work a dozen times. Some things you may want to ask prior to submission are:

- Have I looked for typos of all sorts?
- Have I triple-checked spelling (especially those things that spell checkers cannot pick up, like typing 'form' instead of 'from')?
- Have I checked my line spacing, fonts, margins, etc.?
- Have I numbered all pages, including preliminary and end pages, sequentially? Have I made sure they are all in the proper order?
- Have I checked through the final document to make sure there were no printing glitches (a particular problem with figures and tables)?

Seeking advice

When moving from the first to the final draft, you may need to take the uncomfortable step of seeking feedback. Now you might think this would be a straightforward process, but that is not always the case. You need to know where you are in the process and ask for comments related to your current needs. A good strategy here is to ask your readers to comment on the same questions you need to ask yourself as you work through various drafts of your document. If it is a first draft, you will probably want advice on overall ideas, arguments, logic and structure, while later stages will see you seeking suggestions for consistency, coherence, readability and, finally, copy editing.

Seeking the advice of your supervisor(s) can be invaluable; so too can the advice of colleagues, peers and family. In fact, at some stage, it is worth asking a non-specialist to read your work to see if the logic makes sense to him or her – because it should. And don't forget to try to get a sense of timeframe. It can take some readers several days (even a couple of weeks) to get back to you.

Now knowing who to ask and what to ask is one thing, but being willing to hand over what you have written is quite another. What if your secret fears of not being good enough are validated? Handing over is always exposing, but keep in mind that fears of incompetence are often a crisis of confidence – not a lack of ability. And besides, it is better to find out if you are off track early, than wait until you have invested a huge amount of time heading in the wrong direction. The point is not to delay asking for feedback. The worst thing you can do is hide your draft until you're either inconveniencing someone to read it the day before it's due, or you wait so long that there's no time to revise the document even if you received constructive feedback that very minute.

But let's say you have managed to ask the right person the right questions and you get your draft back. If you are lucky, it is full of constructive, relevant and thought-provoking comments. You should be happy – not only has someone put in a lot of time and effort, but they have provided you with a road map for moving forward. But, of course, you're human. So instead of being happy, you are devastated. In fact, you may feel insulted, frustrated and even incompetent. You are not alone here. We all wish feedback was limited to validation of how clever we are. But that's not useful. Validation simply doesn't move you forward. You need to accept advice and not take criticism personally. If you do, writing up will become an emotional minefield.

So now that you have the advice, what do you do with it? Well, unreflexive incorporation is just as bad as blanket dismissal. You need to mentally take the feedback on board, consider it in light of the source and work through the implications that the advice has for what you are trying to say. And of course this is particularly important if you find yourself getting conflicting advice. Talk to your supervisor/lecturer, but remember that it is your work and you are the one who needs to make the final call.

PREPARING PERSUASIVE PRESENTATIONS

Presentations convey your thoughts, ideas and your work to an audience. It is an opportunity to engage productively with decision-makers, colleagues and stakeholders. It may also one of the most important parts of your small-scale applied workplace-based research project. And the most nerve-wracking. This section deals with how to avoid death by PowerPoint (and conversely, avoiding motion-sickness with Prezi) and how to handle questions with aplomb.

Elements of a powerful presentation:

- *Expertise and knowledge* – Without a doubt you need to know your stuff. You do not have a right to present if you don't know what you are talking about. Knowing your stuff gives you credibility and confidence. But, here is the kicker. *You do not need to tell them everything you know!* Let your knowledge be obvious by showing that you can extract essential, compelling elements; by your confidence; by your flexibility. This is not about your ego. This is not about showing people how much you know. This is about your audience and what they walk away with.

- *Your objective* – You will undoubtedly have an objective related to your study. Say, for example, 'to outline your study and communicate findings'. But, and this is important, *stop and think about what you want your audience to achieve.* Is your goal for your audience to know all the ins and outs of your research process and know exactly what you found? Or could it also be that you want them to be shocked, be motivated, be willing to change behaviors, be willing to get onboard, be a change agent? These should be the things that matter when we are presenting – and the things we often forget. But if you can articulate this type of audience-related goal, it will change how you structure and deliver your presentation. You have no choice but to go from reporting to motivating.

- *Storytelling* – Without a doubt the best presenters know how to **tell a story**. They tell a tale, they build anticipation, they shoot for 'aha' moments, they use anecdotes, and they are not afraid of weaving in appropriate bits of emotion.

- *The power of you* – Here is a fact: *people are motivated by people.* Compare your favorite university lecture-based subject with your most hated. I bet that content is only a minor player in that differentiation. It is the lecturer who motivates and inspires. *And that means you count.* Your presentation needs to have your stamp on it; you need to 'show up'. Now that doesn't mean you should try to be funny if you're not (that will flop!) or try to be authoritative if you're shy (that will only make you more nervous), but do bring out your unique brand of warmth. Think about what your best friend, partner or parents would say is your best quality – authoritative, sincere, funny, warm, wise – and then try to present in such a way that your audience can see that quality reflected in your presentation.

- *Audio-visual aids* – These should support you, not replace you. If you are using PowerPoint slides, aim for no more than one slide for every 2 minutes on stage – less if possible. Try to move away from text-based slides to more powerful visuals. Consider that using a lapel microphone and a wireless mouse allows you to move around and draw focus (and dispel some nervous energy). Hiding behind a podium does not allow you to shine and is less likely to be engaging.

Avoiding death by PowerPoint (for yourself and others)

It is hard to believe, but PowerPoint was once the domain of the elite few. In the 1990s, graduate students had to learn how to use this brand new medium. Now, 400 million licenses later, 'slideware' software has become so ubiquitous that elementary school children have PowerPoint presentation assessments. How do you set yourself apart in a sea of these young up-and-coming go-getters?

First, recognize that PowerPoint is merely a tool. You, the presenter, are the active agent. Think of the software as notes that keep you on-message. It is not a substitute for your persuasion, insights and adaptability. Rather, you should be prepared to give the presentation WITHOUT software should the need arise (and sometimes it does!). For inspiration and examples, see Box 8.5.

BOX 8.5

Great TED talks (www.ted.com)

These TED talks are well worth a look – pay attention to style and try to identify what makes these presenters so compelling.

Sean Anchor (2012) 'The Happy Secret to Better Work'

Philip Evans (2014) 'How Data Will Transform Business'

William Stephen (2015) 'A Talk About Nothing'

Simon Sinek (2010) 'How Great Leaders Inspire Action'

Keren Elazari (2014) 'Hackers: the Internet's Immune System'

Glen Greenwald (2014) 'Why Privacy Matters'

Margaret Heffernan (2012) 'Conflict as Thinking'

John Doerr (2007) 'Salvation and Profit in Greentech'

Ken Robinson (2006) 'Do Schools Kill Creativity?'

Michael Porter (2013) 'Why Business Can Be Good at Solving Social Problems'

Second, less is more when it comes to the number of slides. You have probably seen presentations where the slides rush by as if on a flip-book (bonus points for cheesy swipe and checkerboard transitions between slides). Some speakers appear to be in competition for how many slides they can squeeze in before the buzzer (or people fall asleep/leave). Don't let this be you. Craft a few polished slides and spend time on and between each one. A good rule of thumb is to use no more than one or two slides per minute. This means that a 15-minute presentation should have *no more than* 30 slides. Remember, you need to be the star of the show.

Additionally, do not try to cram in everything; your font needs to be legible from a distance. In fact, limiting words on your slide is a good idea as demonstrated by Figure 8.1. Compelling images are much more effective in a bid to be persuasive.

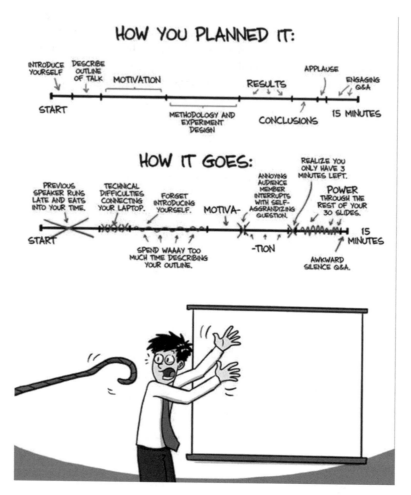

Figure 8.1 Your presentation ('Piled higher and deeper' by Jorge Cham www. phdcomics.com)

Dealing with anxiety

We know that presenting can cause real panic. But guess what? No one else can see that ball in your stomach or the feeling like you are eating your own heart. They can't feel it – unless you let them. That means, you can still feel nervous, but no one has to know. The key is to *look confident*. Research shows that audiences readily conflate confidence with competence. When you speak confidently, others assume that you are competent.

How does one whose heart is eating itself manage to look confident? The easiest way is to stop doing whatever makes you look *unconfident*: nervous pacing, hand wringing, heavy sweating, muffled speech, etc. All of these and more can be hidden, mitigated, or overcome with some clever strategies and preparation.

First, there is no substitute for a dress rehearsal in front of a sympathetic audience (friends, family, roommates). Have one of them video you, or do it yourself using a tripod. You will probably watch this video with dismayed incredulity that your voice 'actually sounds like that'. Also, prepare to be amazed that you used 'um' 35 times while fiddling with your scarf or your tie over the course of 20 minutes. It's ok. Well, it will be. Now you know to pay attention to your hands, and not to wear a scarf. A key is being aware. One student, for example, gave an entire presentation while slowly stepping one toe in front of the other, incrementally shifting in place. The audience was too busy watching her walk on a moving tightrope to really pay attention to anything she said.

The other benefit of a practice session is that others can help you identify potential gaps. Ask your audience what was unclear or unconvincing. Then improve that section AND create a slide at the end of the presentation that provides more details. For instance, an extra slide with cost calculations is always helpful. Commonly, people want to know 'where you got that number'. Be prepared to provide a source or substantiate the estimate. By having these slides at the ready you will strengthen the persuasiveness of your research and bolster your own credibility as a competent professional.

Dealing with audience questions

You may breathe a sigh of relief when your presentation is over. But then during Q & A you get thrown a difficult question that you don't know how to answer. Well, it is important to recognize that *questioning is not an adversarial process*. Rather, a question is the continuation of a conversation. Relish the fact that that your audience member is interested enough to want to continue the dialogue.

The worst case scenario is not a room full of questions, but a room full of silence (like the scenario in Figure 8.1 below). No questions mean your audience is distracted, bored and possibly asleep. With this in mind, you can see questions for what they are – engagement. And you can be thankful when you get one.

Types of questions

Questions and questioners typically fall within three categories.

- *Clarification* (What is that first word on slide 5? What year is that data from? Does your recommendation require any ongoing costs?)
- *Analysis* (How did you decide between the alternative recommendations? How do we know the problem of X is caused by Z? How did you estimate the cost of delaying action?)
- *Gaps* (Did you consider X? I would have considered X, you should consider X.)

The most common questions are simple points of clarification. The response merely requires a quick and simple piece of data and a credible source. Analysis and gap questions necessitate a longer response. The advice here is to hit the high points and encourage the audience to read the full details in your written report. Gap questions tend to arise from genuine interest OR a need to look intelligent. The answer for both is the same: 'Thank you for the suggestion, that's very interesting, and I'll take that on board when reviewing the section on X.' You'll be pleased to know that hostile questioning is exceedingly rare. When unclear about how you should respond, just say, 'I'll have to look into that and get back to you'.

BOX 8.6

When things aren't going to plan

- *Technology failures* – It could be a failure of the software, hardware or Internet connection, but technology dramas can happen. Guard against software issues by saving your PowerPoint presentation on two sources (USB and email/Dropbox); counter hardware failures by bringing your laptop. It's always good to have a back-up of video clips or screen shots of websites on your USB, just in case. All of these suggestions are born of painful experience, trust us!
- *Running out of time* – This is incredibly common. Perhaps a previous meeting or speaker ran late, your audience got caught up in traffic, or due to technology dramas above, everything is running behind. The worst thing you can do is try to get through every slide regardless. We see this all the time. With 5 minutes to go, the presenter tries to fly through 17 more slides. The end result? The audience doesn't remember a thing that was said in that blur of a monologue. When conditions change, change with them. Skip the more minor points (you can always deal with them during questions), and concentrate on the big take-away message.
- *Interruptions* – Fire drills notwithstanding, interruptions are generally easy to deal with. Common interruptions are people coming in late, early questions in the middle of your presentation, or noisy distractions. In the first instance, you may wish to pause for a moment while everyone gets resettled. In the second, answer briefly, then deflect by saying you'll be happy to tackle questions at the end. For the third, just wait. Don't try to shout over crazy distractions. Wait for the ambulance to turn the corner outside, wait for someone's phone to stop ringing. Wait – but not so long that your audience becomes distracted.

A NOTE ON EMPLOYABILITY

Employers are looking for exactly the people who can deliver the professional outputs described in this chapter, particularly those who can do so with confidence and finesse. How can you demonstrate these skills clearly in written and interview form? Luckily I spent the first three years of my professional career as a recruiter and I'm here to help you do just that.

Demonstrating valuable skill-sets on your CV

The first step in enhancing employability is to identify what hard and soft skills you have that are valuable to employers. Soft skills are interpersonal skills like communication, negotiation, critical thinking and time-management. These are valuable skills that cannot be simply taught in a classroom. They are also the first ones to be noticed by an employer in an interview. Are you well spoken? How do you react in group settings? Are you on time?

Hard skills are technical. These typically include software/programming expertise, language skills, formal training (such as Agile, etc.), and in some interpretations, advanced degrees. These are skills that get you to the interview stage. This means that your CV and cover letter should prioritize these. How? You may consider identifying your proficiency in each hard skill on your CV. For languages spoken, if you're fluent in Arabic write that instead of just listing the name of the language. For Excel, say whether you are a basic, intermediate or advanced Excel user. Not sure? If you can create a spreadsheet from scratch, do simple calculations and filter results, you're a basic user. If you can use more complex formulas and create or modify macro commands, you're probably an intermediate user. If you can utilize advanced functions (If, VLOOKUP, IS), manage macros, work with Pivot tables and dabble in basic programming in VBA you're an advanced or expert user. It's worth listing a few of these details to identify what experience you've had that is valuable to the organization.

Other elements of a strong CV that portray you as a valuable candidate include:

- action words;
- quantified success;
- tailored to the job under consideration.

Action words make you the active agent in your CV. For a list of them, see Table 8.3. They are also closely linked to accomplishments, initiatives and results. A common mistake that inexperienced (and even some experienced) professionals make is to use a job description and list of duties for each position in their CV. Don't do it! Job descriptions are vague, dull and usually wrong anyway. Instead, highlight accomplishments. Under the entry for each job, a sentence or two is fine to describe the role. Then use bullet points to identify at least three personal and team accomplishments in that position.

Bullet points should be concise and precise using quantifiable success. Consider the ways you can quantify success on your CV using specific measures: time and money. For instance, instead of listing 'Worked on a project to deliver significant savings to the department', be more specific: 'Helped deliver a project that delivered $145K in savings over 2 months.' Perhaps the numbers are modest and don't seem impressive. This could be the case if you are working with a small company, start-up, government department or non-profit. In this case, utilize the power of percentages. Raising $25K for the International Red Cross would be a minute percentage of their annual goal. However, for a local non-profit, the same amount may be 20% of their annual goal!

Use the appropriate scales to give meaning to the accomplishments that you helped deliver, either as an individual or as a team. Timeframes and team size also merit a mention. If you were promoted within 3 months to a more senior role or into a more prestigious division, include this. If you were part of a small team that delivered a large project, mention that as well.

Once you have a template CV of no more than two pages (if you have less than five years of professional experience), you can adapt it for your job search. Does this mean you need to change your CV for each job for which you apply? Yes and no. Do not completely re-write your résumé for each position, but craft it so that passes the first hurdle – which will be a machine.

If sci-fi has taught us anything, it's that machines are not always our friends. And they are definitely impassable gatekeepers when it comes to job hunting. With

Table 8.3   Action words for your CV/résumé

Leadership and initiative	Analysis	Communication/people skills
Developed	Evaluated	Collaborated
Designed	Assessed	Facilitated
Generated	Measured	Advocated
Launched	Monitored	Persuaded
Initiated	Researched	Supervised
Implemented	Surveyed	Drafted
Administered	Systematized	Wrote
Delivered	Conducted	Edited/Revised
Executed	Forecasted	Mediated
Directed	Conserved	Negotiated
Established	Corrected	Marketed
Reorganized	Customized	Resolved
Increased	Maximized	Mapped
Handled	Diagnosed	Managed
Produced	Extracted	Coordinated
Proposed	Gathered	
Formulated	Inspected	
Recommended	Improved	
	Planned	

the increasing number of applicants for each position, HR and recruitment agencies are increasingly turning to text-matching software to sort through mountains of CVs. These machines use language in the job posting ad to shortlist resumes for human review. Unfortunately, these machines do NOT know synonyms. If the hiring manager is looking for an employee proficient in 'Excel', and you put that you're an expert in 'Microsoft Office software' well too bad. The machine will not recognize the task by any other name, and into the discard pile you go. Thus, when you apply for a position, first identify the key words in the job posting and make sure these *exact words* are reflected in your CV. This is the only way to get in front of a real live person.

Of course, this is not a license to exaggerate your experience; rather, you may need to rephrase some of your accomplishments so that they are recognized by the machine. Remember, anything on the CV is fair game for an interviewer to ask you about during the next stage. So as you craft your CV be prepared discuss the details of your experience and how it's applicable to the current position. Box 8.7 offers a checklist of résumé 'dos and don'ts'.

BOX 8.7

Dos and don'ts for your CV/résumé

The average recruiter or manager looks at your CV (or résumé) for about 12 seconds. Any red flags such as glaring spelling errors will see your CV tossed on the reject pile in less than that. Give yourself the best chance for getting an interview by paying careful attention to what's required.

Do

- Highlight your accomplishments using action words.
- Quantify your success (money/time/lives saved in your project).
- Emphasize transferable skills from your research project (cross-departmental initiatives, engaging with stakeholders, etc.).
- Ensure that your public social media accounts align with your CV (update Linkedin, lockdown your privacy settings on all private social media accounts. Remember everyone can see your Facebook profile photo, and recruiters do check).
- Use/create an appropriate email address for professional correspondence (Stans TheMan1998@cheesydomainname.com does not get interviews, but his CV does get put up on the bulletin board in the Human Resources office kitchen with his name blanked out).
- Read carefully for grammar and spelling mistakes (remember, spell checkers will not save you if you accidentally delete the 'f' from 'shift'!). Better yet, have someone else read it.

(Continued)

(Continued)

Don't

- Use expressions like 'duties included' – that is job description language, not accomplishment-oriented language. And it's dull.
- Claim undue credit, exaggerate your experience or lie (it will be obvious when you can't discuss the project/accomplishment intelligently in the interview).
- Include highly sensitive information on your CV like your Social Security number, tax file number, marital status, number of children (although this once used to be standard procedure). In the age of identity theft, it is becoming common even to exclude your street address; city and state are fine.
- Include high school odd jobs – now is the time to delete all babysitting or by the pool jobs that may be hanging on to your resume.
- List references or referees; that is for a later stage of the process.

Leveraging your project in job interviews

Congratulations. You've passed the text-matching test. You've talked to a human being and progressed to the interview stage. How to get from that first handshake to winning the job as in Photo 8.2?

The interview stage can be intimidating. But remember, if you have got an interview, you are qualified for the job. It helps to know a bit about the interview process itself, so find out as much as you can from HR, previous employees or the interwebs. Try to ascertain if you will be talking to one person, or several. For some graduate or entry-level positions there may be group assessments whereby

Photo 8.2   Leveraging your workplace-based research project in interviews

several applicants work together on a project for an afternoon and then deliver their results. Be prepared to be friendly with the competition. The good news is that you will have probably gained confidence during your work-based placement, and accumulated plenty of material to use in interview questions.

Most managers and interviewers will draw from a traditional pool of questions. Leverage your workplace project experience by incorporating them into common interview questions:

- Tell me a bit about yourself.
- Describe a recent position you've held.
- What projects did you work on? *Think small-scale applied workplace-based research project!*
- Give me an example of a time you influenced a group – *When you got the green light for your small-scale applied workplace-based research project!*
- What accomplishments have given you the greatest satisfaction? *When my small-scale applied workplace-based research project recommendations were taken up by the organization!*
- Tell me about a time you demonstrated leadership.
- Tell me about a time you were a team player.
- Tell me about a time you overcame a challenge at work.
- What experiences/skills do you feel are particularly useful to our organization?
- Have you ever failed at anything (see Box 8.8)?

BOX 8.8

Have you ever failed?

There is only one answer to the 'have you ever failed at anything' interview question. The answer is yes. Yes, you have failed. You have failed because you are a human. Not only that, you are an interesting human that likes to try new things and sometimes those new things don't always work the first time. Not having any failures at this point in your life sends a signal that you prefer to operate within a very tight comfort zone, or actively avoid challenges. Neither of these is attractive to employers. Should you attempt to answer this question with a 'No, nothing comes to mind' the manager may assume that you are boring, too inexperienced, deceptive or have a poor memory.

Why is the organization interested in your honest answer to this question? If you have never truly failed, it is unclear to your potential manager how you will react to failure when it inevitably happens. Will you get angry, become rude or defensive? Will you withdraw, or run away, your self-esteem shattered at the slightest criticism or lost client? The organization is testing your mettle, your resilience and whether they can trust you to maintain composure in front of difficult clients, customers, etc.

(Continued)

(Continued)

Remember to avoid any personal or uncomfortable topics for the failure question (or any professional interview question, for that matter!): 'I tried to get the love of my life back but she's with another guy now.' Inappropriate! Stick to professional examples that have a productive ending: 'I failed at X, but then I took steps Y and Z to correct/overcome/learn.' It demonstrates that you are capable of humility, self-reflection, overcoming obstacles and problem-solving – valuable traits to any employer.

Keep in mind that employers will be interested in how well you write as well as how well you speak. If you produced a professional report or document, you may want to consider providing a brief synopsis or hard copy sample. For instance, the executive summary or a condensed version of your report could demonstrate your writing and organizational skills in a way that simply discussing the project may not. Most employers appreciate the opportunity to peruse these, so bring them with you to the interview (bring multiple copies in case there is more than one interviewer).

Remember that, above all, employers are looking for someone who is likeable, confident, composed, articulate and motivated. An interview is your opportunity to shine, market your skills and prove that you are well prepared for the challenges ahead.

That's all folks!

So that's it! Your research project, and quite possibly your job placement, are winding down. You're on to the next challenge, using the skills you've picked up along the way – organization, persistence, analysis, presentation and persuasion. You should feel proud that your hard work helped to improve an organization – and, who knows, maybe the world, one small-scale research project at a time.

CHAPTER SUMMARY

- Deliverables are the product and outcome of data gathering and analysis. These outputs represent a condensed form of hard work and insight and can take many forms, including essays, reports, policy papers and presentations.
- The first rule of writing is to know your audience. While academic papers have professors for their audience, the audience for workplace-based research is decision-makers, managers, directors as well as colleagues and junior staff.
- Presentations are an opportunity to engage productively with decision-makers, colleagues and stakeholders. Think about motivating your audience to action and welcoming questions as a continuation of the conversation.
- Employers are looking for people who can deliver professional reports, presentations and projects. The key is to demonstrate these skills clearly on your CV/résumé, and leverage them in an interview.

BIBLIOGRAPHY

Adams, D. (1979) *The Hitchhiker's Guide to the Galaxy*. New York: Pocket Books.

Al-Aziz, J., Christou, N., Dinov, I.D. (2010) 'SOCR *Motion Charts*: an efficient, open-source, interactive and dynamic applet for visualizing longitudinal multivariate data', *Journal of Statistics Education*, 18(3): 1–29.

Altman, R. (2012) *Why Most PowerPoint Presentations Suck*. Seattle, WA: CreateSpace.

Anchor, S. (2012) 'The Happy Secret to Better Work', TED Talk, Bloomington, Indiana.

Anderson, C. (2013) 'How to give a killer presentation', *Harvard Business Review*, June.

Andrews, R. (2003) *Research Questions*. London: Continuum International.

Argyrous, G. (2011) *Statistics for Research: With a Guide to SPSS*. London: SAGE.

Arthur, C. (2014) 'Facebook emotion study breached ethical guidelines, researchers say', *The Guardian* (London) 30th June.

Atkinson, P., Coffey, A., Delamont, S., Lofland, J. and Lofland, L. (eds) (2007) *Handbook of Ethnography*. London: SAGE.

Audi, R. (2010) *Epistemology: A Contemporary Introduction to the Theory of Knowledge*. London: Routledge.

Balatti, J., Gargano, L., Goldman, M., Wood, G. and Woodlock, J. (2004) *Improving Indigenous Completion Rates in Mainstream TAFE – An Action Research Approach*. Leabrook, South Australia: NCEAR.

Bazeley, P. (2013) *Qualitative Data Analysis: Practical Strategies*. London: SAGE.

Bazeley, P. and Jackson, K. (2013) *Qualitative Data Analysis with NVivo*. London: SAGE.

Berger, P. and Luckmann, T. (1967) *The Social Construction of Reality: A Treatise in the Sociology of Knowledge*. New York: Anchor.

Bischof, G.H., Warnaar, B.L., Barajas, M.S. and Dhaliwal, H.K. (2011) 'Thematic analysis of the experiences of wives who stay with husbands who transition male-to-female', *Michigan Family Review*, 15(1): 16–33.

Bloom, H. (2006) *Learning More from Social Experiments: Evolving Analytic Approaches*. New York: Russell Sage Foundation.

Boghossian, P.A. (2006) *Fear of Knowledge: Against Relativism and Constructivism*. Oxford: Oxford University Press.

Bogner, A., Littig, B. and Menz, W. (eds) (2009) *Interviewing Experts*. Basingstoke: Palgrave Macmillan.

Booth, W.C., Colomb, G.C. and Williams, J.M. (2008) *The Craft of Research*. Chicago, IL: University of Chicago Press.

Borrell, J. (2008) 'Thematic analysis identifying concepts of problem gambling agency: with preliminary exploration of discourses in selected industry and research documents', *Journal of Gambling Issues*, 22, 195–218.

Bradberry, T. (2014) 'Multitasking damages your brain and career, new studies suggest', *Forbes*, 8 October.

Brown, S.G. and Dobrin, S.I. (eds) (2004) *Ethnography Unbound: From Theory Shock to Critical Praxis*. Albany, NY: State University of New York Press.

Brumfield, B. (2013) 'German Education Minister loses PhD over plagiarised thesis', *CNN*, 6 February. http://edition.cnn.com/2013/02/06/world/europe/german-minister-plagiarism/ (accessed 16 November 2016).

Bryant, A. and Charmaz, K. (eds) (2010) *The SAGE Handbook of Grounded Theory*. London: SAGE.

Bryman, A. (2012) *Social Research Methods*. Oxford: Oxford University Press.

Bumiller, E. (2010) 'We have met the enemy and he is PowerPoint', *New York Times*, 26 April.

Burr, V. (2003) *Social Constructionism*. New York: Psychology Press.

Carey, S.S. (2011) *A Beginner's Guide to Scientific Method*. Belmont, CA: Wadsworth.

Carnegie, D. (1936) *How to Win Friends and Influence People*. New York: Simon and Shuster.

Carroll, L. (2011) *Alice's Adventures in Wonderland*. Ebook: Project Gutenberg. http://www.gutenberg.org/

Cavana, R.L., Delahaye, B.L. and Sekaran, U. (2001) *Applied Business Research: Qualitative and Quantitative Methods*. New York: John Wiley & Sons.

Chakravartty, A. (2010) *A Metaphysics for Scientific Realism: Knowing the Unobservable*. London: Cambridge.

Chandler, D. (2007) *Semiotics: The Basics*. London: Routledge.

Choo, C.W. (1996) 'The knowing organization: how organizations use information to construct meaning, create knowledge and make decisions', *International Journal of Information Management*, 16(5): 23–40.

Clandinin, D.J. (ed.) (2006) *Handbook of Narrative Inquiry: Mapping a Methodology*. London: SAGE.

Coghlan, D. and Brannick, T. (2009) *Doing Action Research in Your Own Organization*. London: SAGE.

Conee, E. and Sider, T. (2007) *Riddles of Existence: A Guided Tour of Metaphysics*. Oxford: Oxford University Press.

Cooper, H.M. (2009) *Research Synthesis and Meta-Analysis: A Step-by-Step Approach*. Thousand Oaks, CA: SAGE.

Corbin, J. and Strauss, A. (2007) *Basics of Qualitative Research: Techniques and Procedures for Developing Grounded Theory*. London: SAGE.

Covey, S. ([1989] 2013) *The 7 Habits of Highly Effective People*, 25th anniversary edition. London: Simon and Schuster.

Creswell, J.W. (2013) *Research Design: Qualitative, Quantitative and Mixed Methods Approaches*. London: SAGE.

Creswell, J.W. and Plano Clark, V.L. (2010) *Designing and Conducting Mixed Methods Research*. London: SAGE.

Cryer, P. (2006) *The Research Student's Guide to Success*. Buckingham: Open University Press.

Danette McGilvray, D. (2008) *Executing Data Quality Projects: Ten Steps to Quality Data and Trusted Information*. Burlington MA: Morgan Kauffman.

Daniel, J. (2011) *Sampling Essentials: Practical Guidelines for Making Sampling Choices.* London: SAGE.

Danto, E.A. (2008) *Historical Research.* Oxford: Oxford University Press.

de Certeau, M. (2002) *The Practice of Everyday Life.* Berkeley, CA: University of California Press.

de Vaus, D. (2009) *Research Design in Social Research.* London: SAGE.

Denzin, N.K. and Lincoln, Y.S. (eds) (2007) *Strategies of Qualitative Inquiry.* Thousand Oaks, CA: SAGE.

Denzin, N.K. and Lincoln, Y. (eds) (2011) *The SAGE Handbook of Qualitative Research.* Thousand Oaks, CA: SAGE.

DeWalt, K.M. and DeWalt, B.R. (2010) *Participant Observation: A Guide for Fieldwork.* Lanham, MD: AltaMira Press.

Dewey, C. (2014) 'How Web Archivists and other digital sleuths are unravelling the mystery of flight MH17', *Washington Post*, 21 July. Available at: https://www.washingtonpost.com/news/the-intersect/wp/2014/07/21/how-web-archivists-and-other-digital-sleuths-are-unraveling-the-mystery-of-mh17/

Dillman, D.A. (2006) *Mail and Internet Surveys: The Tailored Design Method.* Hoboken, NJ: John Wiley & Sons.

Donovan, J. (2012) *How to Deliver a TED Talk: Secrets of the World's Most Inspiring Presentations.* Seattle, WA: CreateSpace.

Dorofeev, S. and Grant, P. (2006) *Statistics for Real-Life Sample Surveys: Non-Simple-Random Samples and Weighted Data.* Cambridge: Cambridge University Press.

Double, R. (2006) *Metaethical Subjectivism.* Surrey, UK: Ashgate Publishing.

Doucouliagos, H. and Ali Ulubaşoğlu, M. (2008) 'Democracy and economic growth: a meta-analysis', *American Journal of Political Science*, 52(1): 61–83.

Ekinci, Y. (2015) *Designing Research Questionnaires for Business and Management Students.* London: SAGE.

Fals Borda, O. and Rahman, M.A. (1991) *Action and Knowledge: Breaking the Monopoly with Participatory Action Research.* New York: Intermediate Technology/Apex Press.

Farquhar, A.B. and Farquhar, H. (1891) *Economic and Industrial Delusions: A Discourse of the Case for Protection.* New York: Putnam.

Ferguson, S.S. (2008) 'Nicotine patch therapy prior to quitting smoking: a meta-analysis', *Addiction*, 103(4): 557–63.

Fetterman, D. (2009) *Ethnography: Step-by-Step.* London: SAGE.

Few, Stephen (2009) *Now You See It: Simple Visualization Techniques for Quantitative Analysis.* Oakland, CA: Analytics Press.

Feynman, R. (1997) *Surely You're Joking, Mr Feynman!* New York: W.W. Norton.

Field, A. and Miles, J. (2010) *Discovering Statistics Using SAS.* Thousand Oaks, CA: SAGE.

Field, A., Miles, J. and Field, Z. (2012) *Discovering Statistics Using R.* London: SAGE.

Fink, A. (2008) *How to Conduct Surveys: A Step-by-Step Guide.* Thousand Oaks, CA: SAGE.

Fink, A. (2009) *Conducting Research Literature Reviews: From the Internet to Paper.* Thousand Oaks, CA: SAGE.

Fishburne, R. (2000) 'The Shadow in Silicon Valley', *The New York Times*, 29 April. http://www.nytimes.com/2000/04/29/opinion/the-shadow-in-silicon-valley.html

Fitzpatrick, J.L., Sanders, J.R. and Worthen, B.R. (2010) *Program Evaluation: Alternative Approaches and Practical Guidelines.* New York: Allyn & Bacon.

Fitzpatrick, K. (2011) 'Stop playing up! Physical education, racialization and resistance', *Ethnography*, 12(2): 174–97.

Fowler Jr, F.J. (2008) *Survey Research Methods*. London: SAGE.

Fox, J. (2014) *The Game Changer: How to Use the Science of Motivation with the Power of Game Design to Shift Behavior, Shape Culture and Make Clever Happen*. Melbourne: Wiley.

Francis, D. and Hester, S. (2004) *An Invitation to Ethnomethodology*. London: SAGE.

Freire, P. (1970) *Pedagogy of the Oppressed*. New York: Herder & Herder.

Friese, S. (2012) *Qualitative Data Analysis with ATLAS.ti*. Thousand Oaks, CA: SAGE.

Friesen, N., Hendriksson, C. and Saevi, T. (eds) (2012) *Hermeneutic Phenomenology in Education: Method and Practice*. Boston, MA: Sense Publishers.

Galvan, J.L. (2012) *Writing Literature Reviews: A Guide for Students of the Social and Behavioral Sciences*. Glendale, CA: Pyrczak.

Garfinkel, H. (1967) *Studies in Ethnomethodology*. Englewood Cliffs, NJ: Prentice Hall.

Gee, J.P. (2010) *An Introduction to Discourse Analysis: Theory and Method*. London: Routledge.

Geertz, C. ([1973] 2000) *The Interpretation of Cultures*. New York: Basic Books.

Gellner, E. (1987) *Relativism and the Social Sciences*. Cambridge: Cambridge University Press.

Gerring, J. (2006) *Case Study Research: Principles and Practices*. Cambridge: Cambridge University Press.

Gillham, B. (2008) *Observation Techniques: Structured to Unstructured*. London: Continuum International.

Giorgi, A. (2009) *The Descriptive Phenomenological Method in Psychology: A Modified Husserlian Approach*. Pittsburgh, PA: Duquesne University Press.

Girden, E. and Kabacoff, R. (2010) *Evaluating Research Articles from Start to Finish*. Thousand Oaks, CA: SAGE.

Gladwell, M. (2008) *Outliers: The Study of Success*. New York, NY: Back Bay Books.

Glaser, B. and Strauss, A. (1967) *Discovery of Grounded Theory*. Chicago, IL: Aldine.

Glucksmann, M. (aka Ruth Cavendish) (2009) *Women on the Line*. London: Routledge.

Goel, V. (2014) 'Facebook tinkers with users' emotions in news feed experiment, stirring outcry', *New York Times*, 29 June.

Goldsmith, M. (2008) 'Preparing your professional checklist', *Bloomberg Business*, 15 January.

Goldstein, K. (2002) 'Getting in the door: sampling and completing elite interviews', *Political Science and Politics*, 35(4): 669–72.

Gorard, S. (2003) *Quantitative Methods in Social Science*. London: Continuum International.

Gorlick, A. (2009) 'Media multitaskers pay mental price, Stanford study shows', *Stanford Report*, 24 August.

Gough, D., Oliver, S. and Thomas, J. (eds) (2012) *An Introduction to Systematic Reviews*. London: SAGE.

Grbich, C. (2012) *Qualitative Data Analysis: An Introduction*. London: SAGE.

Greene, J.C. (2007) *Mixed Methods in Social Inquiry*. Hoboken, NJ: Jossey-Bass.

Greenwood, D. and Levin, M. (2006) *Introduction to Action Research: Social Research for Social Change*. Thousand Oaks, CA: SAGE.

Groves, R.M., Fowler, F.J., Couper, M.J., Lepkowski, J.M., Singer, E. and Tourangeau, R. (2009) *Survey Methodology*. New York: John Wiley & Sons.

Gubrium, J.F., Holstein, J.A., Marvasti, A.B. and McKinney, K.D. (eds) (2012) *The SAGE Handbook of Interview Research: The Complexity of the Craft*. London: SAGE.

Guest, G.S., MacQueen, K.M. and Namey, E.E. (2011) *Applied Thematic Analysis*. Thousand Oaks, CA: SAGE.

Hakim, C. (2000) *Research Design*. London: Routledge.

Hall, G. and Longman, J. (2008) *The Postgraduate's Companion.* London: SAGE.

Hall, S. (2012) *This Means This, This Means That: A User's Guide to Semiotics.* London: Laurence King Publishers.

Hancock, D.R. and Algozzine, R. (2011) *Doing Case Study Research: A Practical Guide for Beginning Researchers.* New York: Teachers College Press.

Hardy, M.A. and Bryman, A. (eds) (2009) *Handbook of Data Analysis.* London: SAGE.

Hartley, J. (2008) *Academic Writing and Publishing: A Practical Handbook.* London: Routledge.

Hemenway, D. (1997) 'Survey research and self-defense gun use: an explanation of extreme overestimates', *Journal of Criminal Law and Criminology*, 87: 1430–45.

Herr, K.G. and Anderson, G.L. (2005) *The Action Research Dissertation: A Guide for Students and Faculty.* London: SAGE.

Higgins, J.P.T. and Green, S. (2008) *Cochrane Handbook for Systematic Reviews of Interventions.* New York: Wiley-Interscience.

Hine, C.M. (2012) *Virtual Research Methods.* Thousand Oaks, CA: SAGE.

Holstein, J.A. and Gubrium, J.F. (eds) (2011) *Varieties of Narrative Analysis.* London: SAGE.

Hood, S., Mayall, B. and Oliver, S. (eds) (1999) *Critical Issues in Social Research: Power and Prejudice.* Buckingham: Open University Press.

Huang, K.T., Yang W. Lee and Richard Y. Wang (1999) *Quality Information and Knowledge.* New York: Prentice Hall.

Hume, L. and Mulcock, J. (eds) (2004) *Anthropologists in the Field: Cases in Participant Observation.* Irvington, NY: Columbia University Press.

Hurston, Z.N. (1942) *Dust Tracks on a Road.* New York: Harper Collins.

IMNRC (2002) *Integrity in Scientific Research: Creating an Environment that Promotes Responsible Conduct.* Washington, DC: National Academies Press.

Irving, H. (2003) 'Trust me! A personal account of confidentiality issues in an organisational research project', *Accounting Forum*, 27(2): 111–31.

Israel, M. and Hay, I. (2006) *Research Ethics for Social Scientists.* London: SAGE.

Jackson, S.L. (2011) *Research Methods and Statistics: A Critical Thinking Approach.* Belmont, CA: Wadsworth.

Jacquette, D. (2003) *Ontology.* Montreal: McGill-Queen's University Press.

Janesick, V. (2007) 'The dance of qualitative research design: metaphor, methodolatry, and meaning', in N.K. Denzin and Y.S. Lincoln (eds), *Strategies of Qualitative Inquiry.* Thousand Oaks, CA: SAGE, pp. 35–55.

Jeynes, W.H. (2001) 'A meta-analysis of the relation of parental involvement to urban elementary school student academic achievement', *British Journal of Cancer*, 85(11): 1700–5.

Joyner, R.L., Rouse, W.A. and Glatthorn, A.A. (2012) *Writing the Winning Thesis or Dissertation: A Step-by-Step Guide.* Thousand Oaks, CA: Corwin Press.

Kaplan, D. (ed.) (2004) *The SAGE Handbook of Quantitative Methodology for the Social Sciences.* Thousand Oaks, CA: SAGE.

Kay, K. and Shipman, C. (2014) 'The confidence gap', *The Atlantic*, May 2014.

Kindon, S. (2008) *Participatory Action Research Approaches and Methods: Connecting People, Participation and Place.* London: Routledge.

Kolb, D.A. (1984) *Experiential Learning: Experience as the Source of Learning and Development.* Englewood Cliffs, NJ: Prentice Hall.

Kozinets, R.V. (2009) *Netnography: Doing Ethnographic Research.* London: SAGE.

Krathwohl, D.R. and Smith, N.L. (2005) *How to Prepare a Dissertation Proposal: Suggestions for Students in Education and the Social and Behavioral Sciences.* Syracuse, NY: Syracuse University Press.

Krippendorff, K. (2003) *Content Analysis: An Introduction to Its Methodology.* London: SAGE.

Krueger, R.A. and Casey, M.A. (2014) *Focus Groups: A Practical Guide for Applied Research.* London: SAGE.

Kruger, J. and Dunning, D. (1999). 'Unskilled and Unaware of It: How Difficulties in Recognizing One's Own Incompetence Lead to Inflated Self-Assessments', *Journal of Personality and Social Psychology*, 77(6): 1121–34.

Kvale, S. and Brinkman, S. (2008) *InterViews: Learning the Craft of Qualitative Research Interviewing.* London: SAGE.

Lee, R.M. (2011) '"The most important technique …": Carl Rogers, Hawthorne, and the rise and fall of nondirective interviewing in sociology', *Journal of the History of the Behavioral Sciences*, 47(2): 123–46.

Leedy, P.D. and Ormond, J.E. (2009) *Practical Research: Planning and Design.* Englewood Cliffs, NJ: Prentice Hall.

Lehmann, E.L. and Romano, J.P. (2010) *Testing Statistical Hypotheses.* New York: Springer.

Letherby, G., Scott, J. and Williams, M. (2012) *Objectivity and Subjectivity in Social Research.* London: SAGE.

Levy, P.S. and Lemeshow, S. (2008) *Sampling of Populations: Methods and Applications.* New York: Wiley-Interscience.

Lewin, K. (1946) 'Action research and the minority problems', *Journal of Social Issues*, 2: 34–6.

Lewins, A. and Silver, C. (2007) *Using Software in Qualitative Research: A Step-by-Step Guide.* London: SAGE.

Locke, L.F., Spirduso, W.W. and Silverman, S.J. (2007) *Proposals That Work: A Guide for Planning Dissertations and Grant Proposals.* London: SAGE.

Lofland, J. and Lofland, L.H. (2003) *Analyzing Social Settings: A Guide to Qualitative Observation and Analysis.* Belmont, CA: Wadsworth.

Lopatto, E. (2013) 'Facebook opens up site data to suicide research', *Bloomberg News* as reported in *Concord Monitor*, 28 January.

Lynch, M. and Sharrock, W. (eds) (2009) *Ethnomethodology.* London: SAGE.

Machi, L.A. and McEvoy, B. (2012) *The Literature Review: Six Steps to Success.* Thousand Oaks, CA: Corwin Press.

Macrina, F.L. (2005) *Scientific Integrity: Text and Cases in Responsible Conduct of Research.* Herndon, VA: ASM Press.

Madden, R. (2010) *Being Ethnographic: A Guide to the Theory and Practice of Ethnography.* London: SAGE.

Madison, D.S. (2011) *Critical Ethnography: Method, Ethics, and Performance.* London: SAGE.

Madriz, E. (2000) 'Focus groups and feminist research', in Denzin and Y. Lincoln (eds), *Handbook of Qualitative Research*, pp. 835–50. Thousand Oaks, California: SAGE.

Malik, S. and Quinn, B. (2013) 'Bank of America intern's death put banks' working culture in spotlight', *The Guardian*, 21 August 2013.

Markham, A.N. and Baym, N.K. (eds) (2008) *Internet Inquiry: Conversations About Method.* Thousand Oaks, CA: SAGE.

Marsh, N. (2010) 'How to make work–life balance work', TedX Sydney, 2010. www.ted.com.

Marshall, C. and Rossman, G.B. (2010) *Designing Qualitative Research.* London: SAGE.

Martin, R. (2010) *Epistemology: A Beginner's Guide.* London: OneWorld Publications.

Mayo, E. (1933) *The Human Problems of an Industrial Civilization.* New York: Viking Press.

McCandless, D. (2014) *Knowledge Is Beautiful.* New York: HarperCollins.

McClendon, M. (1991) 'Acquiescence and recency response-order effects in interview surveys', *Sociological Methods and Research,* 20(1): 60–103.

McIntyre, A. (2007) *Participatory Action Research.* London: SAGE.

McNiff, J. and Whitehead, J. (2011) *All You Need to Know About Action Research.* London: SAGE.

Mertens, D.M. and Ginsberg, P.E. (2008) *The Handbook of Social Research Ethics.* London: SAGE.

Miles, M.B., Huberman, M. and Saldana, J. (2013) *Qualitative Data Analysis: A Methods Sourcebook.* London: SAGE.

Mitchell, M.L. and Jolley, J.M. (2012) *Research Design Explained.* Belmont, CA: Wadsworth.

Moore, M.J. (2015) 'Young banker struggled with quitting Goldman before death', *Bloomberg Business,* 2 June. www.bloomberg.com/news/articles/2015-06-02/young-banker-struggled-with-quitting-goldman-weeks-before-death (accessed 16 November 2015).

Moustakas, C. (2000) *Phenomenological Research Methods.* London: SAGE.

Mulbrandon, C. (2004) Visualizing economics: Designing a persuasive argument. Masters Thesis, Carnegie Mellon University, Pittsburgh, Pennsylvania.

Myatt, G.J. (2006) *Making Sense of Data: A Practical Guide to Exploratory Data Analysis and Data Mining.* New York: Wiley-Interscience.

Nagy Hesse-Biber, S.J. and Leavy, P.L. (eds) (2006) *Feminist Research Practice: A Primer.* London: SAGE.

Neuman, W.L. (2005) *Social Research Methods: Qualitative and Quantitative Approaches.* Boston, MA: Allyn & Bacon.

Nichols-Casebolt, A. (2012) *Research Integrity and Responsible Conduct of Research.* Oxford: Oxford University Press.

Ogden, T.E. and Goldberg, I.A. (eds) (2002) *Research Proposals: A Guide to Success.* New York: Academic Press.

O'Leary, Z. (2001) *Reaction, Introspection and Exploration: Diversity in Journeys Out of Faith.* Kew, Victoria: Christian Research Association.

O'Leary, Z. (2005) *Researching Real-World Problems: A Guide to Methods of Inquiry.* London: SAGE.

O'Leary, Z. (2007) *The Social Science Jargon Buster: The Key Terms You Need to Know.* London: SAGE.

O'Leary, Z. (2014) *The Essential Guide to Doing Research.* London: SAGE.

Oliver, P. (2003) *The Students' Guide to Research Ethics.* Buckingham: Open University Press.

Pan, M.L. (2008) *Preparing Literature Reviews: Qualitative and Quantitative Approaches.* Glendale, CA: Pyrczak.

Patton, M. (2014) *Qualitative Research and Evaluation Methods.* London: SAGE.

Paumgarten, N. (2008) 'Up and down: The life of elevators' *The New Yorker,* 21 April 2008. http://www.newyorker.com/magazine/2008/04/21/up-and-then-down

Pehlke II, T.A., Hennon, C.B., Radina, M.E. and Kuvalanka, K.A. (2009) 'Does father still know best? An inductive thematic analysis of popular TV sitcoms', *Journal of Theory, Research, and Practice about Men as Fathers,* 7(2): 114–39.

Phelps, R., Fisher, K. and Ellis, A.H. (2007) *Organizing and Managing Your Research: A Practical Guide for Postgraduates*. London: SAGE.

Pink, D. (2012) *To Sell Is Human: The Surprising Truth about Persuading, Convincing, and Influencing Others*. New York: Penguin.

Poor, W.B. and Plyhart, R.E. (2004) 'Organizational research over the internet: ethical challenges and opportunities', in E.A. Buchanan (ed.), *Readings in Virtual Research Ethics: Issues and Controversies*. Hershey, PA: Idea Group Inc.

Pratley, A. (2014) *Inside Job: Doing the Work You Want with the Job You Have*. Sydney, Australia: H&P Publishing.

Prior, L. (2011) (ed.) *Using Documents and Records in Social Research*. London: SAGE.

Prusak, L. (2010) 'What can't be measured', *Harvard Business Review*, 7 October.

Punch, K. (2006) *Developing Effective Research Proposals*. London: SAGE.

Pyrczak, F. and Bruce, R.R. (2011) *Writing Empirical Research Reports: A Basic Guide for Students of the Social and Behavioral Sciences*. Glendale, CA: Pyrczak.

Quinlan, C. (2011) *Business Research Methods*. London: Cengage.

Ramazanŏglu, C. with Holland, J. (2002) *Feminist Methodology: Challenges and Choices*. Thousand Oaks, CA: SAGE.

Rapley, T. (2008) *Doing Conversation, Discourse and Document Analysis*. London: SAGE.

Reason, P. and Bradbury, H. (2006) *Handbook of Action Research*. London: SAGE.

Rescher, N. (2005) *Reason and Reality: Realism and Idealism in Pragmatic Perspective*. Lanham, MD: Rowman & Littlefield.

Rettig, S. and Hayes, T. (2012) *Hermeneutics and Discourse Analysis in Social Psychology*. Hauppauge, NY: Nova Science Publishers

Rhoades, E.A. (2011) 'Literature reviews', *The Volta Review*, 111(3): 353–68.

Ridley, D. (2012) *The Literature Review: A Step-by-Step Guide for Students*. London: SAGE.

Robinson, D. (2013) *Introducing Empiricism*. New York: Totem Books.

Robson, C. (2011) *Real World Research*. Oxford: Blackwell.

Rock, David (2009) *Your Brain at Work: Strategies for Overcoming Distraction, Regaining Focus, and Working Smarter All Day Long*. New York: HarperBusiness.

Roethlisberger, F.J. and Dickson, W.J. (1939) *Management and the Worker: An Account of a Research Program Conducted by the Western Electric Company, Hawthorne Works*. New York: John Wiley & Sons.

Rogers, E.M. (1983). *Diffusion of Innovations*, 3rd edn. New York: Free Press.

Rosenbaum, P.R. (2010) *Observational Studies*. New York: Springer.

Rosling, Hans (2006) 'The best stats you've ever seen', TED Talk. www.ted.com/speakers/hans_rosling.

Rossi, P.H., Freeman, H.E. and Lipsey, M.W. (2003) *Evaluation: A Systematic Approach*. Thousand Oaks, CA: SAGE.

Roulston, K. (2010) *Reflective Interviewing: A Guide to Theory and Practice*. Thousand Oaks, CA: SAGE.

Royse, D., Thyer, B.A., Padgett, D.K. and Logan, T.K. (2009) *Program Evaluation: An Introduction*. Florence, KY: Brooks Cole.

Rubin, A. and Bellamy, J. (2012) *Practitioner's Guide to Using Research for Evidence-Based Practice*. Hoboken, NJ: John Wiley and Sons.

Rubin, H.J. and Rubin, I.S. (2004) *Qualitative Interviewing: The Art of Hearing Data*. Thousand Oaks, CA: SAGE.

Rudestam, K.E. and Newton, R.R. (2007) *Surviving Your Dissertation: A Comprehensive Guide to Content and Process*. London: SAGE.

Rumsey, D. (2011) *Statistics for Dummies*. New York: John Wiley & Sons.

Russell, M.A. (2013) *Mining the Social Web: Analyzing Data from Facebook, Twitter, Linkedin, and Other Social Media Sites*, 2nd edn. Sebastopol, CA: O'Reilly Media.

Saldana, J. (2012) *The Coding Manual for Qualitative Researchers*. London: SAGE.

Salkind, N.J. (2012) *Statistics for People Who (Think They) Hate Statistics: Excel 2010 Edition*. London: SAGE.

Saris, W.E. and Gallhofer, I.N. (2007) *Design, Evaluation, and Analysis of Questionnaires for Survey Research*. New York: Wiley-Interscience.

Saunders, M. and Lewis, P. (2012) *Doing Research in Business and Management: An Essential Guide to Planning Your Project*. Sydney, Australia: Pearson.

Schick, T. (ed.) (1999) *Readings in the Philosophy of Science: From Positivism to Postmodern*. Columbus, OH: McGraw-Hill.

Schiffer, M. (1999) *The Material Life of Human Beings: Artifacts, Behavior and Communication*. London: Routledge.

Schreier, M. (2012) *Qualitative Content Analysis in Practice*. London: SAGE.

Schuman, H. and Presser, S. (1981) '"The acquiescence quagmire" in Questions and Answers', *Attitude Surveys*. New York: Academic Press.

Sears, D. (1986) 'College sophomores in the laboratory: influences on a narrow data-base on social psychology's view of human nature', *Journal of Personality and Social Psychology*, 51(3): 515–30.

Senge, P. (1994) *The Fifth Discipline Fieldbook*. New York: Crown Business.

Shulman, J. and Asimov, I. (eds) (1988) *Isaac Asimov's Book of Science and Nature Quotations*. New York: Weidenfeld & Nicolson.

Sidnell, J. (2010) *Conversation Analysis: An Introduction*. New York: Wiley-Blackwell.

Sidnell, J. and Stivers, T. (eds) (2011) *The Handbook of Conversation Analysis*. New York: Wiley-Blackwell.

Silverman, D. (2011) *Interpreting Qualitative Data: Methods for Analysing Talk, Text and Interaction*. London: SAGE.

Sinfield, M. (1995) 'Women with AIDS: a phenomenological study', *Australasian Annual Conference, Society for HIV Medicine*, 16–19 November, 7: 61.

Skerrett, P.J. (2012) 'Multitasking – a medical and mental hazard', *Harvard Health Blog*, 7 January.

Smith, J., Flowers, P. and Larkin, M. (2009) *Interpretative Phenomenological Analysis: Theory, Method and Research*. London: SAGE.

Sofalvi, Alan (2011) 'Health education films of the silent era: a historical analysis', *International Electronic Journal of Health Education*, 14: 135–41.

Spencer, S. (2011) *Visual Research Methods in the Social Sciences: Awakening Visions*. London: Routledge.

Sprague, J. (2005) *Feminist Methodologies for Critical Researchers: Bridging Differences*. Lanham, MD: AltaMira Press.

Stake, R.E. (1995) *The Art of Case Study Research*. Thousand Oaks, CA: SAGE.

Steinmetz, G. (ed.) (2005) *The Politics of Method in the Human Sciences: Positivism and Its Epistemological Others*. Durham, NC: Duke University Press.

Stoudt, B.G., Fox, M. and Fine, M. (2012) 'Contesting privilege with critical participatory action research', *Journal of Social Issues*, 68(1): 178–93.

Swanborn, P. (2010) *Case Study Research: What, Why and How?* Thousand Oaks, CA: SAGE.

Tashakkori, A. and Teddlie, C. (eds) (2010) *Handbook of Mixed Methods Social and Behavioral Research*. London: SAGE.

Ten Have, P. (2004) *Understanding Qualitative Research and Ethnomethodology.* London: SAGE.

Thaler, R.H. and Sunstein, C.S. (2008) *Nudge: Improving Decisions about Health, Wealth and Happiness.* New Haven, CT: Yale University Press.

The Economist (2015) 'The law and unintended consequences: the perils of deliberately sabotaging security', 7 March.

The Guardian (2011) 'German defence minister resigns in PhD immigration row', online. 1 March 2011. www.theguardian.com/world/2011/mar/01/german-defence-minister-resigns-plagiarism (accessed 16 November 2016).

Thompson, C. (2003) 'PowerPoint makes you dumb', *New York Times*, 14 December.

Thompson, S.K. (2012) *Sampling.* New York: John Wiley & Sons.

Thomson, P. and Kamler, B. (2012) *Writing for Peer Reviewed Journals: Strategies for Getting Published.* London: Routledge.

Tortu, S., Goldsamt, L.A. and Hamid, R. (eds) (2001) *A Practical Guide to Research and Services with Hidden Populations.* Boston, MA: Allyn & Bacon.

Trochim, W., Donnelly, J. and Arora, K. (2016) *Research Methods: The Essential Knowledge.* Boston, MA: Cengage.

Trochim, W.M. (2009) *The Research Methods Knowledge Base.* Web page at www. social researchmethods.net/kb/index.php.

Tufte, E. (1997) *Visual and Statistical Thinking: Displays of Evidence for Making Decisions.* Cheshire, CT: Graphics Press.

Tufte, E. (2006) 'The cognitive style of PowerPoint'. Cheshire, CT: Graphics Press.

Van Leeuwen, T. and Jewitt, C. (eds) (2001) *Handbook of Visual Analysis.* London: SAGE.

Vartanian, T. (2010) *Secondary Data Analysis.* Oxford: Oxford University Press.

Visentin, L. (2015) 'Macquarie University revokes degrees for students caught buying essays in Mymaster cheating racket', *Sydney Morning Herald*, 28 May.

Vonnegut, Jr., K. (2000) *Hocus Pocus.* London: Vintage Books.

Wagner, W.E. (2012) *Using IBM® SPSS® Statistics for Research Methods and Social Science Statistics.* Thousand Oaks, CA: SAGE.

Wainer, H. (2000) *Drawing Inferences from Self-Selected Samples.* Mahwah, NJ: Lawrence Erlbaum.

Wainer, H. (2009) *Picturing the Uncertain World: How to Understand, Communicate, and Control Uncertainty through Graphical Display.* Princeton, NJ: Princeton University Press.

Wales, E. and Brewer, B. (1976) 'Graffiti in the 1970s', *Journal of Social Psychology*, 99(1): 115–23.

Wallerstein, I. (2001) *Unthinking Social Science: The Limits of Nineteenth-Century Paradigms.* Philadelphia, PA: Temple University Press.

Ward, A. (2013) 'The neuroscience of everyone's favorite topic: themselves', *Scientific American*, 16 July.

Webb, E.J., Campbell, D.T., Schwartz, R.D. and Sechrest, L. (1998) *Unobtrusive Measures: Nonreactive Research in the Social Sciences.* Dallas: Houghton Mifflin.

Weber, M. ([1904] 1949) 'Objectivity in social science and social policy', in M. Weber, *The Methodology of the Social Sciences.* New York: Free Press.

Wengraf, T. (2001) *Qualitative Research Interviewing: Semi-Structured, Biographical and Narrative Methods.* London: SAGE.

Wertz, F., Charmaz, K., McMullen, L., Josselson, R., Anderson, R. and McSpadden, E. (2011) *Five Ways of Doing Qualitative Analysis: Phenomenological Psychology,*

Grounded Theory, Discourse Analysis, Narrative Research, and Intuitive Inquiry. New York: Guilford Press.

White, P. (2009) *Developing Research Questions: A Guide for Social Scientists.* Basingstoke: Palgrave Macmillan.

Wholey, J.S., Hatry, H.P. and Newcomer, K.E. (eds) (2010) *Handbook of Practical Program Evaluation.* Hoboken, NJ: Jossey-Bass.

Willer, D. and Walker, H. (2007) *Building Experiments: Testing Social Theory.* Stanford, CA: Stanford University Press.

Witte, J.C. (2009) 'Introduction to the Special Issue on web surveys', *Sociological Methods & Research*, 37: 283–90.

Wodak, R. and Meyer, M. (eds) (2009) *Methods of Critical Discourse Analysis.* London: SAGE.

Wolcott, H.F. (2008) *Ethnography: A Way of Seeing.* Lanham, MD: AltaMira Press.

Wolcott, H.F. (2008) *Writing Up Qualitative Research.* London: SAGE.

Yau, N. (2012) *Visualize This: The Flowing Data Guide to Design, Visualization and Statistics.* Indianapolis, IN: Wiley.

Yin, R.K. (2014) *Case Study Research: Design and Methods.* Thousand Oaks, CA: SAGE.

INDEX